Towards Transaction Cost Regulation

Institutional Change in Agriculture and Natural Resources
Institutioneller Wandel der Landwirtschaft und Ressourcennutzung

Governing Sustainability in India

edited by/herausgegeben von
Volker Beckmann & Konrad Hagedorn

Volume/Band 51

Ranjan Kumar Ghosh

Towards Transaction Cost Regulation

Insights from the Indian Power Generation Sector

Shaker Verlag
Aachen 2014

Bibliographic information published by the Deutsche Nationalbibliothek
The Deutsche Nationalbibliothek lists this publication in the Deutsche
Nationalbibliografie; detailed bibliographic data are available in the Internet at
http://dnb.d-nb.de.

Zugl.: Berlin, Humboldt-Univ., Diss., 2014

ISBN 978-3-8440-3263-5
ISSN 1617-4828

Shaker Verlag GmbH • P.O. BOX 101818 • D-52018 Aachen
Phone: 0049/2407/9596-0 • Telefax: 0049/2407/9596-9
Internet: www.shaker.de • e-mail: info@shaker.de

Aim and Scope of the Series

„Nothing endures but change". Heraclitus the Ephesian (ca. 535–475 BC)

Institutions, defined as "the rules of the game", are a key factor to the sustainable development of societies. They structure not only the multitude of human-human interactions of modern societies, but also most of the human-nature interactions. Poverty, famine, civil war, degradation of natural resources and even the collapse of ecosystems and societies often have institutional causes, likewise social and economic prosperity, sustainable use of resources and the resilience of socio-ecological systems. Agriculture, forestry and fisheries are those human activities where the interdependencies between human-human and human-nature interactions are perhaps most pronounced, and diverse institutions have been developed in history to govern them.

Social and ecological conditions are, however, ever changing, which continuously challenge the existing institutional structure at a given point in time. Those changes may be long-term, like population growth or climate change, medium-term, such as new technologies or changing price relations, or short-term, like floods or bankruptcies, but all of them pose the question whether the rules of the game need to be adapted. Failures to adapt timely and effectively may come at a high social cost. Institutional change, however, face a principal dilemma: on the one hand, institutions need to be stable to structure expectations and effectively influence human behaviors; on the other hand, they need to be adaptive to respond to the ever changing circumstance mentioned above. Understanding stability and change as well as developing adaptive institutions and effective, efficient and fair mechanisms of change are, therefore, of central importance for societies and an ongoing research challenge for social scientists.

If we want to improve the effectiveness, efficiency and adaptability of institutions, it stands to reason that we have to develop a good understanding of the causes, effects, processes and mechanism of stability and change. This is the aim of the series "Institutional Change in Agriculture and Natural Resources," which attempts to answer the questions "How do processes and mechanism of institutional change actually work? What and who are the main determinants and actors driving, governing and influencing these processes? What are the economic, political, social and ecological consequences? How can adaptive institutions be designed and developed, and what governance structures are required to make them effective?" These are the questions at the heart of the series. The works published in this series seek to provide answers to these questions in different economic, social, political and historical contexts.

Volker Beckmann and Konrad Hagedorn
Ernst-Moritz-Arndt-Universität Greifswald und Humboldt-Universität zu Berlin

Focus of the *Governing Sustainability in India* subseries

Deep transformations of interconnected social, ecological and technical systems are taking place in many regions of the world, requiring complex processes of institutional change. In India, such processes of transformation are particularly intense. As in many other countries, the main drivers there can be found in population growth associated with demographic change and economic growth, closely interlinked with technological change. Especially in Indian society, this often occurs in contexts of high population density, extreme resource scarcity, weak carrying capacity of ecosystems and harmful pollution. The growing economy calls for reliable energy provision and increased energy efficiency while, at the same time, also needing to cope with climate change.

The ICAR subseries Governing Sustainability in India provides a collection of studies on such action situations in both rural and urban areas. Rural areas are increasingly affected by the above-mentioned problems, as people's livelihoods there often depend directly on well-functioning bio-physical systems. They suffer from soil erosion, declining water tables, loss of biodiversity, impacts of climate change and other crucial problems. In Indian cities meanwhile, particularly its emerging megacities, urbanization is proceeding rapidly, leading to increased demand on natural resources. Changing lifestyles and economic growth are increasing energy consumption and greenhouse gas emissions. Climate change impacts, worsened by such urban developments, are already causing extreme weather events such as floods, heat waves and droughts.

In such action situations, crafting institutions can be the key to achieving sustainable development. The young researchers presenting their analyses in this subseries have accepted this challenge and engaged in excellent, in-depth studies. A variety of related issues were analysed, including enhanced energy efficiency, power-generation efficiency, policies for renewable energy, political discourses for promoting biofuels, sustainable traffic solutions, sustainable food chains, localized food systems, food accessibility for the urban poor, electricity provision for irrigation, microcredit organisations to combat poverty, governance of water allocation, industrial water pollution abatement, collective action in watershed management, rehabilitation of displaced farmers, and local service delivery. We are very grateful to the authors for having employed well-developed analytical frameworks, enlightening theoretical approaches and multiple methods to contribute to our common knowledge base. They have been working together with many partners in India and elsewhere, to whom we also want to express our special gratitude.

Volker Beckmann and Konrad Hagedorn
Ernst-Moritz-Arndt-Universität Greifswald & Humboldt Universität zu Berlin

Acknowledgments

Like any graduate researcher I also started with a dream of conducting meaningful and cutting edge work, unaware of the challenges which lay on my path. Yet, when I look back upon completion, what strikes me most is the inseparability of the contribution of guides, peers and well-wishers in this tedious sojourn. Konrad Hagedorn's profound concern, patience and attention to my overall well-being were simultaneously a motivation and an assurance. If this work is of any pragmatic utility then it is an ode to his organization, openness and ability to stimulate critical thinking. It is no exaggeration to say that my success would remain elusive without the active and encouraging involvement of Vinish Kathuria. He was like a captain who steered the ship through stormy weather. I feel honored to have worked in such close contact with an academic of such erudite scholarship and simplicity. It was another great stroke of luck for me to have got the support of Daniel Cole during my stay at the Ostrom Workshop at Indiana. His stunning command over an incomprehensively wide range of subject matter will remain an inspiration much beyond graduate academic life.

It is said that 'walking with a friend in the dark is better than walking alone in the light'. I think this is so true of my friends and colleagues at both Humboldt and Indiana. I cannot but express my most warm feelings for Jens Rommel and Christian Kimmich, who more than being fantastic colleagues, have been wonderful friends. Without their feedback at every stage I would never have made the progress I did in my work. Srinivas Reddy Srigiri's personal friendship and shared interests ensured a comfortable stay not only in academic life but also outside. I am grateful to Christine Werthmann for providing critical financial support for field research. Important support also came from other 'Megacity-Hyderabad' colleagues like Ramesh Chennamaneni, Dimitrios Zikos, Julian Sagebiel and Philip Kumar.

My prime learning about institutions came from excellent, stimulating lectures of Daniel Bromley, Kate Farrell and Konrad Hagedorn. Dan Bromley's enduring friendship and ease of access will remain an invaluable asset for all time to come. To Kate I owe my philosophical foundations, deeper understanding of epistemology and one of the most fulfilling learning experiences ever. Perhaps my initiation into the field of New Institutional Economics would never have been complete if I didn't have the opportunity to closely associate with Lee Benham who has been extraordinarily kind and concerned about my career development ever since. Of the many other important influences (directly or indirectly) outside Humboldt which helped me shape my research ideas and provided inspiration in the same measure, Acharya Vishnugupta (Chanakya), Ronald Coase, Oliver Williamson, Elinor Ostrom, Alexandra Benham, Pablo Spiller and Russell Pittman deserve special mention.

I offer my special gratitude to Sigrid Heilmann, Ines Jeworski and Renate Judis for their infinite patience, help and concern at every stage of my stay at the department. I can hardly ever repay their debt, especially of Ms. Heilmann's persistent efforts to organize the finalization procedures. The journey would have been incomplete at worst and dull at the best without the friendship and support of all my colleagues from Ress but especially Andreas Thiel, Philipp Grundmann, Wiebke Hampel, Lars Berger, Sergio Villamayor, Seema Singh, Bhaskar Poldas, Bhuvana Vignaesh, Ahmad Hamidov, Sai Kumar B.C., Phungmayo Horam and my special partners-in-crime, Mario Torres, Keerthi Kiran and Vikram Patil.

I dedicate this work to my entire family and especially my parents, Mr. A.C. Ghosh and Mrs. Geeta Ghosh, my uncle Dr. B. C. Ghosh, my parents-in-laws, Mr. and Mrs. Ajit Das, my brother Sugoto Ghosh and sister-in-law Preety Priya, my sister Rajashree Ghosh and brother-in-law, Kumarjit Sengupta, my sweet nephew Swarnav and lovely niece Dwaitaa, my sisters-in-laws, Rashmi Priya and Shiwika Priya and their families. The list can go on endlessly, however the one person whose extraordinary patience and loving support served as a foundation for my entire enterprise is my wife, Reema Priya. I have no words to express this except an inadequate 'thank you'.

I am very thankful to my friends who gave close support before and during this period: Viney Sharma, Manibhushan Kumar, Yugank Goyal, Sanjeet Rai, Vaibhav Parel, Jai Pandya, Abhijit Saha, Veena Tirupathi, K. Vasu, Mayank Thakur and Shilpi Bhargava. My final expression of gratitude is always to my teachers who have shaped my journey of life: Radhanath Swami, Anjan Bhattacharya, Govinda das, Gauranga das, Gaur Gopal das, Vishwajeet Sanyal, Konrad Hagedorn, Vinish Kathuria, K.S. Kavi Kumar, Kate Farrell, Nilanjan Banik, Alok Dash, A.A. Nambi and Arabinda Mishra.

Financial support for this work came from DAAD and German Ministry of Education and Research (BMBF) through its 'Future Megacities' program and is gratefully acknowledged. Special thanks to the editors of ICAR series, Volker Beckmann and Konrad Hagedorn and the publishers, Shaker Verlag. All remaining errors are mine.

Berlin, November 2014   Ranjan Kumar Ghosh

Table of Contents

List of Tables

List of Figures

1. Introduction and Problem

As long as there are shortages in the electricity sector, this talk of competition has little meaning

- *Prabir Purkayastha*

Last few years have seen widespread electricity deregulation in both transition and developing countries. Deregulation is a type of regulatory reform where there is partial or complete elimination of regulation, so that economic performance can be enhanced (Kim and Prescott 2005). In reality however, deregulation almost never entails a complete elimination of regulation or regulatory structures. The meaning of deregulation, as used in this thesis, therefore, refers to a greater role for the market and lesser for state intervention. So what is the economic rationale behind electricity sector deregulation? Conventional wisdom suggests that investments and efficiency in the power sector can be increased by deregulating the electricity market and making it competitive. Entry of new firms and the unbundling of vertically integrated monopolies will eventually lead to lower prices and higher productivity (Joskow 2008). The 'neo-classical prescription' of electricity deregulation is that generation should be privatized completely and transmission and distribution being natural monopolies be regulated but privately owned. Some call this the 'top down' reform model (Hunt 2002). The main components of this model are: a stand-alone transmission company; privately-owned, competing generation companies that bid into a bulk/wholesale power pool; supply competition for all or part of the retail market; third-party access to transmission and distribution on non-discriminatory, transparent terms; and an independent and transparent regulator.

Figure 1-1 presents a picture of this 'top down' reform model. However, there are many *ex ante* necessary conditions for this restructuring to take place and for electricity markets to be functional. Hansen (2008) summarizes from the literature some of the main features which helped US and UK make this successful transition. The absence of these features creates problems if developing countries plan to deregulate. First, unless there is a stable and functional grid, buyers and sellers cannot come together. Second, robust regulatory capacity is needed with skills and manpower to regulate complex networks. Third, there has to be robust institutional framework in the form of legal systems and contract law enforcement. Fourth, distribution companies need to be physically and financially strong. Fifth, demand growth has to be slow and controlled and some excess capacities before the reforms are initiated. Clearly, India did not fulfill most of these criteria when the process of deregulation began in the early 1990s. Yet the power sector in India was deregulated and brought under independent regulation. What has been the impact of this? While the thesis makes an attempt to investigate this in great details, the next section begins with a brief history and the context of Indian power sector deregulation.

1.1 Genesis of Indian Power Sector Reforms

Prior to 1991, Indian power sector was characterized by the ownership of electric utilities by the federal state electricity boards (SEBs)[1]. They were 'loosely' regulated, vertically integrated, and were natural monopolies, with the primary control in the hand of the federal state governments. The industry structure in the pre-reform phase included two important legislations: the Indian Electricity Act 1910 and the Electricity Supply Act 1948. Under the Act of 1910, most of the electricity generated and supplied was owned by private licensees and local governments. However with the 1948 Act the industry was nationalized and all the functions of generation, transmission and distribution were brought under state control. Thus state electricity boards (SEBs) were created and the sector got a vertically integrated structure. This followed the logic that public utilities perform the best when they are regulated natural monopolies. The primary control was in the hand of the state governments which also set the tariffs, a crucial aspect of the whole industry. There were significant achievements in terms of generating capacity which increased 50 times at an annual growth rate of 9.2 percent during the years from 1948 to 1991 (Dubash and Rajan 2002). Around the mid-seventies two giant central government owned utilities were formed which are still among the best performing power companies in the world, the National Thermal Power Corporation (NTPC) and the National Hydroelectric Power Corporation (NHPC). For instance, in 1997-98 the plant load factor (PLF) of NTPC was 11 percentage points higher than the national average, and in 2012-13 it was 13 percentage points higher than the national average. NHPC produces roughly 18.77 percent of total electricity generation in India. However, the SEBs kept on sinking through increased financial gaps. Of many reasons the primary cause has been identified in the literature as the high political subsidization or free provision of electricity to agriculture, based on unmetered consumption (Dubash and Rajan 2002).

---

[1] The 'democratic state' of India is federal in nature similar to the US where there is a centrally elected government and also different elected governments at the federal state level. While some duties fall exclusively in the purview of the federal states, some are concurrent to both, the state as well as the center. These SEBs are/were operated at the federal state level with limited central government intervention.

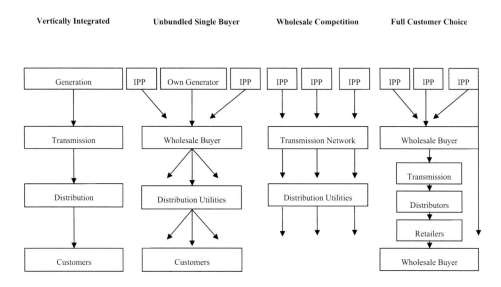

Figure 1-1: Top-down reform model

Source: Own diagram based on Hansen (2008)

Additionally, poor management practices, theft and loss due to industrial high tension lines, corrupt and inefficient staff mainly leading to non-payment of dues, meant that the SEBs became loss making liabilities (Purkayastha 2001). Finally the macroeconomic crisis of the early 1990s made an impending deregulation inevitable. The objective of this program was to unbundle the traditionally state owned public utilities into separate generation, transmission and distribution functions. The first phase, during the early nineties, was of generation reform where the sector was opened up to allow private players to participate in generation. The Electricity Laws (Amendment) Act, 1991 provided a legislative route where Independent Power Producers (IPPs) could establish and run generation plants and sell the output to the SEBs through long term contracts. There was a plethora of incentives offered in order to induce as much investment as possible. Some important ones included a guaranteed 16 percent return on equity, expedited clearance procedures and escrow arrangements for non-payment of dues by SEBs. As a result within 3 years of amendment, 243 contracts were signed for a capacity of 90,000 MW. But soon dissent grew and the plans failed to materialize. The IPPs became tired of bureaucratic delays, non-implementation and fear of non-payment from SEBs. There were also questions raised at the economic viability of the projects. As a result by 2001 only 3200 MW worth of capacity achieved financial closure

(PMGER 2007). So in spite of an immense enthusiasm in the beginning and investments to the tune of US $ 100 billion lining up in the first three years, the fizz ended soon and only a fraction of it materialized (Dubash and Rajan 2002). One possible explanation was the absence of a regulatory system and hence clear guidelines to be followed either by the investor or by the government authorities.

Once a realization of this came, the Indian parliament passed the Electricity Regulatory Commissions Act in 1998 to bring the whole power sector in India under independent regulation. Thus the Central Electricity Regulatory Commission (CERC) was established in August 1998. The Act also mandated that each state establishes its own State Electricity Regulatory Commissions (SERCs) which many of them did. The functions of the CERC and the SERCs can be broadly categorized into three distinct roles: The *core role* which includes tariff regulation, monitoring quality of service, adjudicating disputes, enforcing licensing conditions, monitoring compliance and redressing grievances; A *recommendatory role* which includes recommendations for approval of licenses; and an *advisory role* under which it advises the government on related matters (Rao 2004). Further institutional reforms came in the form of the landmark Electricity Act in 2003 which repealed all the previous acts and put the whole agenda of power sector administration and reforms under a single frame. Some of the key features of this act were removal of licensing requirements for generation, freedom to produce captive power, government ownership of transmission utilities with provision for private licensees, regulation of trading by state regulatory commissions, open access in distribution etc. However, these reforms too faced lots of hurdles and the next section discusses them briefly.

1.2 Persistent Problems

The process of deregulation has neither been smooth nor even close to being successful in India. In fact this has been true of most the developing countries where this process was introduced (Singh 2010: p. 4197). Even in the case of liberalized mature markets, there has been a problem of investment and there seems to be far from a satisfactory model based on market signals which can resolve this. These mature markets have been able to bypass this fear because they operate in a condition of overcapacity. However, for developing markets the problem of investment is far from marginal as there is high rate of and sporadic demand growth and higher uncertainties (both supply and demand related). Moreover, experiences from Chile, Argentina, Colombia and Brazil do not prove either that the de-integrated model has been helpful for increased investment (Finon 2006). There is a growing discontent with the view that the British model of electricity restructuring is ideal for the Indian scenario (Thomas 2005). One recent discussion of open access in electricity markets in India, by an associate of the Indian planning commission, also acknowledges that the British experience cannot be followed very easily (Dasgupta 2013). The main reason being the fact that in India there is a situation of excess demand. Additionally, there is also the situation of security-of- (fuel) supply. There are even suggestions that in the developing countries reforms should be designed so that the commitment for protection of investments is through coordination by public governance (Finon 2006). Moreover the reforms should be such that investment related risks are minimized through long-term contracts. Returning to the case of India, Table 1-1 shows how the main objective of reforms i.e. of replacing the share of public-owned generation with privately owned generation has not been achieved even as late as the year 2012. The share of private generation in the total is only 27.1% whereas that of public owned generation (including the state and the central sector[2]) has been 72.8%.

Table 1-1: Generation (in Megawatts) by mode and ownership as of 2012

	Hydro	Thermal			Nuclear	RES	Total
		Coal	Gas	Diesel			
State	27380	49457	4965.32	602.61	0	3513.72	85918.65
Private	2525	23450.38	6713.5	597.14	0	20989.73	54275.75
Central	9085.4	39115	6702.23	0	4780	0	59682.63
Total	38990.4	112022.38	18381.05	1199.75	4780	24503.45	199877.03

Source: Own calculations based on CEA Power Scenario, 2012

There are several bottlenecks which block the efforts to bring in competition in the sector, as summarized by Singh (2010). Transmission access and pricing is one of the major problems which continue to persist. The transmission pricing system is only focused towards cost recovery without adequate concerns for giving appropriate investment signals. Whether an electric feed into the transmission grid is congestion-increasing or congestion-reducing, they are charged the same tariff. This is on top of the fact that transmission capacity is itself very limited. There are no incentives to expand transmission capacity to ease the load. Privatization of transmission capacity is not expected to work as there are no markets to resolve problems arising due to network externalities. Therefore, it continues to remain state-owned and does not keep up with the expansion in generation. Another important bottleneck arises out of the partially

---

[2] State sector is that which is owned by federal SEB or companies, for example, the Andhra Pradesh Electricity Generation Company Ltd. (APGENCO). Central sector is that which is owned by the central Indian government, like the NTPC.

liberated fuel supply sectors. There is hardly any market for key fuel inputs: coal and natural gas. Although there has been allotment of pit-head captive coal mines allotted to power companies, so as remove their dependence on state-owned supply, it is not adequate. Availability of natural gas, although on an increase, continues to be plagued with uncertainties (Singh 2010). Additionally the design of market mechanism is not adequate for competition as the regulators are not equipped to prevent the misuse of market power (Purkayastha 2001; Singh 2010).

Although an institutional change in the form of Electricity Act 2003 introduced new provisions in legislation so as to improve the industry structure and make the regulatory regime more flexible (Bhattacharya 2005), the results have not been as expected. Sinha (2005) analyses the specific features of the EA 2003 which are aimed at introducing competition in the power sector namely, open access and multiple distribution licensees in the same area. Basically open access allows a consumer to choose a supplier other than the distributor in its area. However in the presence of cross subsidy, implementation of open access leads to the problem of cream skimming with new licensees preferring only high end cross subsidized consumers. As compensation there is a levy of a cross subsidy surcharge but the impact of the surcharge has been to "neutralize the force of competition provided by open access" (Ranganathan 2004). Apprehending this, the Act emphasizes a timely phasing out of cross subsidies to avoid this burden but political compulsions seem to have prevented a realization of this and also in near future. Another way in which the effect of open access is dampened is through the arbitrarily high pricing of transmission charges by the regulator (*ibid.*). Nair (2008) cites some cases in which regulatory capture has led to anti-competitive practices. In Rajasthan excess wheeling charges were levied to discourage captive units from selling power to third parties. There was a similar instance in the case of Andhra Pradesh regulator. The same regulator was once engaged in trimming down generation tariff to improve the financial health of state owned utilities.

Moreover, there are problems with the model of independent regulation too. Literature identifies several of these. The regulatory architecture of Indian electricity regulation commissions is such that it hardly allows any autonomy or independence. The central and state governments make appointments of the staff and approve the budgets of the commissions. They also have the authority to issue directives on policy matters to the commissions. There is very limited discretion of the regulator (Nair 2008). For example, there are several elements of fuel cost pass through in generation tariff, which is beyond the regulator's purview but which seriously undermines its credibility. Thus, there are many analysts who think that the current regulatory framework is more of a design problem (Dubash 2008; Nair 2008). Predominant ownership of the utilities by the government, lack of democratic accountability and political dictation in fixing tariffs are some obstacles on the way of effective regulation. As has been seen earlier, the key objectives of deregulation have not been achieved in the prime target i.e. the generation sector. However, the distribution sector is no different. The pattern of government ownership of utilities has had a negative impact on competition in the distribution sector too (Nair 2008). Typically the distribution utilities were unbundled across large geographical areas with a mix of different consumer segments. This was largely an administrative approach and failed to promote competition. Ideally, the units should have been much smaller and large urban areas would be segregated from rural areas avoiding the problem of cross subsidization. This would eventually generate more competition for bulk power supply and allow retail tariffs to reflect the relative efficiency of firms thereby making a case for yardstick competition (*ibid.*).

While there is a strand of very insightful literature discussing the dynamics of Indian power sector reforms and independent regulation (Kannan and Pillai 2001; Dubash and Rajan 2002; Rao 2004; Bhattacharya 2005; Shanmugam and Kulshreshtha 2005; Lal 2006; PMGER 2007; Dubash and Rao 2008; Nair 2008; Sen and Jamasb 2010), they have either focused on the political process and practice, or incentive alignments or the effectiveness of regulatory policies. However, regulatory incentives affect the performance of public utilities only when regulatory governance is in place (Levy and Spiller 1994). Thus it is imperative that regulatory performance cannot be understood independent of the institutional determinants of regulatory governance. Dubash (2008) provides valuable insights into the institutional context of independent electricity regulation in India. The first attempt towards independent regulation happened in Orissa starting early 1990s. The SEB was unbundled and management reforms were introduced. The regulators were mandated to take over the tariff function of the government and their prime goal was in balancing investor and consumer interests. In doing so, the Orissa regulatory agency was legislated as an autonomous body. However, reality turned out to be quite different. While the government lost control over tariff setting as a political tool, neither did the regulators raise tariff to attract investors (*ibid.*).

Thus the main purpose of setting up regulators, which was to send credible signals for private investment (credible commitments) rather than solely protecting consumer interests, was not served. Dubash (2008) cites two important flaws in this type of a regulatory design. First, it was expected that an apolitical regulatory sphere can be created merely by legislating one. That state regulators are an extended branch of the government itself is a widely known fact. Second, the regulation of state owned generation and distribution utilities is an "idiosyncrasy" in that it is a strange case of 'a state agency regulating another state agency'. Dubash and Rao (2008) conduct an empirical analysis of 'regulatory practice' by examining regulators in three specific cases of Andhra Pradesh, Delhi and Karnataka. Their first conclusion is that political and institutional contexts play a crucial role in the evolution of regulatory design. Electricity regulation is generally an extension of the earlier establishment.

Selection of regulators and staff is heavily influenced by the government, with most of them retired from high ranked government cadre under the Indian Administrative Services (IAS). Their second conclusion is that regulation is as much political as techno-economic. Though technical criteria are present, they are not dominant. Decisions are often individual-specific, variable and entrenched in the political networks from which the staff is drawn. Thus the process is heavily politicized and tied to electoral outcomes resulting in a non-transparent and imbalanced negotiation of political pressures. Thirdly, they find that there is little progress towards the stakeholder model of independent regulation where "independence is ensured not through isolation, but through being subject equally to the voice and representation of all stakeholders" (Dubash and Rao 2008). There are some positive examples, most notable among which, is the active scrutiny of power purchase agreements in Andhra Pradesh. Whereas strong and supportive governments provide for a more effective regulation, given the entrenchment of electricity in national politics, a regulatory framework with an active stakeholder engagement could provide an alternative route.

This discussion has, therefore, pointed out that the problems of reforms are as much a problem of the way independent regulation is designed as it is of an appropriate incentive structure. Moreover, the process of regulation is not independent of institutional and political considerations. So what is the institutional criterion for successful reforms and what are its determinants? The next section delineates how the thesis is structured into different segments so as to answer some of these critical and often unexplored inquiries.

1.3   Thesis Structure: Key Questions and Leitmotif

Given the current status of electricity reforms, although normative concerns like the appropriate market mechanism to promote competition among utilities have surfaced in the general literature, this thesis uses a *positive* approach. The question asked is: if a minimum rate-of-return is sufficient for generating credible commitments (Newbery 1999), then why in spite of the presence of such an incentive structure, investments are low, inefficiencies are high and tariffs have not been normalized? The preliminary hypothesis is that this is because credible commitments depend on appropriate *ex-post* governance structures rather than on *ex-ante* incentive structures. And assessment of an appropriate governance structure requires a shift from the presumption of efficient markets to a comparative institutional analysis. The remaining thesis explores this intuition from various empirical and theoretical perspectives and is structured as follows:

Chapter 2 deals with the issue of which framework of analyzing regulation would be appropriate given the aims and principles of *positive* research? In doing so, first the core debates on economic regulation are discussed. Then, the conditions under, and the history of, the origins of utility regulation is presented which draws attention to the inconsistencies and the tautological nature of the mainstream economic theories of regulation. Then the key elements of the approach of 'institutions of regulation' are delineated which emphasize that the success of economic regulation (or deregulation) depends on the extent to which it matches the institutional environment and thereby minimizes the various transaction costs involved in the governance of the entire sector. Chapter 3 lays the methodological foundation for the entire thesis. Emphasis is on a shift away from the neo-classical deductive approach to a more Coasean environment with its emphasis on abduction, empirical field work and non-reductive micro-analytics. This chapter also explains the plural methods as used for tackling different types of questions in the thesis.

After this the section of empirical investigations begins. To study the impacts of power sector reforms and analyze the linked transactional complexities, the thesis is divided into three separate empirical pieces of work based on the three natural subdivisions of the electricity generation sector:

   a. Private generation utilities,
   b. State-owned generation utilities, and
   c. Private generation non-utilities (also known as captive power plants)

In Chapter 4, the impact of deregulation on private utilities is studied. Since the level of investment is quite low and there is small-N problem with regards to plant level data, the question asked is: what explains the problem of private investment in the generation sector? Contrary to predictions of the economic theory of competition, why has the basic, and arguably the most important objective of deregulation not been met? In trying to answer that a comparative transaction cost analysis of private investment in the states of Andhra Pradesh and Gujarat is performed. Chapter 5 studies the impact of reforms on non-utility generation of electricity, mostly by manufacturing firms for self-consumption. The question asked is: why do some firms produce their own electricity while others do not? Chapter 6 tests the prediction that the overall efficiency of the electricity generation sector should increase post deregulation. The question we ask is: has deregulation positively impacted the efficiency of state-owned thermal power plants in India? The recurrent theme in the three empirical segments is the inability of the sector regulators to reduce, or at least bring down to manageable levels, the costs generated at the various nodes of electricity related transactions. This forms the basis of the contention that regulation needs to move beyond the sole objective of bringing about 'fair competition' to 'minimizing transaction costs' through appropriate governance structures. Hence the need for a new transaction cost regulation framework.

In Chapter 7 the problem of regulatory commitment is revisited and the role of information in the standard Newbery model is examined. Using an ordinal game-theoretic framework - linking action situations – it is shown that in the short run increased public information lead to reduced level of commitment and investments. However, in the long run this can be solved if the regulators make public interest moves. This is however contingent upon the institutional mechanisms for information production. Chapter 8 concludes with lessons from earlier parts of the thesis and also lays down the essence of a transaction cost regulation framework which prescribes vertical integration (or re-regulation) as viable alternative governance structure to competitive markets, till the time the sector does not reach the frontiers of sufficiency.

2. The Institutions of Regulation: Governance over Incentives

Overview

This chapter provides justification for the claim that the mainstream theories of regulation, which have often assumed institutions to be given, do not adequately provide for regulatory analysis. Hence the need for a more evolved institutional analysis – i.e. transaction cost regulation. In this chapter the path of evolution in utility regulation research is laid down and it is argued why the schools of thought which pre-ceded institutional theories had gaps which need to be addressed at the methodological level. Such a methodology is an *abductive* and *micro-analytic* approach to the study of economic problems. Navigating through the key streams of thought in economic regulation, a brief history of why and how utility regulation actually originated and the problems of assuming away institutions, the last sections of this chapter explains the elements of the 'institutions of regulation' approach which provide the avenue to analyze the governance aspect of electricity and regulatory reforms.

2.1 Main Streams of Economic Research on Regulation

Though there is no consensus on an exact definition of regulation (den Hertog 2010), regulation basically means an act of restraining a market actor's behavior so as to either increase overall social efficiency or redistribute rents. Hertog summarizes the basic intent of regulation by defining it as 'the employment of legal instruments for the implementation of social-economic policy objective' (*ibid. p. 3*). Regulation could be both economic and social in nature (Viscusi et al. 2005). Social regulation is in the areas of environment and resource use, protection of consumer rights, labor rights, health and safety and so on. But for our purposes we focus only on economic regulation where individuals or organizations are compelled by the government to comply by certain market related behavior. Further, economic regulation can be sub-divided into two categories: *structural* regulation and *conduct* regulation (Kay and Vickers 1990). Structural regulation deals with market structure and its regulation, for example, by rules on entry or exit or by rules on which services to supply and which not. Conduct regulation, on the other hand, concerns itself with the behavior of producers and consumers such as through price controls, product labeling, quality standards, compliance with intellectual property regimes etc. Another distinction, although of limited consequence, is between regulations and legislations. Through legislation, regulatory powers are decentralized to agencies or officials who then use such legislated rights to come up with specific rules, also known as regulations.

2.1.1 'Normative Analysis as a Positive Theory': Dominant Paradigm

The economic literature on regulation could be categorized into two theoretical approaches: the *positive* approach and the *normative* approach. The normative approach deals with the ways in which regulation should be designed or structured so as to maximize social welfare. In doing so it is close to the concept of optimal taxation (Newbery 1999). But such a normative approach could be criticized on the same lines as welfare economics which is difficult to be put to practice. This is shown by the impossibility theorem (Arrow 1951) which states that there is no way by which voting can lead to aggregation of individual preferences into a single social preference. However, social welfare could reflect ethical judgments if not individual preferences (Rawls 1971). Newbery (1999) argues that independent regulatory commissions (in his case the British Monopolies and Mergers Commission) often work on this principle where the members are supposed to act in keeping with public interest and impartiality in judgments. The welfare economic approach can be traced back to Vilfredo Pareto[1] whose concern was deviation from the competitive market conditions and social efficiency (Hägg 1997). Regulatory studies using this principle basically deal with the comparative costs and benefits of specific regulatory policies which are required to correct for market failures. The sources of market failures could be externalities, natural monopolies, failure of competition or information asymmetries. Till the 1960s this was the pre-occupation of economists with regulation which has been aptly titled by Joskow and Noll (1981) to be 'normative analysis as a positive theory'. The emphasis was on a *normative* corrective interference of the government, through direct or indirect regulatory policies, to correct for the *positively* analyzed market failures. Alternately, these are also known as the *public-interest theories of regulation* because 'it holds that regulation is supplied in response to the demand of the public for the correction of inefficient or inequitable market practices (Posner 1974: p. 335).

According to Joskow and Noll (1981) this approach to regulation was concerned mainly with three issues: price and entry regulation in competitive industries; price and entry regulation in monopolistic industries; and qualitative regulation like environment, health, product-quality etc. They summarize the research on all these aspects and we discuss only the key elements from those. By 1960s it was shown effectively by empirical research, which mostly used comparisons of equilibrium prices, costs and production quantity, that price and

---

[1] It needs to be underlined that in reality, more than the strict Pareto criteria of efficiency, less stringent Kaldor-Hicks criterion are useful in assessment of regulation as they describe better the conditions of approaching optimality where compensating (or the possibility of doing so) those who get worse off is the criteria of allocative efficiency. An important point is that this criterion does not necessitate that the losers be actually compensated but that an objective measure of loss substitutes the subjective valuation of losses (Ogus 2004).

entry regulations in agriculture, transportation and energy industries led to economic inefficiencies. Inefficiency was observed through higher production costs and prices as well as slower technological development (Snitzler and Byrne 1958; Stigler 1971; Joskow 1973; MacAvoy and Noll 1973). However, Joskow and Noll argue that most of these studies were plagued with data incommensurability and methodological deficiencies. For example, although MacAvoy and Sloss (1967) and Spann and Erickson (1970) study the effects of ICC (Interstate Commerce Commission) on railroad prices the data was so backdated in history that it was not comparable to the contemporary effects of the time. The additional problem was non-availability of data on unregulated firms often leading to hypothetical comparisons. Another problem was that most of these studies assumed product homogeneity and discounted for the effects on product quality while measuring the cost of regulation. Studies by Douglas and Miller (1974) for airlines, Boyer (1977) and Levin (1978) for surface transportation showed that the assumption of homogeneous product quality could lead to overestimation of the costs of regulation. These studies pointed out that prices and costs were not true indicators of the costs of regulation when product quality varied because service quality was usually inferior in unregulated firms.

Coming to the issue of price and entry regulation in monopolistic industries, (neo-classical) economic theory is quite clear that monopolies create economic inefficiency. Probably nothing is more popular than the A-J (Averch-Johnson) effect (Averch and Johnson 1962) which stresses that it is not easy for the regulatory commission to observe the actual cost structure of the regulated industry as a result of which the regulated firm produces output at higher than the minimum cost. This is inefficient and by inducing competition, such inefficiency can be avoided. As Joskow and Noll (1981: p. 11) note, 'the A-J explanation for the metafact that regulated monopolies appear to be excessively capital-intensive industries has become conventional fare in the economics literature'. Yet, studies have shown (Bailey and Malone 1970) that the results of the A-J effect can change if the model is specified differently using variant objective functions and constraints. Other papers by Klevorick (1971), Bailey (1973) and Sheshinski (1971) argue that cost minimization cannot be the only criteria of measuring regulatory efficiency and they show that some amount of regulation is 'always optimal'. Joskow further challenges the assumptions of the A-J model which are far removed from the realities under which a regulated monopoly operates. The first assumption which is misplaced in the A-J model is that regulators regulate profits while in reality the regulator fixes the prices and not the rate-of-return. Second assumption that the regulator does not observe the true costs is also not very accurate as in reality the regulator has the authority to disallow cost recoveries for production inefficiencies. The assumption that investor firms have short planning horizons in comparison to the intervals between regulatory reviews and that the firm can respond quickly to unanticipated changes is also flawed. Given the heavy capital intensity and long gestation periods of public utilities, the planning horizons are longer than the regulatory intervals. Although there is some empirical support for the A-J hypothesis, McKay (1976) showed that the results are suspect.

Another preoccupation of the normative research on regulation has been with regard to the sustainability of a natural monopoly i.e. whether there exists a second best (or optimal) price which can act as an entry barrier into the sector where a natural monopoly exists. Work by Faulhaber (1975), Panzar and Willig (1977) and others have shown that there cannot be any set of optimal prices which prevent entry in a market of natural monopoly and hence it is not sustainable unless it charges a price which is higher than its average costs. It will also be unsustainable when there are diseconomies of joint production, high inter-product substitution effects and product-specific scale economies. However, this literature ignores some critical assessments which make the unsustainability arguments weak (Joskow and Noll 1981). First, the assumption of perfect regulation which enforces least cost production by monopolists is unrealistic. Second, it is assumed that entrants do not have an optimal product mix portfolio and that they produce only a subset of what the incumbent monopoly does. Third, it is assumed that the incumbent will not respond to a new entry by cutting its losses through a decrease in the product mix, thereby making the entrant price untenable. Moreover, the assumption of sub-additivity, which is at the core of the logic of natural monopoly, is more theoretical than real. Sub-additivity of a cost function is when the cost of producing the whole basket of goods together is smaller than when they are produced separately. In reality, regulators know the range of products over which the cost function is diminishing.

One branch of the normative literature which has 'atypically' been successful in practical world is the work on variable (peak-load) pricing (Houthakker 1957; Boiteux 1960; Kahn 1970) i.e. pricing in a situation where short term demand and supply fluctuate. This success owes itself to methodological variance in which the economists working on these issues actually engaged themselves - with reality more than mere theoretical deductions (Joskow 1979a, 1979b) as shown by the fact that 'half of the references cited in this section were written by people who were willing to work with utility managers and whose research is to some degree the result of successive confrontations of theory with reality...(where) greater attention has been paid to bringing the assumptions of the models ever closer to the realities of operating a utility, and nearly all of the papers recognize the problems and costs associated with implementing a perfect pricing scheme and even provide some additional analysis on locating...the *"optimally imperfect"* scheme' (Joskow and Noll 1981: p. 20). This is an example of our claim of a non-reductive substantive methodology, a subject we will return to in greater details in a subsequent chapter of the dissertation.

The stream of research discussed so far analyzes regulation based on the presumption that it is supposed to increase social welfare and hence is called as 'normative analysis as a positive theory'. This normative research, better known as the public interest theories of regulation, tend to rationalize the existing regulatory institutions whereas positive research, as we will discuss later, appear to explain existing regulatory institutions (den Hertog 2010). The public interest theories have been criticized from other perspectives as well. The theory that monopolies lead to market failures and inefficient solutions is contingent upon the fact that the models assume away transaction costs. If transaction costs are included, then the models do not clearly predict that monopolies will lead to inefficiencies (Dahlman 1979; Toumanoff 1984). Market failures are often corrected by market mechanisms themselves through development of institutions. Externalities can be internalized by the market itself (Cheung 1978), markets can be used to even supply public goods like lighthouses (Coase 1974b) and adverse selection can be resolved through brand names, issue of guarantees or advertising campaigns (Nelson 1974). In the same vein, theories which predict that government regulation is effective have also been criticized by those who believe that partial efficiency need not necessarily lead to overall social welfare as there could be distortions in product or labor markets (Ng 1990). Another important criticism of public interest theories is that they are incomplete because neither do they explain how legislative actions translate into social welfare (Posner 1974) nor do they specify the costs and benefits of regulation to specific industries.

2.1.2 Special Interests

As a response to the limitations of the normatively oriented public interest theories, in the 1970s there was a wave of positive explanations about 'why regulation exists' which came mostly from political economists and is popularly known as the *private interest theories of regulation*. The earliest in this family of theories is the capture theory which according to Posner (1974) is 'a process by which interest groups seek to promote their (private) interests and was propelled by 'Marxist' ideologies and 'muckrakers' which alleged that the 'capitalists control the institutions of our society'. Another version of capture theory stems from political scientists (Bentley 1908; Leiserson 1946; Truman 1951; Bernstein 1955; Ziegler 1964; Huntington 1966) according to whom 'over time regulatory agencies come to be dominated by the industries regulated (*ibid. 341*)'. However, Posner criticized this branch as lacking any sound theoretical foundation, not having much empirical support or not being indistinguishable from the public interest theories. More recently there have been some explanations based on dynamic capture theory which uses the perspective of the agency (Martimort 1999) and emphasizes that industries capture regulators because of information asymmetry. Yet this is not related to the earliest versions of capture theory as we will see later.

The most important positive 'Theory of Economic Regulation' was given by Stigler (1971) and also began a school of research on regulation also known as the 'Chicago Theory of Regulation' or the *special interest theory of regulation*. Stigler's theories were built upon the explanations of political mechanisms which related the constituent's preferences of regulatory policies to the outcome: mainly the voting process and preferences of the pressure groups. The median voter theorem of Black (1958) and Downs (1957) predicted that it was the preference of the median voter which would influence the political outcome and that this marginal voter would shift its preferences according to the political agenda. However, the assumption of one-dimensional political scale in the theorem is unrealistic as political agenda and actors come in a package. Further, developments in game theory showed that there existed no stable political coalition and that any coalition was subject to defeat by another rival coalition (Plott 1967; McKelvey 1976; Schofield 1978). This cast a doubt on the view that democratic process would lead to a stable political environment which would come up with regulatory policies favorable to the public interest. Increasingly, the public interest rationale for the existence of regulation was shrouded in uncertainty. This shifted the focus of the political scientists on 'interest groups' initiated by a discussion of Bernstein (1955) who studied independent regulatory commissions in the US and argued that commissions actually ended up protecting those same industries which it was supposed to regulate in favor of the public interest. A clear evidence of this was given by Kolko (1965) who studied railway regulation and found that the regulators were actually serving the interests of the railway owners. Later on Downs (1957) came up with the theory that voters were powerless in reacting to the political outcomes as the cost of information was very high for them. This gave another reason for failure of public interest protection. Subsequently, Olson (1965) came up with a strong theoretical precept, as per his logic of collective action, that it was the size of the pressure group which determined its ability to influence regulatory outcomes. In essence the powerful insight was that better organized interest groups such as industry associations, cartels or religious organizations have a distinct advantage over the interest of dispersed consumers.

Stigler formalized these insights into his 'economic theory of regulation' which visualized the political process as a market and predicted that politically influencing industries would be able to gain favorable regulation which would be protectionist in nature and prevent competition. And this would be possible because of the better organization of such pressure groups. As Stigler puts it, '(a) representative cannot win or keep office with the support of the sum of those who are opposed to: oil import quotas, farm subsidies, airport subsidies, hospital subsidies, unnecessary navy shipyards, an inequitable public housing program, and rural electrification subsidies….(w)hen an industry receives a grant of power from the state, the benefit to the industry will fall short of the damage to the rest of the community (Stigler 1971: p. 10-11). As can be seen in Figure 2-1, interest group A has lower marginal costs of organizing the pressure group and also has higher marginal benefit of doing so as compared to the interest group B. As a result the level of influence is higher for interest group A at C_A whereas that of interest group B is lower at C_B. Usually producers organize themselves better than consumers and hence yield better chances of regulatory influence. Moreover as consumers are dispersed, per head cost of regulation is too low to motivate costly organization. Yet, in the same issue in which Stigler published this influential article, Posner (1971) criticized it by explaining how regulation often benefited consumer too. He gave the example of utility and infrastructure services like gas supply, water supply, rail transport, electricity etc. where although the cost of service is higher in rural areas the prices charged are the same as urban consumers cross subsidize them. This negated Stigler's predictions.

Peltzman (1976) extended Stigler's theory of regulation and proposed that politicians choose regulation to maximize *political support*. So even as higher regulated prices draw support from industries, lower prices draw political support and votes from consumers. Peltzman's concern is therefore of efficient regulation which is able to optimize between votes lost and gained due to price regulation. There is an interesting literature on the other variants of Stigler's and Peltzman's theory (Jean-Luc 1977; Keeler 1984; McChesney 1991). Another significant contribution from the Chicago school came through Gary Becker who highlighted competition among interest groups to exert higher political pressure and hence influence (Becker 1983, 1985b, 1985a). Those interest groups who are more efficient owing to their differential abilities can exert higher pressure leading to transfer of wealth from the low efficient groups to them. But because this leads to deadweight losses, the pressure on low efficiency groups to become more efficient increases and therefore equilibrium is reached. Some deductive insights from the Chicago theorists is that competitive industries are better suited to gain from regulation as compared to consumers, and that regulation will most likely be present in sectors where there are market failures. In essence, Chicago theorists see regulation as *redistributive* rather than *corrective*.

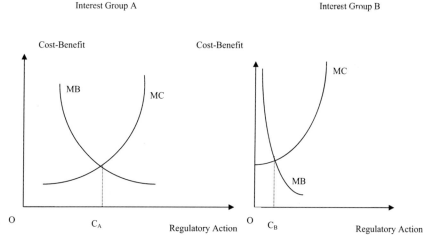

Figure 2-1: Interest group representation

Source: Based on Baron (2000) and den Hertog (2010)

However, the special interest theories of regulation have drawn criticisms on various fronts. The first one comes from Noll (1989) who argues that the Chicago theories are tautological. One can simply understand a tautology to be a self-explanatory proposition, which hinges only on the assumptions it is built upon. Noll contends that merely by showing who bears the cost and who enjoys the benefits of regulation, one cannot prove that they have been the reason driving regulation. Put simply, Noll's criticism points to a basic flaw we discussed earlier also in the case of public interest theories, that such explanations are not truly *positive* science. Another criticism is that the special interest theories have been very difficult to test empirically. Although Stigler and Friedland (1962) showed that regulation did not have the desired impacts of either lowering of prices or lowering profits of monopolies, later research showed different results (Zerbe and Urban 1988; Peltzman 1993). In fact as stated by Potters and Sloof (1996), it is very difficult to put the special interest theories to empirical test as it is almost impossible to decipher which pressure group has exerted maximum influence.

Another serious drawback of the special interest theories is that they quite conveniently assume that interest groups always and easily influence electoral outcomes and that these groups control legislators who become their wish-fulfilling machinery. Many of these are not so simple to prove in the empirical world. As den Hertog (2010) notes that there is lacking insights on at least three counts which make these theories incomplete: a) the motivation and behavior of various actors like voters, legislators, government agencies etc. b) interactions between the various actors involved, which we will call the 'supply side of regulation' and are discussed in details in the later sections, and c) the mechanisms which link interest groups to regulators. This has also led to some criticism by the public choice theorists who state that organized interest groups are not the only ones who can obtain favorable regulation (Wilson 1974, 1980). In fact, Wilson points out that interest group politics are relevant only when the costs and benefits of legislation are concentrated. When both costs and benefits are diffused then either majoritarian politics or client politics become activated. Public choice theorists open the black-box of bureaucracy and distinguish the differential impacts which agency structure and composition will have on regulation. This weakens the argument that only interest groups lead to regulation. Weingast (1981), although agrees that independent agencies do not have significant role, nonetheless states that there are other consumer and environment related groups that have as much political power as the other better organized traditional interest groups. Another criticism by the public choice theorists come from the Virginia school (Buchanan et al. 1980; Tullock 1993) who point out that Chicago theorists disregard the inefficiencies of regulation. The Virginia school emphasize on rent seeking which means "spending scarce resources on political action by individuals and groups to obtain monopoly rights or other favors granted by the government (den Hertog 2010: p. 33)". They emphasize that the social costs which arise due to rent-seeking should be added to the basket of inefficiencies due to regulation. However, the Virginia school has been criticized for overestimating the welfare losses (Samuels and Mercuro 1984). So whether it was public-interest based or private interest based explanations, most of these theoretical propositions were based on neo-classical assumptions such as perfect rationality of the actors, zero transaction costs, utility maximizing behavior and treatment of the political process and the firm as a black box. None of which adequately represent the empirical reality. While there was a plethora of literature on the costs and benefits of regulation, there was no comparative assessment of the costs and benefits of the institutional arrangement alternative to regulation. Given the fragility of the assumptions (making it tautological) and no empirical basis to support that regulation was an inferior solution based on a comparative assessment (making it normative); there was still no true 'positive' explanation of *why* regulation existed? But to arrive at a positive theory of regulation, we need to first look historically into why and under what conditions regulation actually evolved.

2.2 Brief History of Public Utility Regulation

2.2.1 The Theory of Natural Monopoly

We have seen that by the decade of 1960s and 1970s, a significant volume of literature grew which showed theoretically that regulation led to inefficiencies and the sector could be better organized through de-regulation and competition

(Demsetz 1968; Priest 1993). Demsetz (1968) in particular showed that 'there were no conditions under which regulation by commission could be guaranteed to optimize social welfare' (Priest 1993). The theory of natural monopoly states that a single firm can produce the total market demand at lower cost than any combination of two or more firms. A sustainability condition in a natural monopoly market with a single output is that average costs will fall as output expands, which means that the marginal or the incremental cost will be lower than the average cost. The usual average cost curve of a firm is as shown in Figure 2-2. Up to Q', the average cost of output keeps falling and displays economies of scale but beyond that the average cost curve starts rising and it becomes uneconomical for the firm to produce any output level beyond Q'. Then other firms come in to satisfy the market demand beyond that level. However, in the case of a natural monopoly the average cost of a firm keeps falling in the long run and can alone meet most of the market demand as shown in Figure 2-3.

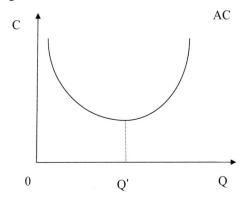

Figure 2-2: Average cost curve and economies of scale

Source: Own diagram

The argument given by economists in favor of regulation was that public utilities like, electricity, gas and water displayed natural monopoly characteristics. They could be provided at a lower cost by a single firm than by a set of competing firms (Grossman and Cole 2003). This would avoid duplication of infrastructure and avoid sunk costs of competing firms. Natural monopoly characteristics was therefore, a case of market failure and an efficient provision of such essential commodities was possible through natural monopolies working under state monitored regulation which would restrict its market power and reduce deadweight losses (the area OAB in Figure 2-4). Under monopoly, the price charged by the utility would be P_m which is much higher than the competitive price P_c. However, by putting a price ceiling (by the regulator) to P_r, the area for the deadweight loss can be reduced.

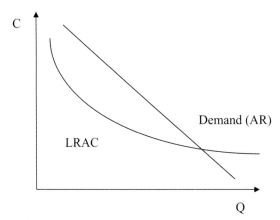

Figure 2-3: A monopolist's long run average cost curve (LRAC)

Source: Own diagram

Demsetz (1968) challenged the logic that this was the best way to resolve a natural monopoly problem. In fact, Demsetz argued that monopolists are prevented by market conditions themselves to charge monopoly prices without even the need for intervention through regulation. The theory of natural monopoly predicts that two firms cannot survive when the average cost per unit keeps falling because one firm will expand production to reduce the selling price and hence eliminate the other. This helps the incumbent firm achieve market power and subsequently charge monopoly price. However, Demsetz points out to at least two problems in this line of argument. First, bidding rivals need not share in the total production with the incumbent firm as they can directly contract with the buyers and the best bidder can win a patronage. Secondly, monopoly price may not be a natural outcome of an unregulated market as the number of rival bidders can be large and hence the final contracted price could be low enough to match the average cost. Therefore he proposed that even if competition cannot be introduced at the level of production, the management of a natural monopoly could be awarded to a franchisee based on competitive bidding. This way efficiency could be increased as it would lead to low price and better management. This was a powerful argument and not only did it push the logic of regulation to the limits but also lay the foundation of the future work of Stigler. Stigler proposed the 'theory of regulation' which was essentially an interest group theory, underlining state coercion as the reason why regulation existed. However, what Demsetz had proposed as some theoretical case of a franchisee contract based model, actually existed even before regulation by commission was introduced (Priest 1993). It existed from the early 19th century up to early 20th century when it was replaced by regulation. Although the franchisee model worked quite well it had several problems (*ibid.*). But before we understand that it is important to know how the electricity sector evolved over time.

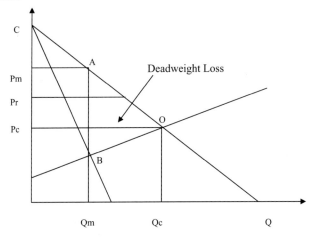

Figure 2-4: Problems of natural monopoly and deadweight losses

Source: Own diagram

2.2.2 Franchisee Model, Edison and John R. Commons

In the beginning (late 19th century and early 20th century) electricity sector was organized as a set of large-scale vertically integrated utilities which were either state-owned or privately owned (Rose and McDonald 1991; Joskow 2008). They were regulated in a rate-of-return style through government controlled commissions. The origin of this form of public utility regulation lies in the US which was at the center of all forms of electricity sector evolutions and continues to remain so (although the dominant model of deregulation as currently applied in most of the developing countries has its origin in UK, a subject we will return to later in the thesis). It may come as a surprise to some that the original implementation of rate-of-return regulation through public commissions was done under the influential Wisconsin institutional economist, John R. Commons (Hausman and Neufeld 2002; Grossman and Cole 2003). As Hausman and Neufeld (2002: p. 1050) put it:

> "The evolution of the electric-power industry in the United States has been heavily influenced by the institutional structure under which it has operated. Beginning in the

first decade of the twentieth century, electric utilities in an increasing number of states were subjected to rate-of-return regulation".

In fact, the concept of a rate-of-return public utility regulation originated in the management of railroads. That was transplanted to the regulation of electric public utilities. There has been a debate about the real motivation behind regulation of both railroads and the public utilities (Stigler and Friedland 1962; Anderson 1981; Kennedy 1991). Some proposed the public interest theories which suggest that such regulation was introduced to protect consumer interests while some invoked the capture theories which suggest that it was essentially to preserve the monopoly status and hence rents. Both these debates however focused on pricing and market structure as key drivers. But as Hausman and Neufeld (2002) point out interestingly, that the actual reason for favoring of state regulation was to raise enough capital through financial solvency of utilities (*ibid. p. 1051*):

> "The problem of raising capital in the early days of the electric utility industry (prior to the adoption of regulation) was enormous, a condition that may have retarded the nation's electrification, and one that has not been fully appreciated. Regulation reduced the risk of investing in an electric utility, thus making utility bonds and stocks more attractive, increasing the availability of capital, and lowering its price. Consumers benefited as well because increased investment enabled the production of more electricity, which, in an era in which there were substantial economies of scale, lowered its price".

This argument has a striking resemblance to the conditions and situations facing those economies where the electricity sector has been recently liberalized and brought under independent regulation. The main reason why electricity sector, for example in India, needed to be reformed was to generate enough capital so as to make the sector financially viable. Yet the relevance of vertical integration subject to state-regulation has been completely sidelined. This is a point to which is discussed later in Chapter 4 (Problem of Private Investment), where we make similar arguments. For the time being, it is worthy to note that this historical similarity is often overlooked. Starting from Thomas Edison himself in 1882, all private owners of electric utilities emphasized on the capital intensity of electricity production as its main handicap. For example, as these figures from the US Department of Commerce and Labor show that for a period up to 1902 the total investments made by electric utilities were to the tune of $483 million whereas the profits earned were only $16 million per annum. How did the utilities raise funds for continued investment? One way was by paying equipment suppliers in the form of capital stocks and bonds which were subsequently held in the form of investment trusts that combined stocks from many utilities. This gave rise to the utility holding companies whose profits depended exclusively on the efficient management of the operating utilities. But there was hardly any industrial structure for electricity. Most of the utilities were small and franchise based, facing competition from each other as well as from self-generating firms. Although majority of the utilities were privately owned around 23% were municipality owned (*ibid.*). The period from 1900-1906 was of consolidation and creation of vertically integrated utilities mainly driven by the problems of stiff inter-franchisee competition, lack of ability to reap economies of scale and the difficulties in raising capital. Another problem was extraction of rent by the municipalities as the utilities needed to take special permit from the municipality so as to get the rights to use public streets for transmission. This gave the municipalities a kind of regulatory power and a way to increase consumer benefits through bargaining for low price. This added to the financial woes of the utilities. This also foreshadowed what later would be termed by economists as a case of ex-post political opportunism through expropriation of utility rents (Spiller and Tommasi 2005). In a way, municipal regulation was a pre-cursor to the rate-of-return regulation.

However, the existing problems set a tone among private utility owners to move away from the franchisee model and towards the preservation of a monopoly status of utility 'whose charges would be set by public regulators to be based on cost plus a reasonable profit'(McDonald 1962). This point was so far ignored by students of regulation who presume anti-trust or natural monopoly considerations to be the main motivation behind this. Yet, the main argument for this form of regulation was to make raising capital easy by lowering interest rates through adequate returns on utility stocks. As there were strong opinions for and against regulation, a 21 member committee was set up to study the merits and de-merits of both the models. A three volume report came out as a result of a detailed study of the utility sectors of both US and the UK. Some members were supportive of the municipal franchisee model whereas some were very critical sighting assurance of investor returns as key criteria (Hausman and Neufeld 2002: p. 1059):

> "Manager and investor must have guarantee that where they have sown they may reap.... Give a company the perpetual and exclusive franchise enjoyed by the municipality, with reasonable protection and regulation, and its bonds will sell as well as the bonds of the city for money borrowed on plant and franchise".

At this point, John R. Commons used the insights from the report to draft a Wisconsin law in 1907 which established state commissions to regulate electric utilities. As Commons states in his autobiography (Commons 1934: p. 120), 'I adopted nearly the whole of the recommendations signed by nineteen of the twenty-one members of the investigating committee of the Civic Federation'. The same year New York passed a similar law and the movement spread rapidly. In a span of few years most of the states in US adopted the model on independent regulation through a guaranteed 'rate-of-return' over the cost of production. It is clear from these historical facts that the chief motivation of state regulation and its acceptance by the electricity utilities were to ease the financial risk and reduce borrowing costs and not preserve market power as is often claimed by theorists in favor of de-regulation. However, did the introduction of regulation actually lead to the intended benefits? Hausman and Neufeld (2002) tested this using data of electric utility bonds for the period 1910 to 1919. They also studied relation between regulation and output using state level data from 1902 to 1927 so as to study the relation between regulation and output. Indeed, they found evidence that state-regulation did lower borrowing costs and also led to an improvement in output as a result of higher investment and lower indebtedness (*ibid.*).

2.2.3 The 'End of Natural Monopoly' and Williamson's Challenge

This brings us back to Demsetz's argument, which although appeared original and appealing during the decade of 1960s, interestingly, seems to have been historically redundant. The franchisee contract model preceded regulation and was eventually given up due to its inherent difficulties. Yet, there was no clearly laid down information about the more important reasons why such a model turned out to be inefficient. In fact there was no theory explaining contractual hazards and the associated high transaction costs. Perhaps this was one reason why the movement of deregulation spread very quickly following a voluminous research agenda by micro-economists attacking the inefficiencies of regulation (Winston 1993). The basic economic logic of Demsetz was to replace sitting commissions with market processes (Priest 1993: p. 304): However, Demsetz's theoretical proposition would be valid only under two assumptions. Firstly, there needs to be a legal regime where a governmental body has absolute rights over the decision to grant or deny the rights of operation to the utility. Secondly, a property rights structure whereby a governmental body owned the capital plant and would then offer franchisee rights to others. However, in the pre-regulation days when franchisee model did actually exist, these conditions did not exist and Demsetz's franchisee model would not have worked at all. There was no legal regime which imposed entry barriers and the municipality did not have exclusive rights over the utilities. Moreover, most of the public utility services were owned by private capital and government hardly made any expenditure in this regard.

Williamson (1976) and Goldberg (1976) posed a serious challenge to Demsetz's logic that the theory of natural monopoly is deficient and competition is possible though auctioning the right to serve (franchise bidding). They showed the limits of this proposition in the presence of specific investments and significant uncertainty for the case of cable TV franchising. In fact Williamson's paper turned out to be one of the most influential works which laid the foundation for a deeper analysis of transaction costs and comparative institutional arrangements. Williamson argued that merely showing that regulation is flawed was not sufficient to prove that it was inferior mode of organizing a transaction. One had to compare it with the deficiencies of the alternative mode which in this case was franchisee bidding. In doing so Williamson looked into contractual details in what he calls a 'micro-analytic' approach. Demsetz in his abstract analysis and in order to simplify his logic had stripped away some 'irrelevant complications' (Williamson 1976: p. 77) like uncertainty, irrational behavior or durability of distribution systems. He also assumed that there would be many non-collusive bidders for the contract and that 'long term contracts for the supply of (nonutility services) are concluded satisfactorily in the market place without the aid of regulation' (Demsetz 1968: p. 64). But Williamson differed with the idea that contracts are complete and free of *ex-post* hazards. Whether they were once-for-all contracts, incomplete long-term contracts or re-current short term contracts, bounded rationality and uncertainty would lead to the hazards of opportunism. The contracts cannot be specified to an extent where monitoring is costless. Owing to contractual incompleteness and the hazards associated with it, Williamson proposed that regulation will be a viable alternative (Williamson 1976: p. 61-103):

"At the risk of oversimplification, regulation may be described contractually as a highly incomplete form of long-term contracting in which (1) the regulatee (*sic.*) is assured an overall fair rate of return, in exchange for which (2) adaptations to changing circumstances are successively introduced without the costly haggling that attends such changes when parties to the contract enjoy greater autonomy... (a)n unbiased assessment of the abstract properties of alternative modes will be facilitated by examining the transactional attributes of each in microanalytic detail. It will be useful for this purpose to regard rate of return regulation as a highly incomplete form of contracting in which the prospects for windfall gains and losses are strictly limited and, in principle and sometimes in fact, adaptations to changing circumstances are introduced in a low cost, non-acrimonious way. The frequency and extent to which such adaptations are required and the differential ease with which these are effectuated by alternative modes are important in making an informed comparative institutional choice".

Williamson not only laid down a theoretical proposal that under conditions of high transaction costs, contracts will eventually be incomplete and regulation would be a preferred mode of organizing such complex transactions, but with this paper, also opened up a new world of 'economics through the lens of contract'. The essence of this approach is a *comparative institutional assessment* which stresses that various institutional arrangements exist so as to minimize the transaction costs. This was indeed a truly 'positive' explanation of why regulation existed: because for certain transactions and under specific conditions, it minimizes the costs of exchange which would otherwise be insurmountable under a non-regulatory institutional set-up such as franchisee bidding or deregulated markets. As we shall see in the next section Levy and Spiller (1994) use this 'lens of contract' to study the problem of regulation.

They take transaction as a unit of analysis and treat regulation as a design problem, bringing the focus back to regulatory governance from regulatory incentives.

2.3 Regulatory Governance

What do we actually mean by regulatory governance? In the spirit of Williamson's concept of economic governance, Levy and Spiller (1994) seminal paper distinguishes between regulatory governance and regulatory incentives. While the later basically deal with rules related to utility pricing, subsidies etc. the former is defined as "the mechanism that societies use to constrain regulatory discretion and to resolve conflicts that arise in relation to these constraints" (*ibid. p. 205*). Why is regulatory governance so fundamental to evolving power markets? This can be easily understood, if we take the example of new private investment in power generation utilities. The investments are asset-specific (with little or no alternative use), there are significant economies of scale in electricity production and the product is widely consumed. Specific investment means that a substantial portion of that is sunk (due to low potential for alternative use) and hence there is a lock-in where, once committed, the firm may be willing to operate at even lesser than average costs. Economies of scale imply that tendencies for natural monopoly will always be at the boundaries. Moreover, wide consumption means that the set of consumers will match the set of voters, thus implicating political interests. These three factors combined, increase the probability of government trying to expropriate rents through administrative means (for example, limiting pricing flexibility) (Spiller 2010). In such a case by keeping prices low, the governments can garner political support while deflating the incentives to invest. Hence, unless there is an assurance against expropriation through regulatory commitment, investments won't take place (Spiller and Tommasi 2005). Such an assurance comes from stable market rules i.e. institutions and hence is a governance issue.

Actually, the governance and incentive aspects together constitute the design of regulation. Standard economic theories of regulation have dealt mainly with the demand side i.e. regulation as a product desired by stakeholders. But new institutional economics perceives it as a design problem (Çetin 2009) and hence sees the *supply of regulation* as a product of the complex interaction among the institutions of regulation (Spiller and Tommasi 2005). In fact regulation is viewed as entrenched in the complexities of a country's public policy. While the Chicago school (Stigler 1971) views rent seeking and distributional effects as crucial to public policy outcomes, the institutional view holds that a country's institutional endowment (i.e. political and social systems) determine the nature of the regulatory institutions and hence the sectoral performance. It similarly differs from the 'Incentive Theory' school (Laffont and Tirole 1993) by emphasizing that the optimal contracting schemes are also dependent on the institutional environment. The seminal paper in this was by Levy and Spiller (1994) which defines regulatory governance as the framework of regulation. This inspired research into the determinants of the regulatory process with the underlying theme that regulatory governance is heavily influenced by the institutional endowments of a particular country. The composition of institutional endowments is based on five types of classification by (North 1990):

i.   The legislative and executive institutions, which means the *mechanisms* by which legislators are chosen, laws are made and implemented.
ii. The country's judicial institutions, meaning the mechanisms which lead to judicial supply.
iii. The country's informal norms and customs which influence or constrain individual and collective behaviour.
iv. The character of contending social interests including the role of ideology.
v.   The administrative capabilities of the nation and its institutions.

Levy and Spiller (1994) has also drawn attention to the requisite regulatory arrangements essential for sustained private investment. A key insight from this strand of research was that the success or failure of a regulatory structure (primarily in attracting sustained investment but not restricted to that) will depend on how well it fits the prevailing institutional endowments. For example if the regulatory governance takes the form of independent regulation in an institutional environment which does not facilitate true independence of the regulator from the political actors or the legislative, then this will hamper the credibility of the whole regulatory system. In an extension of the work by Levy and Spiller, Stern and Holder (1999) study the role of informal accountability in the regulatory process in the spirit of points iii and iv above, while Levy and Spiller focused on the formal accountability of the regulatory institutions related to points i and ii. The Levy and Spiller framework provides a detailed analysis of the relationship between the regulatory design and a nation's institutional environment. Typically, there are two types of political actors, one interested in short term gains (being myopic) whereas the other having a vision for long term benefits. Limiting political powers have a cost though, in terms of the inflexibility to respond to exogenous shocks. And the benefits accrue if policies are more stable and predictable creating a better environment for investments. The politicians interact among themselves in the manner of a game, bearing conflicting interests. Regulatory institutions are contractual outcomes of this game aimed at limiting powers of the political actors. When the actors have an infinite horizon and are patient, the outcome is a stable Nash equilibrium where the public policy will be flexible, limiting political opportunism and promoting trust towards investment. But when the political actors are myopic (having high discount rates), policies will be guided by short term distributive and political gains, leading to an unstable outcome. Under this outcome, rules that emerge will be inflexible and less adaptive to technological or economic shocks. Hence regulatory policies will be *inadequate* in providing investment safeguards. It is in these institutional environments that policy makers will enter into agreements limiting their *ex post* powers. But these need strong enforcement mechanisms, in the absence of which own political interests would drive the equilibrium to simple, inflexible rules which may not adjust well either to economic shocks or politics.

The basic proposition of this strand of argument is that regulatory policies are highly dependent on the institutional environment. In order to study the characteristics of these elements which determine the institutional environment one needs to analyze variables like "key political actors, determinants of their payoffs, institutional veto points, variables determining who holds those institutional veto points and at which point in time (related to parameters of stochastic description of the political process), horizons of key political actors and their determinants, institutional features (constitution, budget procedures, informal practices) that facilitate unchecked moves by some actors, independence and strength of Supreme Court or equivalent, characteristics of the bureaucracy" (Spiller and Tommasi 2005). And these are the *institutional* sources of regulatory commitment.

2.3.1 Regulatory Commitment

An appropriate regulatory design tries to balance the trade-off between commitment (for example, limiting government opportunism) and flexibility. This design in turn is highly influenced by the institutional environment. For example in well-functioning democracies regulatory policies like incentive schemes can be operational due to the sufficient independence with the regulators, whereas in less democratic states this may not be possible. Thus the resultant regulatory governance will be defined by the existing institutional endowments. Their relevance is more when it comes to network industries where specific investments are required, unless there is an assurance against expropriation, investments won't take place in the absence of strong regulatory governance. Of the different features of governance observed *first* is the delegation to independent agencies. Spiller and Urbiztondo (1994) propose that "the probability of observing independent agencies is higher in systems characterized by divided government". However, when legislature is weak and political rotation is high, bureaucracy will be highly politicized and hence there will be lower degrees of independence. *Second* is the design of administrative processes. The ability and the mandate of the court to review all administrative agencies' policies are very important for the participation of interest groups in the regulatory process. A *third* feature is independence of the judiciary. As per theory, in the presence of unified governments political subjugations of courts will be higher as compared to parliamentary systems with multi-party coalitions. *Fourth* is the question of 'policy making transparency' which requires 'the existence of a set of institutions that cannot be exogenously created'. The purpose of transparency is to facilitate the active participation of interest groups in the administrative process.

In reality many countries with more or less unified forms of government (e.g., Japan, UK, and Mexico) have patterns of private ownership of utilities and have adopted contract law as the chosen mode of regulatory governance. The advantage of this system is that any change will involve the contracting parties. This however comes at a cost of inflexibility where a contract once drawn, administrative changes cannot be made easily. When courts see license-based regulatory contracts as binding, they will not fail as a source of regulatory stability. Thus contract based regulation is a mechanism to provide protection against opportunism in both cases of weak as well as strong government systems, which generally have either highly unstable or highly rigid policies. So when there is change in the political preferences or regimes, leading to legislative changes investment is insulated. In situations where regulation is already based on contract law, changes would have to be done including the contracted firm in the process. This additional veto power to the investor is another safeguard. This is the reason why many countries adopted this system of contractual regulation. Thus "institutions of regulations arise to deal with basic transaction problems among policy makers" and how effective or credible regulatory structures are depends on "the nature of the institutional environment, and the way it affects the policy makers' capacity to enter into complex inter temporal agreements among themselves...agreements that have direct consequences for firms' investment incentives and performance" (Spiller and Tommasi 2005: p. 538). Basically it is about credible commitments and hence, leitmotif of the thesis.

To sum up so far, the theoretical discussions have drawn insights mainly from two different (though related) approaches: the literature on 'institutions of regulation' in the tradition of Levy and Spiller (1994), followed by important studies on this (Stern and Holder 1999; Spiller and Tommasi 2005; Çetin 2009; Spiller 2010) and transaction cost economics (Williamson 1976, 1985; Dixit 1996). Providing it the taxonomy of transaction cost regulation (TCR), Spiller (2013) contends that this approach gives a ground breaking opportunity to analyze (positively) the institutional reasons for why empirically the standard form of regulatory governance (based on UK and US models) has been successful in some instances but has been in troubled waters in many emerging and developing economies. It can also be useful in prescribing institutionally compatible regulatory governance systems which are stable or sustainable. It brings back the focus on the institutional determinants of regulatory commitment, which otherwise in the neo-classical literature can be achieved by merely an assured rate-of-return (Newbery 1999). And based on the theoretical discussion above, it can be deduced that the supply of regulation is not only a static outcome of the complex interactions between the institutions of regulation but a dynamic outcome of complex transactions (having temporal dimensions) between the *actors* involved in the regulatory process. Moreover, the structure of regulatory governance comprising of such actors is a multi-level one, in which the independent regulator is only one element. Additionally, there are key *emerging actors* (akin to third parties, for example civil society groups representing consumer interests) whose influence on regulatory supply needs to be investigated for a greater insight into the institutional endowment of a specific system.

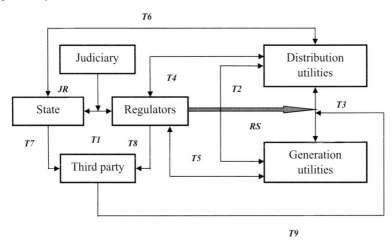

Figure 2-5: Supply of regulation

Source: Own diagram

2.3.2 Supply Side of Regulation

Figure 2-5 presents a stylized illustration to visualize the propositions stated above. The arrow RS indicates the output of the regulator i.e. regulatory policy or the supply of regulation. The other arrows map the transactions between different actors. T1 is mainly the political and bureaucratic transactions between the elected government and the independent regulators. There exists a kind of political contract between them which has principal agent component. These contracts are implicit (or unwritten) in nature but enforceable. T2 shows the transactions that take place between the regulators and the utilities. This takes the form of a regulatory contract, which is again implicit in nature. T3 represents the transactions that take place among the utilities, for example between the distribution and the generation companies. T4, T5 are those transactions which take place among the regulator and the individual utilities outside the regulatory contract. This assumes special significance in those situations where the unbundled utility is state owned. These will involve bureaucratic interactions. T6 maps the relations between the state and the generation utilities. These transactions are of economic and political nature and have a tendency towards rent seeking. JR shows judicial transactions which is technically meant to review regulatory decisions in terms of their constitutional validity. T7, T8 and T9 represent the role and transactions of the third parties with the state, the regulators and the utilities. Definition of third parties is context specific, but generally they are understood to include civil society groups (representing consumer interests), the media or private interests.

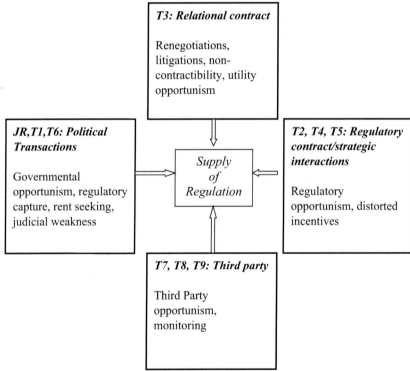

Figure 2-6: Ex post contractual hazards

Source: Own diagram

However, implicit or explicit contracts to regularize these different transactions, and sometimes within different levels, does manifest significant hazards. A simple illustration of this hazard is presented in Figure 2-6. For example, the transactions symbolized by T1, T6 and JR are political in nature and present the threats of governmental opportunism, regulatory capture, rent- seeking or judicial weakness. T2, T4 and T5 fall under implicit principal agent regulatory contracts (Stern and Holder 1999) invoking strategic interactions and risks of regulatory opportunism or distorted incentives. T3 representing explicit relational contracts between utilities (like the power purchase agreements) pose the threats of renegotiations, litigations, non-contractibility and utility opportunism. T7, T8 and T9 can lead to third party opportunism in case they represent private interests but can also play the role of additional monitoring in case they represent genuine consumer interests. Hence our theoretical set-up proposes, as shown by these simple stylized illustrations, that the supply of regulation is not merely a product of the deliberations[2] of a benevolent welfare maximizing regulatory agent, but an outcome of a set of complex transactions between various actors enmeshed within a dynamic institutional environment. Not only do all of these transactions have some impact or the other on the ultimate regulatory outcome, but they also change over time, creating additional complexities. Thus regulatory supply cannot be understood independent of the multiple levels of contractual hazards which arise due to the complex structure of multi-level regulatory governance

2.4 Summary

It then boils down to the question of whether the reform process in India generates adequate levels of commitment through minimizing contractual hazards and related transaction costs. Although the theoretical foundations for investigating this have been laid down, this is essentially an empirical question. The thesis therefore never loses emphasis on that. Moreover, to maintain a specific focus investigations are restricted to the generation segment. This is consistent with the fact that the key motivation for initiating power sector reforms was to ramp up the generation capacity in a way that all demand can be met. Thus, the performance assessment of this particular segment will be an adequate indicator, although further research should use similar analytical tools for the other components of the electricity supply chain. In the next chapter the methodological approach used to answer the various questions raised throughout the thesis is laid down. Differentiating between methods and methodology, the approach of New Institutional Economics (NIE) as practiced by its founding fathers is explained.

---

[2] It is to be noted that a general criticism of the traditional economic theories of regulation could be the fact that the role of discourses in shaping the internal interpretation of an institutional structure is often overlooked. While this is not the objective of the current thesis, it is acknowledged that the literature needs to account more of this in the future.

3. Methodology: Coase, Pragmatism and Micro-analytics[*]

Overview

Over the last few decades New Institutional Economics (NIE) has evolved as one of the most popular branches in economic sciences. Judging by its empirical success in the field of public policy - its brazen openness to insights from other disciplines, the ability to relax unrealistic neo-classical assumptions, and still make a set of coherent economic predictions - this trend is likely to only slant upwards. Yet, and precisely because of its strengths as listed, there is the risk of a methodological blurriness which may erode the unique appeal of NIE. It may get subsumed under standard and methodologically narrower but clearer, traditional approaches in economics. In this chapter we therefore make an attempt to delineate and for the benefit of the general student of economics, the distinct methodological convictions of two of the founding fathers of NIE, Ronald Coase and Oliver Williamson. We show how they used methods to approach economic problems which were empirical, substantive, micro-analytic and non-reductive. This is in contrast to the traditional neo-classical economic methodology which is *deductive* and relies more on theoretical construction than on empirical observation. But NIE's unique methodological and realistic appeal, we argue, lies in *abduction*, the ability to move from empirical observation to theory-building.

3.1   Introduction

'It requires a very unusual mind to undertake the analysis of the obvious' (Posner 1993: p. 205). Remember Newton and gravity, Einstein and relativity? Arguably, Coase and transaction costs fall in the same category. When Coase was writing his first important article (The Nature of the Firm, 1937) rational choice theory was not the ruling paradigm in economic theory, formal modeling of economic activity as a major program was yet to develop, the concept of econometrics as the dominant empirical method of testing economic predictions did not exist, World War II had not begun and Oliver Williamson was only 5 years old. By the time he wrote his latest article 'Saving Economics from Economists' (Coase 2012), economics had re-incarnated several times, his work had inspired more than one Nobel Prize and global sustainability had become a real concern. What has, however, not changed is his conviction that economics is *essentially* substantive and that a useful economic methodology is *necessarily* empirical.

---

[*]   A version of this chapter has been presented at the First WINIR Conference, September 11-14 in London. Modified parts of this chapter are under review as a journal article in The Cambridge Journal of Economics as of 20th October, 2014

In his 1974 article 'The Lighthouse in Economics', Ronald Coase launches an attack on the standard theoretical approach to economic problems. Classical economists have often used the example of lighthouses to explain the public good problem and have concluded that they *have to be* provided by the government. Yet, as Coase notes, none of them actually studied the provisioning of lighthouses historically, which were in fact often provided by private enterprises. Coase notes his surprise that,

> "(H)ow is it that these great men (...Mill, Sidgwick, Pigou, Samuelson) have, in their economic writings, been led to make statements about lighthouses which are misleading as to the facts, whose meaning, if thought about in a concrete fashion, is quite unclear, and which, to the extent that they imply a policy conclusion, are very likely wrong? . . . Despite the extensive use of the lighthouse example in the literature, no economist, to my knowledge, has ever made a comprehensive study of lighthouse finance and administration. The lighthouse is simply plucked out of the air to serve as an illustration . . . This seems to me to be the wrong approach" (Coase 1974a: p. 211).

In a similar vein as the 'lighthouse' example, Coase (2006) points out to the inaccuracy of the Fisher Body-GM merger case, a widely used example in the field of industrial organization which explains 'hold-up' as a reason for vertical integration. Coase's core purpose is not how lighthouses should be organized and financed[1], or about the veracity of opportunistic behavior in explaining vertical integration. Rather it is about the proper use of examples. In fact it is about methodology. Yet, very little work has been done on the 'methodological and conceptual foundations' of institutional theorists such as Coase, Williamson and others (Mäki et al. 1993: p. 5). Although there has been some genuine interest (Posner 1993; Mäki 1998; Hsiung 2001; Wang 2003) on the methodological aspect of Coase's work, we feel it deserves greater emphasis.

Therefore, in this chapter, we not only re-emphasize the empirical nature of economic methodology in Coasean terms but also show through the example of Williamson, how this could also lead to theory development and without the need for abstraction. However, this demands a paradigm shift in methodology (from deduction to abduction), and in the use of methods (from singularity to plurality). The rest of the chapter is structured as follows: in Section 3.2, we begin by clarifying what methodology means in Coasean terms and how it can be often confused with methods. We then explain why Coase's approach (or

---

[1] There is some criticism that even as Coase made valid observations on the provisioning aspect of British lighthouses, he was not quite accurate on the financing aspect (Bertrand 2006) has shown that lighthouses were made profitable due to a protectionist regime of the British Crown and were not after all so 'private' as Coase claimed. However, Bertrand also acknowledges that this criticism was also based on application of the Coasean method of analysis i.e. historical case studies. In a sense the criticism granted the larger point Coase was making about methodology through his lighthouse example.

methodology) makes for an interesting case. In Section 3.3, we describe how Coase's approach has inspired one of the most successful fields in economic theory: the new institutional economics and transaction cost economics (TCE) in specific. The section describes how Williamson's approach was radical to the previous attempts at reducing complexity and making it pragmatic in a real sense. We examine Coase's own convictions and show how, even if unintended, they have similarities with a deep philosophically grounded tradition: pragmatism. In Section 3.4, we argue why this substantive and empirical view demands methodological pluralism, including the use of case studies. In Section 3.5 we conclude by proposing that unless NIE is on guard against any compromise on its clear methodological stand, it stands the risk of losing its unique appeal and the cutting edge.

3.2 Economic Methodology: A Brief Overview

Although often used interchangeably, the terms methodology and methods are different and have specific connotations. In the words of Mark Blaug:

> "A fatal ambiguity surrounds the expression "the methodology of . . ." The term *methodology* is sometimes taken to mean the technical procedures of a discipline, being simply a more impressive-sounding synonym for *methods*. More frequently, however, it denotes an investigation of the concepts, theories and basic principles of reasoning of a subject..." (Blaug 1992: p. xxv).

Methodology is a *theory* about the *rules* of scientific method (Popper 1959: p. 49). Simply put, methodology is the study (or a theory) of methods and hence at least philosophically, if not rhetorically, different. Specifically, economic methodology has been engaged for the most part with 'questions of theory confirmation or disconfirmation of empirical theory choice' (Hausman 1989)[2]. In other words, economic methodology is about trying to make sure whether a piece of economic work is good science or not. Hausman provides (in his own words), a 'tendentious' survey of economic methodology (*ibid.*) by stating four key methodological positions prevalent in the literature: the *deductivist*, the *positivist* (Popperian), the *predictionist* and the *eclectic* views. We begin by a discussion of those that are dominant in the mainstream economic literature. Hausman attributes *deductivist* methodology mainly to John Stuart Mill, in whose view matters of economics ('political economy' as it was known at that time) were so complex, and influenced by so many causal forces, that induction was not an adequate method to study them. Induction is concerned with 'properties of all members of a class based on an examination of a subset of that class' (Bromley 2006). It is the process, as Bromley suggests, of going from

---

[2] Since economic theory has been somewhat detached from real world messy issues, Hausman's reference here is to 'economic methodology' and not economic ontology in general.

case (assumptions) to result (observed phenomena) to rule (general proposition). The classic inductive proposition (*ibid.*), -all swans are white- is based on an assumption being confirmed by an observation of a subset of swans leading to a general rule. However, swans in Australia are black (*ibid.*) and therefore the rule based on induction does not apply outside the observed subset. Mill, and the deductivists, point to this inability to observe the entire set as a limitation of the inductive methodology to study economic problems. Marshall, although opined that induction and deduction should be used as per the requirement, had an inclination for induction. As stated by Coase (1975: p. 28), 'Marshall himself, of course, was a great collector of economic facts not only from such sources as Government reports but also from visits to factories and from questioning businessmen and workers'.

Deductive methodology on the other hand is concerned with results (outcomes) being derived out of certain assumptions (or rules) without the need to actually look into the actual subject of interest. To use Bromley's syllogism (Bromley 2006: p. 89): If the *rule* (axiom) is that 'all the beans from this bag are white'; if the *case* is that 'these beans are from that bag (with a label white)'; then the *result* is that 'these beans are white'. So the result is deduced from the rule and the case without the need to actually look into the actual colors of the beans. Bromley then gives a parallel from international trade theory where assumptions (rules) could be that consumers are self-interested and rational, and that factors of production are freely mobile. Based on these assumptions the economist builds a model and deduces the result that there is gain from free trade when each country produces the good in which it has comparative advantage. This claim is then empirically tested for its accuracy and precision.

The positivist methodology (a part of logical positivism) stems from Karl Popper's stand that it is almost impossible to demonstrate that something is true, but it is possible to show that something is not true. This gave rise to *falsificationism* where Popper stated that scientific propositions are those that can be, at least theoretically, falsifiable. This distinguishes them from mere 'statements' or unfounded claims (Blaug 1992). This approach is critical of the assumptions in deductivist logic, which according to positivists, are qualified claims which are not falsifiable. Hausman gives the example of a statement: '*ceteris paribus,* variable inputs will diminish'; which, because of its vagueness, lacks empirical content and is unfalsifiable. Positivism has led to the most acceptable form of statistical inference, widely applied through econometric methods, where the statistical test is designed not to prove the core hypothesis, but to disprove the contradictory 'null' hypothesis. An alternate hypothesis is accepted as valid when the null hypothesis cannot be rejected within a certain probabilistic range.

Predictionism, is a part of positivism, most famously associated with Milton Friedman and his work 'The Methodology of Positive Economics' (Friedman 1966). Friedman's three basic propositions were (Caldwell 1993): realism of a theory's assumptions does not matter for its assessment; predictive adequacy should be the main criteria for a theory; simpler theories are more preferable than those that are complex. He asserts that the goals of a positive science are predictive, not at all explanatory and that a 'theory which enables one to make reliable predictions is a good theory' (Friedman 1966: p. 7).

Even if not the focus of this chapter, but it is easy to show that Friedman's propositions are fundamentally problematic. Friedman misses the point that it is the assumption that provides the explanation for the prediction. The realism of assumptions is important because prediction is very context-specific. For any assumption it is always possible to find a valid prediction in some context or the other. But in a different context those same assumptions may not be able to lead to the same predictions. However, if in any context the assumptions are shown to be realistic, then there is a justification and high likelihood to pre-suppose that it will work in other contexts too, without finding it necessary to actually test them in a different setting. It is not difficult to imagine that this is one key reason why most of the economic policies which work very well in Western economies do not give the same results in developing countries.

3.3   Coasean Methodology and New Institutional Economics

3.3.1   Elements of Coase's Methodology

Where does the approach of Coase fall in all of this? We argue that although Coase was not consciously adhering to any particular methodological stream, in his own ways he paved the way for a methodological approach which was not only inclusive of some of the key elements across those discussed above, but also helped *simplify* and *broaden* them. A critical feature of Coase is that he uses a *benchmark* approach. In his 1937 paper, The Nature of the Firm (Coase 1937) he uses the market mechanism as a benchmark to compare how and why a firm exists and in his 1960 (Problem of Social Cost) paper, he uses the condition of zero transaction costs as a benchmark to explore how resources will be utilized in the real world (Hsiung 2001).

However, Coase in his *Problem of Social Cost* paper (Coase 1960) is 'not a doctrinaire adherent to laissez-faire' (Posner 1993: p. 202); rather his insistence is on comparing the costs of government intervention and not merely assuming them to be zero. His persistent resistance to government intervention should be seen in this methodological context, of comparative assessment, rather than an alleged personal inclination for private arrangements. Thankfully, this has indeed inspired a more general comparative institutional analysis program especially as pursued by Williamson and the transaction cost economists (Williamson 1991, 1998; Aoki 2001; Madhok 2002; Rosser Jr and Rosser 2004). The core idea is to look at various forms of industrial organization (markets or vertically integrated firms) and see which minimizes total costs (including transaction costs) compared to others[3]. This program has been widely recognized as an 'empirical success story'[4] (Williamson 1996) and also appears to be Coase's methodological *leitmotif* i.e. comparing the costs of alternative arrangements. In fact this so-called benchmark approach is an extension of the concept of opportunity cost where Coase perceives the preferred institutional arrangement to have a higher opportunity cost than its immediate next alternative. But the difference in Coase's approach from other game-theoretic based comparative institutional analytical approaches (Aoki 2001) is that the choice and constraint set are not derived from economic theory but gathered from knowledge about those that real economic actors face. This makes its appeal unique and applicable.

It is interesting to view Coase's stand as compared to that of Gary Becker (Hsiung 2001), who has not only been his colleague at the University of Chicago and a fellow Nobel laureate but also one who took upon himself to expand the domain of economics by applying economic methodology to problems erstwhile considered outside the bounds of economics. Hsiung shows that although Becker's approach appears to be more general owing to its use of mathematical reasoning (in the tradition of Robbins), it is the approach of Coase which is more general and fruitful in understanding how the economy works. Since Becker's focus is *human behavior*, it requires the assumptions of stable preferences, utility maximization and an idea of the equilibrium. However, since Coase only applies a benchmark for comparative analysis, these assumptions can be dispensed with, expanding the scope of empirical investigation. The result can be seen in the ways in which Coase's two famous articles (1937, 1960) have influenced the fields of industrial organization and law and economics (*ibid.*). The reason why Coase is immensely popular in the legal tradition is because "...the legal scholars may be suspicious of the concepts implicit in the rational choice model, such as rationality, maximization, and equilibrium: by contrast, Coase's benchmark approach is intuitive, is simple, and can be applied easily....." (Schwab 1989).

In terms of applicability too, Hsiung argues and we agree that, Coase has an edge over Becker, although the contributions of Becker in expanding the domain of economics is irrefutable as he brought into a formal analytical framework those factors like, discrimination, social income and marriage among others. But for the general reader it is difficult to accept those concepts as being driven by maximization principles and towards some kind of equilibrium. Coase's

---

[3]   Williamson's concept of transaction costs as an operational tool to design efficient governance structures could be a highly stylized version of the reality where often the sequencing of rules and forms governance precedes analysis of such costs. Therefore, the element of alignment is a more convincing principle compared to design, when it comes to applying TCE.

[4]   Williamson, like Coase, is another 'lighthouse', whose contribution to methodology we will discuss in details below.

benchmark approach on the other hand, is entirely positive and doesn't emphasize value or normativity. In the spirit of Coase's methodology, Hsiung uses Becker as a *benchmark* to make the elements of Coase's approach explicit! Our intention, however, in using this comparison is that Becker represents to a certain degree the *deductivist* (in the tradition of logical positivism) mainstream methodology in economics, also known as the formal one (Wang 2003), which has been dominant over the past century or so. On the other hand, Coase's approach represents a fairly different approach to economic problems which is more empirical, pragmatic and uses what some would call the process of *abduction* (Bromley 2006). This is a topic we will return to in a later section.

The second aspect of Coase's approach is his lack of enthusiasm for 'high economic theory'. While Coase is certainly not completely dismissive of economic theorizing, it is reasonable to believe that he is not very satisfied with the way it has shaped up in recent times. If he was at all against all forms of theory then his criticism of the old institutional school as "waiting for a theory or a fire"[5] (Coase 1984: p. 230) would appear rather strange. In fact, judging from his influence on economic theory, Coase is among the most original theorists of the 20th century and hence cannot be anti-theory. Instead, what explains this position is the emphasis he puts on "economic theories being realistic" (Wang 2003). Although there have been concerns about whether Coase is a realist or not (Mäki 1998), Wang (2003) proposes that Coase's 'primary methodological message lies in his heterodox view of the subject of economics...(which) insists that economics has a unique research subject, i.e., the real world economic system'. This is distinct from the received view which views 'economics as a subject-free discipline characterized by a specific approach with universal applicability'. While the latter view is called the formal one, best epitomized by Gary Becker who believes that 'what most distinguishes economics as a discipline from other disciplines in the social sciences is not its subject matter but its approach' (Becker 1976: p. 5), Coase's view could be called as a substantive view defining economy in terms of its substantive or material (or empirical) concerns i.e. the subject matter. For Coase it is clear that the subject matter and the type of questions asked should be a priority over methods or techniques used to analyze them, which according to him, will follow logically and in thematic accordance. This is also in tune with the view Marshall had on economic methodology (Coase 1975) and is an indicator that Coase is more inclined towards plurality in the choice of methods. That Coase had a wide exposure to a variety of subjects and liked studying different things when at college is a marker to his extra-disciplinary leanings, and has had a deep impact in his methodology (Coase 1988). For Coase, the *research question* is of

---

[5] This view of Coase has been contested (Williamson, 1995) and we will return later to how there are methodological similarities between Coase and some prime followers of American pragmatism (Bromley, 2008; Bromley, 2006).

utmost importance. This is exemplified by his own pursuit in trying to find out as a young student at LSE, the answer to a very interesting research question: Why do firms exist when markets can coordinate all the activities (at least as per price theory)? The methodology which followed included a young Ronald Coase travelling to the US from England on a travelling scholarship, visiting various industrial firms (including Ford and General Motors and their suppliers), meeting key informants and investigating through cross-examination, logic and observation until he found the answer (*ibid.*):

> "Whether a transaction would be organized within the firm …. or whether it would be carried out on the market by independent contractors *depended on a comparison of the costs of carrying out these market transactions* with the costs of carrying out these transactions within an organization, the firm. As I said in my letter of October 10, 1932, my approach succeeded in linking up organization with cost".

The point of departure in Coase's approach as compared to the deductive or the inductive processes is the fact that it puts more faith on (empirical) *observation* and lesser on (theoretical) *inference*. While we do not, for a moment, hold any disparaging view of the other methodological approaches[6], being well aware of their own utilities, this special character of Coasean methodology i.e. of reliance on observation, to our mind, makes it very useful and hence of undeniable importance to economic researchers. At this point we summarize three important messages which come out so far from our discussions about the Coasean methodology:

a. Study of economic system is substantive and empirical. There is a need to look at real problems (or surprises) and analyze them.

b. There has to be a focus on comparative assessment of different economic or social arrangements.

c. The right type of research question is critical and the methods or techniques used to answer them should spring from them, and not the other way round.

In the next section, we show how these precepts have been exemplified and used towards achieving a highly successful research objective by Oliver Williamson.

3.3.2 Williamson's Pragmatic Methodology

The phrase 'New Institutional Economics' was coined by Oliver Williamson (Coase 1988) in order to differentiate from the 'old institutional economics' associated with great intellectuals like John R. Commons, Wesley Mitchell,

---

[6] In fact even Coase is himself quite respectful of the traditional approaches in economics (Coase, 1998: p. 73): "…in saying this I should not be thought to imply that these (traditional) analytical tools are not extremely valuable".

Thorsten Veblen and others. Coase, in his 1998 article in the *American Economic Review*, summarizes the new institutional program succinctly (*ibid. p. 73*):

> "Adam Smith explained that the productivity of the economic system depends on specialization (he says the division of labor), but specialization is only possible if there is exchange-and the lower the costs of exchange (transaction costs if you will), the more specialization there will be and the greater the productivity of the system. But the costs of exchange depend on the institutions of a country: its legal system, its political system, its social system, its educational system, its culture, and so on. In effect it is the institutions that govern the performance of an economy, and it is this that gives the "new institutional economics" its importance for economists".

He continues on to predict that when this complex set of interrelationships, between (and in reference to) various institutions, have been uncovered "then all of economics will have become what we now call 'the new institutional economics'" (*ibid. p. 73*). However, for this to happen a *different approach* (which he did not specify but what we call an *institutional methodology*) needs to be adopted: "it (the change) will come as a result of economists in branches or subsections of economics adopting a different approach, as indeed is already happening" (*ibid. p. 74*). It is only natural that we bring in Oliver Williamson at this point who not only operationalized very successfully (along with other peers working on transaction cost economics) the key ingredient of Coasean methodology i.e. comparative institutional analysis, but also brought it closer to making it a substantial methodological program.

In spite of the fact that Williamson does not entirely agree with Coase's views on substantive economics (Williamson 1994) and believes that economics is 'distinguished more by its approach than by its subject matter', the methodology adopted by Williamson matches to a great degree to that of Coase. Williamson's transaction cost economics (TCE) is essentially empirical (substantive), applies the benchmark approach of comparative assessment, emphasizes on the framing of the right question (which in his case was: what are the boundaries of the firm?) and applies plural techniques ranging from case studies to orthodox statistical methods. The Williamsonian point of departure is, however, the *predictive* intent of TCE. This guided Williamson towards a building a theory which could predict the characteristic transactions under which a particular mode of organization would evolve. Essentially, if an asset was specific and facing the threat of contractual hazards, then conducting that transaction would be risky in a market and vertical integration would be the preferred mode of organizing such transactions. Similarly when a transaction could be done outside a firm at least cost, the boundaries of a firm would be set. Coase pointed a finger towards this direction in his 1937 paper on 'a gap in economic theory' and threw light (as does a lighthouse often) towards *transaction costs*, but did not build up a theory which had predictive empirical content. In our opinion, Williamson successfully continued the methodological tradition of Coase. The ship had sailed by the lighthouse!

Yet, Williamson is not a certified methodologist and did not make much significant comments about it till he elaborated his views in his 2009 article in the *Journal of Economic Methodology*. In that article he mixes three important viewpoints to lay out, and to our knowledge for the first time, what he calls a 'sketch' of a 'pragmatic methodology': that of Solow, Friedman and Nicholas Georgescu-Rogen. From Solow he borrows the three precepts of: keep it simple – get it right – make it plausible, which are re-substantiated by the opinions of Friedman and Georgescu-Rogen. Keeping it simple entails stripping away the inessentials so as to 'focus on the first order effects'. Getting it right means making it logical and making it plausible means to keep it as close to reality as possible. Here Williamson invokes Friedman who says '(m)ost phenomena are driven by a very few central forces. What a good theory does is to simplify, it pulls out the central forces and gets rid of the rest' (Friedman, in Snowdon and Vane (1997: p. 196). This is essentially a response to complexity and ways of dealing with it. As we saw earlier complexity was one of the reasons why people like Mills thought it was unviable for methods of induction to work in economics.

But it is interesting to note a critical *deviation* in Williamson. The only way earlier economists conceived of simplifying complexities was through an increased use of abstract mathematics. Friedman made three propositions with respect to methodology: that realism of theory's assumptions do not matter for its assessment; predictive adequacy should be the main criteria for judgment and; simpler theories are more preferable than those that are complex (Wong 1973). Although Friedman was critical of too much mathematical abstraction these proposition allowed economists to delve more into mathematics (Caldwell 1993). Once that becomes a methodologically dominant paradigm, the next steps prescribed by Solow become contradictory and self-denying. While mathematical constructions can be often logical and 'right', they need not match data or reality. Coase (2006) quotes Niels Bohr whose response to purely mathematical reasoning would be that 'you are not thinking, you are just being logical'. Coase also quotes Pigou's description of Marshall who, '(although) a skilled mathematician …used mathematics sparingly. He saw that excessive reliance on this instrument might lead us astray in pursuit of intellectual toys, imaginary problems not conforming to the conditions of real life' (Coase 1975). In the face of increased use of mathematical abstraction, instead of 'pull(ing) out the central forces and get(ting) rid of the rest', the opposite may happen. This is the primary risk of *reductionism*, a meta-methodological approach which primarily solves complex *physical* phenomena but has found substantial acceptance in economic methodology too. 'Everything is simple and neat – except, of course, the world' (Goldenfeld and Kadanoff 1999). Even in the world of physical science there is an acceptance of the deficiencies of reductionism, specially its inclination for oversimplification (Gallagher and Appenzeller 1999; Farrell et al. 2013). So what did Williamson do so different? Instead of reducing complex phenomena into abstract mathematical formulations, he used a 'micro-analytic' approach by moving away from (what Coase would call) 'blackboard economics' to a fine reading and observation of empirical world. This is the *pragmatic* twist in Williamson's methodology. The fourth precept of Williamson (in addition to the three of Solow), 'derive refutable implications to which (often microanalytic) data are brought to bear' (Williamson 2009: p. 146), only followed naturally. This precept of a predictable, refutable hypothesis led to a theoretical framework which operationalized the core intuitions of Ronald Coase and John R. Commons. In our opinion, Williamson's *micro-analytic* methodology is under-appreciated although its importance cannot be overemphasized. In fact, micro-analytics is not a popular term (yet) in economic methodology and does not have any specific literal connotation. It basically means rotating the lens and looking at the finer micro details of any phenomenon. Any question or puzzle can have not only various hypothetical explanations but also have them at various levels. Let us take for instance a historical question, 'Why did the Berlin Wall Fall[7]'? One answer could be because the period of cold war was ending and it was increasingly unsustainable for the Eastern Bloc to continue with its post-war policies. In fact this was the reason most of us knew as young kids or teenagers in other parts of the world. Another explanation could be that Gorbachev was responding to Reagan's challenge of bringing down the wall and the artificial barriers. Further investigation would reveal that Hungary loosened its border controls with Austria in the latter half of 1989 which led many East Germans escaping to the West. The East German government responded by prohibiting further travel to Hungary and this was one of the reasons which led to series of strong but peaceful demonstrations in Berlin, Leipzig and other places. The exodus of refugees in Czechoslovakia put pressure on the administration there to allow exit through their crossing points over to the West. In response the East German authorities decided to modify the proposal to allow private travel to the West. This was by no means any indication of bringing down the wall or to allow free passage to all East Germans. It was simply meant to allow private travel through the various check-points subject to border crossing rules. But the East Berlin party boss, Günter Schabowski, who was entrusted to announce this minor modification turned out to be less informed about this change (and luckily so) than he was supposed to be. He announced this policy in a press conference and when asked about the exact time of implementation, just casually responded (for lack of any specific updates from his superiors) that 'it was with immediate

---

[7] It is only a matter of 'coincidence' that as I write this, I am sitting right by where the Berlin wall stood at one time!

effect'. It was a mistake unparalleled in history[8]. So which is the correct answer? Actually all of them, but the interesting thing is that the finer we go into the micro-details the greater and richer the analysis becomes. And sometimes, it throws surprises: communication error can merge countries!

The point we are trying to drive through these apparently rhetorical comparisons is simple. The finer one looks into a phenomenon, the deeper explanations become. Williamson did this by looking into the minute contractual details of transactions; Coase did it by visiting component suppliers. Williamson's micro-analytic approach looks at the dynamics of transactions, the transactors and the rules which govern these bilateral relationships. That, this approach is far removed from the world of 'blackboard economics,' should be quite apparent by now. As Williamson notes in his own words (Williamson 1976: p. 74):

> "I attempt here to examine franchise bidding issues in somewhat finer microanalytic detail than has been done previously….it was necessary to examine the contracting process in greater detail than had been done previously to discern the types of difficulties which market mediated exchange encounters and, relatedly, to establish in what respects and why internal (collective or hierarchical) organization offers an advantage".

3.3.3 Abduction and Pragmatism

So far we have seen that although beset with marginal differences, the approach of both Coase and Williamson are similar and appear neither deductive, nor inductive but rather abductive. We contend that this is a very important *methodological harbor* in economics. At the risk of repetition, let us revisit the example of beans and bags from Bromley (2006). Earlier we saw that deduction works something like this: *rule* (axiom) is that 'all the beans from this bag are white'; if the *case* is that 'these beans are from the bag'; then the *result* is that 'these beans are white'. In *abduction* the order is changed. The starting point is the result, from which one reaches to the case via the rule. First a result is observed – these beans are white; then the rule says – all the beans from this bag are white; then the case is derived that – therefore, these beans are from the bag. Abduction is therefore, 'a class of inference that yields explanatory hypothesis for observed phenomena…(w)hereas deduction produces empirical claims that might result in theoretical propositions, abduction starts with particular observed empirical circumstances (the result) and then invokes specific axioms (the rule), and the case (assumptions, and applicability postulates) to produce propositions (testable hypothesis) with the intent of explaining those observed circumstances' (*ibid. p. 96*). Surprise in an observed phenomena is the trigger in an abductive

---

[8]   West German News Program,, "Gunter Schabowski Press Conference," *Making the History of 1989*, Item #704, http://chnm.gmu.edu/1989/items/show/704 (accessed June 14 2014, 2:22 am).

approach and the *why* question takes pre-eminence over the *how* question. Why do firms exist? Why some firms make while others buy? These were the questions Coase and Williamson asked and not 'how do firms optimize among factors of production to maximize profits'. As Bromley (2006: p. 99-100) states, '(w)e can regard Ronald Coase's (1937) pioneering work on nature of the firm to be an example of abduction. In this instance, Coase was clearly motivated by surprise – the existence of firms in the face of deductive belief from classical economics "proving" that the efficiency properties of markets would render firms inefficient and therefore unnecessary'.

Abduction can also be understood as diagnosis[9]. In the words of Charles Sanders Peirce, abduction is a 'method of hypothesis' where the task is to construct plausible explanations for observed regularities or irregularities (*ibid. p. 96*). This is a critical element of pragmatism as associated with Peirce and Dewey. Pragmatism is about reasons. According to pragmatism, utility is not a reason for a choice. It is a justification. Bromley (2008) uses the example of someone ordering for snails in a restaurant: if the question is asked, 'why did you order snails?' the answer 'because it maximizes my utility' is not the reason. Once the choice is made, *ex-post* both the choices could be attributed to utility maximization. If the question was instead, 'why did you *not* order snails?' the answer would be again 'because it maximizes my utility'. Therefore, this answer does not actually provide a reason or an explanation for 'choosing' snails:

> "Utility is not a reason—it is merely an index of something that most people (non-economists) call happiness or satisfaction. Indeed before the marginalist revolution, the word "utility" in economics meant exactly what utility means to most everyone— useful, instrumental, practical. Pareto used the word that way, and he used the term "ophelimity" to denote some index of satisfaction or gratification (Cooter and Rappoport 1984). Under the influence of W. Stanley Jevons, economists moved away from the awkward ophelimity and let the word utility connote gratification. Clarity suffered" (Bromley 2008: p. 2).

If there ever is a doubt on whether Coase is a pragmatist or not then this analysis answers in the affirmative. Whether he was consciously so? - is neither clear nor important. What is important is that his benchmark approach is useful in *explaining*. Counter that with Becker's approach where everyone acts so as to maximize utility. What would be (and what is indeed) the answer for the question: Why do firms exist (...over markets)? Standard explanation would be: because firms maximize profits. But as per the logic of pragmatism, that is an *ex-post* justification. However, the answer that they exist because *they reduce*

---

[9] Without digressing too much into the approach of Elinor Ostrom, another luminary applying principles similar to that which can be termed Coasean, it is worthwhile to note that she applied a diagnostic methodology which was largely abductive in spirit (Ostrom 2007).

transaction costs is an *ex-ante* reason; it explains *why* certain transactions would be carried out in a certain way at the first place.

In the next section we discuss how in order to adopt the methodological approach of Coase, there needs to be a greater use of plural methods in economics, going beyond quantitative techniques over to qualitative methods like case studies. But before that, we examine the existing use of qualitative research in economics other than the large body of institutional economic work inspired by Coase, Williamson, Ostrom and other luminaries.

3.4 Qualitative, Case Study and Field Research

The beginnings of modern economics owe itself to Adam Smith's visit to the pin factory (Helper 2000). Yet, modern economics itself is more engaged with mathematical modeling and deductions from secondary information sources. Helper's insights stem from an National Bureau of Economic Research (NBER)/Sloan foundation funded a project on productivity change with an emphasis on field visits and informally known as 'Pin Factory' project. The importance of field visits is made clear in the words of Martin Feldstein in his address during the January 2000 meeting of the American Economic Association (Feldstein 2000):

> "We found that the managements at the companies we visited were generally eager to show their facilities, to tell us about their management practices, and to explain why they did certain things and how their practices have changed over time. They were also generally open about answering our questions. We would discuss not just the production process itself but also things like the compensation systems used to motivate workers, the criteria on which incentives were based, the sources of ideas for new products, and new processes. We also talked about why productivity-increasing changes were introduced. Among the reasons we heard were: pressure or requirements from industrial customers, the impact of a merger or of being acquired, and the pressures resulting from increased financial leverage or external competition. In short, the sources of change included a wide range of things that seemed obvious to us – *only after someone told us* (emphasis added).....(w)hen I have described this project to non-economists, they were invariably surprised that the process of visiting companies, looking at production, and asking questions is an unusual part of economic research. It seemed like such a natural thing to do. But as economists all know, it is unusual. We economists are generally accustomed to getting our insights by reading economic literature, going to seminars, and thinking hard about problems. We elaborate these insights in more or less formal models and then sometimes test these theories with aggregate statistics into micro data. But we rarely go and look and ask. I think that it is a pity. Looking and asking provide insights and suggest hypothesis – and can shoot down wrong ideas – in ways that go beyond introspection and reading".

Helper gives the example of Landers et al. (1996) paper where they modeled the role of observability constraints on the incentives to work inefficiently long hours. The actual insights came from Rebitzer talking to lawyers and workers. So instead of depending on (sometimes) tautological constructs of the objective function and constraints, they can be found out directly from real economic actors. Another advantage of field work, according to Helper, is that 'fieldwork allows exploration of areas with little pre-existing data or theory'. She gives example from her own dissertation work where her perception of the 'make or buy' decisions in US automobile industry changed a lot after making plant visits and she realized that information exchange and commitment were important for supplier performance, an insight she would have missed otherwise. Fieldwork also facilitates the use of correct data. Helper cites the work of Ichniowski et al. (1997) to demonstrate that it was plant visits which helped them ascertain and collect data on steel finishing lines and the impact of innovative human resource policies. Moreover, 'fieldwork provides vivid images that promote intuition' as Lazear (1996) states in his work '(i)t's one of my most –cited papers – I think it's because everyone can imagine those guys working harder to install windshields once they're on piece-rates, and it's an image they remember a lot more than the regression coefficients' (Helper 2000: p. 2).

Qualitative research has not been as prominent as the quantitative ones in modern economics although the promise it holds are high. In fact there is an increasing use of mixed methods where both qualitative and quantitative methods are used (Kanbur and Shaffer 2007; Starr 2012). One can see Starr (2012), for a survey of important qualitative research in economics but the key point stressed there is that the difference between qualitative and quantitative methods is not so much about words and numbers as is about open vs. closed end approaches. As we saw above, abductive approaches tend to be more open ended than the deductive approaches. This is because the emphasis on the '*why*' question lends itself to an *ex-ante* flexibility of responses from subjects. It is open to surprises. Open ended qualitative questionnaires or observations provide a scope for this. Once important insights stem from such an approach, quantitative methods could be used to complement and verify more generalized claims related to those insights. However, "..assum(ing) a priori that the researcher knows the specific informational items that played a central role in the subjects' behaviors, perceptions and/or decisions (Starr 2012: p. 3)" often blocks lateral flow of new insights. But doing credible qualitative work can be quite challenging and for a good discussion about the concerns and ways to overcome, the readers are directed to Starr (2012), Kanbur and Shaffer (2007), Bertrand and Mullainathan (2001) and other related pieces of work.

One important method in qualitative research is case studies and its importance lies in that it compels economists to be empirical. Today's empirical studies (based on econometrics) are not empirical in the Coasean sense. What they do is to refute or confirm quantitative relations between variables. The 'why' question is left to theory. In practice, empirical studies are used to justify theory – theory predicts some relation between variables, which can be tested by conducting an econometric analysis. Coase's critique of Friedman (Coase 1982) is that this is not what economists actually do. As Williamson suggested, you need a theory to beat a theory. This contradicts Friedman's approach and confirms Coase's. Given the selection bias (we only present econometric analysis that confirms our favored theory), we can understand why this approach is so futile, if not broken. But for economists who believe in "the methodology of positive method", this is the only way to do empirical studies. The conventional critique of case study (the small N problem, lack of replicability) misses the point. The value of a case study is mainly theoretical – a good case study changes the way we look at the problem (for example, Coase's study of lighthouse, Cheung's study of bees, etc.). In Coase's methodology, theory-building and facts-finding cannot be separated, whereas for believers in positive methodology, you first come up with a theory, and then subject it to testing. What we wish to emphasize here is that plurality of methods or mixed approaches are often more congenial to the Coasean/pragmatic methodology.

3.5 Conclusion

We began by stressing that methods should not be confused with methodology as the latter is a theory about the knowledge and use of methods. The critical elements of a Coasean methodology were then laid down which stems from Coase's belief that the study of an economic system is substantive and should use empirical observation, comparative assessments and plural methods. We then explain how Williamson not only followed a similar approach but added a pragmatic predictive element to develop a verifiable and highly successful branch of economic theory called transaction cost economics. But this was made possible because of his focus on the micro-analytics of contractual details and was a key turning point in the history of economic methodology, significantly different from the deductive and mathematical abstraction approaches used otherwise by the neo-classical economists. This is in spite of the fact that some of the founding fathers of neo-classical economics, like Marshall, were themselves skeptical of deductive approaches and feared mathematical abstraction will one day take over the study of real economic system. We contend that a micro-analytic, non-reductionist approach is a more insightful way of reducing complexities than mathematical abstraction. The empirical success of new institutional and transaction cost economics is evidence of that. All this can be fairly encompassed under the methodological basis of *abduction*, as viewed by Bromley, which asserts that economic inquiry begins with empirical observation and then uses specific axioms to produce testable propositions which explain economic phenomenon. This of course demands more openness towards plural methods which include qualitative approaches of inquiry. In other words, whether it was Adam Smith's visit to the pin factory or Coase's visits to industrial plants, we know where the action lies. And unless

NIE is on guard against any compromise on this, there is a risk of losing its unique appeal. In the next section, we briefly explain how plural methods have been used in various segments of the thesis to conduct empirical investigation into the research questions.

3.6 Summary of Empirical Methods Used

As has been seen in the discussion above, the essence of a Coasean methodology is that it is empirical, substantive and abductive. Combined with the Williamsonian non-reductive and micro-analytic approach, it gives the general methodology of NIE. Consistent with this, in chapter 4 a comparative institutional case study method is used where the cases of investor utilities and the institutional arrangements in the Indian states of Andhra Pradesh and Gujarat are studied. A micro-analytic approach of studying the utility contracts (also known as power purchase agreements, PPAs) in great details is applied. Various regulatory documents and risk protocols of utility companies have also been scrutinized. It is essentially a qualitative and comparative method which helps look at finer details which can be lost in quantitative analysis. In chapter 5, a quantitative empirical analysis is performed in keeping with the nature of the research question which is about finding out the determinants and their impact on the likelihood of electricity self-generation. But before such an analysis was done, detailed focus-group interviews and expert interviews were conducted over a period of several months in order to derive empirically the relevant factors which could influence the firm decision. Subsequently a primary survey was conducted under challenging conditions in the state of Andhra Pradesh where decision-makers in manufacturing firms were interviewed face-to-face and asked to fill survey questionnaires. The collected data was analyzed using discrete choice econometrics which involved estimation of a binary-choice model where the dependent variable took values of one, when a firm had an installed backyard power plant, and zero when it had no such backyard power plant.

Chapter 6 asked the specific question of the role of regulatory governance in thermal power efficiency and was primarily a measurement issue. The analysis aimed at answering the 'what' question and a quantitative parametric analysis was best suited for this. A stochastic frontier inefficiency effect model was estimated to calculate the plant level technical efficiency scores. The reason parametric specification was preferred over a deterministic approach is because such a flexible functional form (translogarithmic in this case) allows for random errors in deviation from the efficiency frontier. These errors can be then modeled to find out the determinants of technical inefficiency. In our analysis one of the determinants was an index of regulatory governance. This index was constructed based on secondary data collection from verified government sources. The plant-level data for the production function was also sourced from authorized government sources. With this theoretical and methodological background, the next chapter marks the entry to the empirical section of the thesis.

4. The Problem of Private Investment: A Comparative Transaction Cost Analysis*

Overview

After two decades of attempts to deregulate the Indian power sector and bring in more competition, the question we are asking is: why has private investment not flooded in as expected? We analyze the problem using an economics of governance framework which suggests that various organizational arrangements: markets, hierarchies and hybrids align themselves to minimize transaction costs. We subject our observations to the privately owned gas based power plants in two Indian states - Andhra Pradesh and Gujarat. The Andhra Pradesh Independent Power Producers (IPPs) suffered because the government reneged on its soft commitments to provide gas, leading to contractual hazards whereas the IPPs in the state of Gujarat performed better because they had insulated themselves against such risks by securing private gas supply contracts. Our analysis shows that the problem of private investment will persist as long as the costs of governance (adaptation to *ex-post* contractual hazards) are high. Under such a scenario, rather than moving towards a market based system, the sector will move towards organizational arrangements which are closer to vertical integration.

4.1 Background and Problem

It is now well acknowledged that the Indian power sector has seen lesser than the expected inflow of private capital when compared to its reform siblings, the Latin American economies (Singh 2005). This is especially worrying for the generation segment. At the time of initiating deregulation, investment in electricity generation was mostly by the government and there were no policies to encourage private investment (Audinet and Verneyre 2002). But currently there are policies to attract more private investment[1] and there has indeed been some improvement in the share of private sector participation in generation. The share of privately owned generating capacity has increased from 12.7 % of the total generating capacity by the end of the 10th plan period (2002-2007) to 27.1% at the end of the 11th plan period (2007-2012). However these figures include contributions from hydro-based, nuclear based as well as renewable

---

* A preliminary version of this chapter was presented at the 34th Annual Conference of the International Association of Energy Economics (IAEE), June 19-23 in Stockholm, Sweden. A previous version of this chapter is available online as USAEE Working Paper No. 13-110. Modified parts of this chapter are under review as a journal article in Energy Strategy Reviews as of 20th October, 2014.

[1] For policies to attract private investment, kindly refer to Sections 7 and 9 of the Electricity Act, 2003.

supply based generation. Our concern with private investment is in the thermal generation segment because its current share is the highest at 65.8 % of the total installed capacity. This share is likely to remain high. According to projections even in the best case where the share of nuclear and renewable sources increase, thermal share will remain at 63 % in 2052-53 (Grover and Chandra 2006). But thermal also includes diesel. Since diesel is used by small captive power units and hence is not the fuel source for large-scale private power plants, any analysis looking into dynamics of private investment should exclude this. When we discount for all this and calculate only for thermal capacity based on gas and coal (the real major avenues of private investment) then also we find an increase in the share from 6.4 % to 15% in the last ten years.[2]

However, a closer look into the trends only in coal and gas reveals a different picture. During the 11th plan period (2007-12) the capacity addition through private investment in gas based power generation was to the tune of 2530.5 MW (megawatts). However, the proposed capacity addition, i.e. investment in the 12th plan period (2012-2017) is zero! While in coal the private investment was to the tune of 18,649 MW in the 11th plan period, in the 12th plan period it will be 43,270 MW, which is more than the double. The question then arises why there is no private investment in gas-based generation forthcoming? Could this be because the projections for gas supply are not very optimistic? Even if that were the case, in spite of an increase in coal based investments, why have the profiles of private sector IPPs (independent power producers) still rated as high risk (Ghosh et al. 2011)? In this chapter we apply a transaction cost reasoning to give an explanation to this problem of private investment by looking at the *ex-post* contractual perspective. We are motivated to do this because the *ex-ante* incentive structure for investment is framed more centrally and is more or less similar for most IPPs, irrespective of their state-based location[3]. Yet we observe variation in their performance. Our contention is that it is not the incentive structure only that matters but what happens ex-post entering into a contract and having made the investment commitment. In what is known as the 'fundamental transformation' (Williamson 2002), a contracting party with significant asset specific investments could face an ex-post hold-up situation due to opportunistic

---

[2] These figures are own calculations based on Central Electricity Authority (CEA), Government of India, reports: All India Electricity Statistics, General Review 2008 (CEA, 2008); Power Scenario at a Glance, 2012 (CEA, 2012).

[3] The 'democratic state' of India is federal in nature similar to the US where there is a centrally elected government and also different elected governments at the federal state level. While some duties fall exclusively in the purview of the federal states, some are concurrent to both, the state as well as the centre. Rules for setting regulatory tariffs are decided centrally by the central regulators, CERC, and states are mandated to implement them.

behaviour or contractual incompleteness. That also determines the performance and hence signals for future investments.

The remaining chapter is organized as follows. In Section 4.2, we begin by explaining the exact nature of this problem. The investment problem is different in matured power sector of the developed countries and evolving power sectors of the developing countries, which have to face sporadic and accelerated demand growth. While capacity adequacy during peak period is the guiding paradigm of matured markets, developing markets face more a problem of base-load investments (Finon 2006). In Section 4.3, we explain why we use an economics of governance approach to explain this problem and also lay down the essential elements of its theory and relevance for electricity sector performance. In Sections 4.4 and 4.5 we discuss the case of IPP investment in two Indian states - Andhra Pradesh and Gujarat – which provide contrasting insights from investments. Both the states have comparable electricity situations in terms of demand structure but have divergent institutional arrangements for operation. The purpose is to show in micro-analytic details the presence of contractual hazards and their commensurating disastrous consequences in Andhra Pradesh. Then using the case of Gujarat we show how they have a better design to avoid and respond to such hazards. In Section 4.6, we explain why the same trends may continue for any fuel based production wherever there are risks of contractual hazards. The implication of this is either investment slows down or generation companies would vertically integrate so as to minimize upstream and downstream risks. The discussion about coal supply risks and upcoming large scale power plants substantiates this. However, this evidence is only indicative and more empirical research on various components of the Indian power sector using this economics of governance framework will improve the validity of this claim.

4.2 Nature of the Investment Problem

The market mechanisms in matured electricity sectors (i.e. of US and Western Europe) are geared to solve the problems of system reliability (which is an undisputed collective good) and capacity adequacy during peak demand (Finon 2006). The problem basically boils down to coordination of investment in peak and base load equipment so that the combined investments are profitable. The problem is not of fulfilling the market demand at a reasonable cost. The usual way by which the investment problem of mature electrical sectors is resolved is through investment incentives for base load capacity which ensures capacity adequacy at peak. According to pro-market theories, such incentives will automatically come from the market, which will signal the optimal level of investment in base and peak through competitive prices (Crew and Kleindorfer 1986). As a result, investors, based on market signals, would use 'low investment cost-high operating cost' equipment for peak load and 'high investment cost-low operating cost' equipment for base load (Hunt 2002). This kind of market mechanism for investment in peak and base load capacity leads to high price volatility and hence uncertainty on returns to investments, leading to potential 'hold-up' of investment.   Transaction Cost Economics (TCE) theorists suggest that this 'hold-up' problem can be avoided through long-term contracts or vertical integration, as short term contracts do not guard against price risks (Pittman 2007).

Empirical evidence shows that the progress in investments in production in UK from 1990 to 2000 was a result of long-term arrangements (Finon, 2006). When these long term contracts are not easily implementable due to opportunism of the purchasers (*ibid. p. 609*), vertical integration of production and supply becomes a feasible option. Examples from several European countries show that reformers have actually organized the market structure in a way so as to reduce this problem of investment. Interestingly, Belgium, France, Spain, Sweden and Germany have kept their vertically integrated status. England, Norway and Italy have gone for de-integration but recent experiences from Britain have shown that there has been re-integration after the merchant plants went bankrupt (*ibid. p. 609*).

In the developing world the nature of the investment problem is entirely different. It is about adequate investment for annual supply of electricity, rather than optimal investment in base and peak load equipment. The aim of electricity reforms in many developing countries including India was to bring in short term private capital. The underlying idea was gradual replication of the British model where ultimately hourly prices would reflect peak and annual capacity, and thereby provide the right signals for investment (Thomas 2005). The first stage is the 'single buyer model' where the distributor (a public utility) is the lone buyer and a monopoly seller and the producer enters into contracts with this public utility. Most of the countries, India in particular, have not been able to move beyond this first stage. The reason is that the single buyer model needs a set of institutional pre-conditions for success (Bhattacharyya 2007). This model works through power-purchase agreements (PPAs) which have 'take or pay'[4] clauses and also tariff clauses which come in a 'cost-plus' form[5]. In the presence of these clauses a series of derived contracts exist from the building and procurement stage up to the selling stage. These clauses protect investors from various sectoral risks (Glachant and Hallack 2009). This single buyer model has advantages when compared to the market signal model as it allows for planning and avoids scarcity situations. The prices in the single buyer model are stable and the risks of the investors are shared by the large buyer or guaranteed by

---

[4]   A strict 'take or pay' clause means that buyer has to pay for the contracted capacity irrespective of whether there is any off-take or not. The seller is also committed to provide the required volume.

[5]   Cost plus model is where the utility earns a reasonable rate of return (typically in the range of 16-20 percent) over and above capital expenditure and variable costs.

public budget and/or passed on to the consumers. However, the single buyer model is limited by the institutional and macroeconomic environment rather than by its own internal structure. Especially when the institutional environment is not stable, then the single buyer model runs into difficulties. The single buyer utility is caught between the high price as per PPA and the low ability of the buyers to pay it. Even in the early stages of Californian power sector reforms this was a major problem which led to bankruptcy of distribution companies. While a volatile wholesale market was created in California there were price controls at the retail level for investor-owned utility, which meant that the price variations could not be passed on to the consumers (Sweeny 2002). Due to political economy considerations, regulators are unwilling to change tariffs and buyers are unwilling to improve their performance. Because of the strict 'take or pay' clauses many contractual costs are passed on to the public budget or sometimes on to consumers, which may be politically unviable. These lead to transaction costs. There are also other macroeconomic risks to the single buyer like currency risks and purchase of imported fuel. In essence although 'take or pay' contracts minimize risks of IPPs, it increases the risks of buyer and guarantors.

The most cited case for the single buyer model and its associated problems in India is Enron's investment through the Dabhol Power Corporation (DPC) in the state of Maharashtra, in the beginning phase of India's reform process in electricity. DPC avoided demand risks by a 'take or pay' PPA with the single buyer i.e. state owned Distribution Company. However, this was overturned by a new government in the middle of the project (Dubash and Rajan 2001). Ramamurti (2003) attributes the failure of the Dabhol project to government reneging. The mistake of Enron project was that it relied too much on contractual design overlooking the risks of government reneging due to other political and economic factors. He states three main reasons for government reneging: economic uncertainty, obsolescing bargain and political change. Economic uncertainty could arise from, say, change in input prices or demand. They could also be macroeconomic in nature like currency devaluation. Obsolescing bargain means that governments find some deals costly/risky *ex-post* although *ex-ante* they were attractive (Vernon 1971). Investors face this risk due to their sunk and asset specific investments (Levy and Spiller 1994; Ordover et al. 1994). Once the investments are made, they cannot move out and the government behaves opportunistically. These could also be specified in contractual terms but many a times governments use legislative powers to change the terms of the clauses. A recent example of this is forced renegotiation of terms by Chad government with a donor agency for the Chad–Cameroon oil pipeline (Gould and Winters 2007). Lastly, political change could come in the form of an election or coup. When *political* regimes *change,* the actors involved change (ministers, bureaucrats etc.) and the new actors could reverse the decisions made by previous governments. These are *ex-post* contractual hazards, which are costly for the investors and ultimately passed on to the end consumers.

The preceding discussion thus emphasizes two points. First, the nature of investment problem in India is different from those of the *mature* electricity sectors of the industrialized countries. While the problem in a *mature* set-up is to balance investments in base and peak load equipment, in India it is of assured investments for secured annual supply of electricity which is able to fulfill the rapid growth in demand. That there is a serious supply problem in India can be seen from Fig. 4-1 which shows the trends in peak demand shortage (in MW) over the last 10 years. In the financial year 2010-11, the peak demand shortage was 9.8 % (Rallapalli and Ghosh 2012). Second, there are risks of *ex-post* contractual hazards. In the next section we elaborate on a transaction cost based approach, also known as economics of governance, which suggests that the problem of private investment will persist as long as the costs of governance (adaptation to *ex-post* contractual hazards) are high.

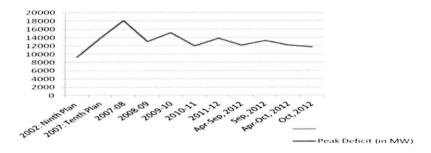

Figure 4-1: All India peak deficit over time

Source: Own compilation based on CEA, 2012

4.3   Why Economics of Governance?

The chief reasons for the low level of private investment in the Indian power sector are generally attributed to an inadequate legal framework, delays in getting regulatory approvals, poor financial health of the state electricity boards (SEBs) and politicization (Sharma et al. 2005; Singh 2005; Corbeau 2010). The prescriptions of standard competition theories then revolve around scenarios where these bottlenecks will eventually give way to a more idealized system and towards full blown market based electricity prices. But the fact that these bottlenecks impose significant costs and economic actors work around minimizing them, escapes traditional economic analysis. That these costs matter can be seen from the fact that while the major theoretical debates in deregulation have focused mainly on ownership i.e. state or private, empirical experience has shown that the problem lies more in how the sector is governed (Nakhooda et al. 2007). However, to identify such costs which cannot be easily quantified, a micro-analytic perspective (Williamson 1976) is needed. The study of economic governance is one such an approach.

One of the earliest ideas on the economic study of governance came from John R. Commons, who suggested that "the ultimate unit of activity…must contain in itself the three principles of conflict, mutuality and order" (Commons 1932) and that unit is a 'transaction'. In this sense, governance is the means by which order is brought in a transaction by mitigating the conflicts and realizing mutual gains. Based on this, Williamson (2005) defines economic governance as the study of good (private) order and workable arrangements. Another closely linked definition is that it is those set of devices used to bring order in transactions through defining property rights, contracts and other enforcement mechanisms (Dixit 1996). The economics of governance literature draws from transaction cost economics (TCE). TCE takes a micro-analytic view of economic organization and looks at it as a contracting problem. According to Williamson's discriminating alignment hypothesis (Williamson 1998), governance structures align themselves to minimize the costs which arise out of the particular attributes of a transaction. Since TCE follows the assumptions of bounded rationality, in presence of uncertainty, the crucial physical attribute of asset specificity generates complexities of a degree where governance, or institutions of private ordering like long term contracting, is the only viable option. However when transactions are complex, the presence of bounded rationality and uncertainty means that future events cannot be foreseen, hence contracts are almost always incomplete. When the costs of adapting to the *ex-post* changes under long term contracting also become very high, vertical integration of production becomes the default option. Suffice to state for the electricity sector, that markets can develop only when contracts between producers, suppliers and buyers are credible. If the institutional environment (the mechanism of rule production and enforcement in a society) is such that contracts are not credible, then the costs imposed by such a governance structure are high and economic actors internalize transaction costs through vertical integration (Spiller and Tommasi 2005).

Electricity sector governance is broadly about the rule of law (formal institutions) and the certainty of investment conditions in electricity markets (Dubash 2002). According to Joskow (1998) potential private investors in new generation capacities look for stable market rules and long term contractual commitments. Once investors enter into contracts with buyers for power purchase, both the parties are then governed by the terms of the contract. Any change in the terms of the contract which imposes *ex-post* costs is therefore called governance cost. The sources of these changes in the terms of contracts are the usual bottlenecks (listed earlier) of an economic system, which we refer to as a part of the institutional environment. These costs could come in the form of high priced alternate fuel (in case of non-availability of fuel), low retail prices, regulatory reversals and litigation, losses on stranded assets etc. We contend that unless the risks of such costs are minimized either through a highly committed regulatory set up or through court enforced long term contracts, private investors will not enter the generation segment. And if they do, it will be through organizational arrangements which include some form of vertical integration.

In the next section we look at two cases of private investments in the states of Andhra Pradesh and Gujarat respectively, which testify this logic. Although the states have comparable electricity demand structure, they have divergent institutional arrangements for operation. The section will reveal through a micro-analytic study of contractual hazards in Andhra Pradesh and the structural management of those by Gujarat, how institutional divergence leads to differences in performance.

Table 4-1: Comparison of AP and Gujarat electricity scenario (in %)

	Share in All India Installed Capacity		Share of Private Sector in Total Capacity		Share of State Sector in Total Capacity		Share of Industrial Consumption	Share of Agricultural Consumption
Year	2007	2012	2007	2012	2007	2012	2007	2007
Andhra Pradesh (AP)	6.8	8.1	21.4	24.5	78.6	75.5	36.5	42.7
Gujarat	6.2	11	30.1	57.9	69.9	42.1	41.3	25.4

Source: Own compilation based on CEA (2008) and CEA (2012)

4.4 The Cases of Private Investment in Andhra Pradesh and Gujarat

Both Andhra Pradesh and Gujarat have historically been two of the most developed and industrialized states in India. As can be seen from Table 4-1, the share of industrial consumption is high in both Andhra Pradesh and Gujarat. In 2007, the share of both Andhra Pradesh and Gujarat in total Indian generation capacity was almost similar (Gujarat being marginally lower). But by 2012 the share of Gujarat increased almost by double at 11 % whereas that of Andhra Pradesh was at 8.1%. Even striking was the fact that while the share of private sector increased only by 3 percentage points for Andhra Pradesh, it increased by 28 percentage points in Gujarat during the period 2007-2012. While in Andhra

Pradesh the private sector installed capacity increased from 1927.4 MW in 2007 to 3948.71 in 2012, in Gujarat it increased from 2459.2 to 12713.44 MW for the same period. To explain the reasons for this divergence, we start with the case of Andhra Pradesh in the next sub-section.

4.4.1 Investment in Andhra Pradesh: Supply and Contractual Hazards

First we look at the case of independent power producers (IPPs) investing in generating capacity in Andhra Pradesh for the last 15 years. Andhra Pradesh is widely considered as a leader in electricity reform and its regulatory agency, Andhra Pradesh Electricity Regulatory Commission (APERC), is deemed as the 'best practice' in electricity regulation (Dubash and Rao 2008). Apart from that Andhra Pradesh was also among the first ones to restructure its *erstwhile* naturally monopolized power sector. A pro-reform state government during the decade of 1990s initiated a program of inviting private participation in generation[6].

Table 4-2: Features of current PPAs

S.N	Name of the IPP	Entry Route	Capacity (MW)	Year of First PPA	Year of Final PPA	Year of COD#	Initial Allotment of Gas (MCMD)	Number of Renegotiations
1	GVK	MoU	220	1998	2003	2006	1.1	2
2	Gouthami	Bidding	464	1997	2003	2006	1.96	2
3	Konaseema	Bidding	445	1997	2005	2007	1.60	3
4	Vemagiri	Bidding	370	1997	2007	2006	1.64	3

Note: # COD - Commercial Operation Date; Mcmd: million cubic metres per day

Source: Various PPAs (power contracts) and APERC reports

Typically the IPPs enter into power purchase agreements (PPAs) with the state distribution utilities. These are generally long term contracts ranging from 15 to

---

[6] In the beginning the government allowed firms to set up their gas based power plants mostly through the Memorandum of Understanding (MoU)[6] route and few through competitive bidding. 119 MoUs were signed for power plants during the period from 1991 to 1995 to create an estimated capacity of 7841 MW of power (PMGER, 2003). However, only three power plants could become operational at the end of the decade, namely GVK's Jegudupadu Combined Cycle Gas Turbine (CCGT), Godavari CCGT of Spectrum and Lanco's Kondapalli CCGT for a combined capacity of nearly 800 MW. In the second phase some new IPPs entered through the bidding route, namely Gouthami's Peddapuram Power Plant (later taken over by GVK Industries Ltd.), Konaseema EPS Oakwell Power Ltd. and Vemagiri Power Generation Ltd.

23 years. However, these IPPs have had to face contractual renegotiations several times even before they started operating. Important features of these IPPs which faced huge delays in operation and underwent the process of contractual renegotiations have been listed in Table 4-2.

Gas supplies improved from April 2009 due to increased availability from the KG Basin (KG-D6) and Reliance Industries Limited (RIL) committing regular supply of gas to the IPPs. The increased supply of gas from KG-D6 to the IPPs in AP has definitely helped them begin production on a regular basis which was not possible under the earlier GAIL supply. But this hasn't eliminated supply uncertainties[7]. The future projections also do not seem very favourable from KG-D6. Additionally there are issues related to the Gas Utilization Policy of government where power sector is not on the highest priority for gas supplies (Jain and Sen 2011).[8] The only option for IPPs in such scenarios, as was implemented once during early 2012, is for RIL to buy imported re-gasified liquefied natural gas (R-LNG) and supply to the IPPs. The price for this gas comes to about $22 mmbtu compared to $5 mmbtu price for local KG-D6 gas. This is economically unviable and hence cannot be a long term solution.

Table 4-3: Supply divergence in gas allocation

Year	Allocated Gas (in MCMD)	Actual Supply of GAIL gas (in MCMD)	% of actual to allocated
2003-04	4.85	3.69	76.08
2004-05	4.85	3.633	75
2005-06	4.85	3.439	71

Source: APERC Common Order, 2009

---

[7] The potential from KG-D6 was pegged at 337 billion cubic meter (bcm) and could potentially double India's gas production. It was expected to reach the plateau production of 80 million standard cubic meter per day (mmscmd) in 2011-12 (Corbeau, 2010). However, the realization has been less than expected. In 2011, the peak reached was 28 mmscmd (a shortfall of over 65%) (Borawake and Anand, 2011); (PMGER, 2011). This gas supply uncertainty also adversely affected the IPPs and their PLF (plant load factors) fell to 65% by November, 2012. The IPPs suffered not only on the count of PLF decline but also incurred losses due to higher heat rate and auxiliary power consumption. The four IPPs require 7.21 mmscmd for full production but they received only 4.54 mmscmd (i.e., only 60% of their requirement) (Mitra and Kumar, 2012).

[8] As per the current Gas Utilization Policy for New Exploration Licensing Policy (NELP) D-6, gas based power plants rank third in the order of priority after existing gas based urea (fertilizer) firms and gas based Liquefied Petroleum Gas (LPG) extracting firms. http://www.oxfordenergy.org/wpcms/wp-content/uploads/2011/05/NG_50.pdf

Table 4-4: Extra burden to utilities of open market purchase

Year	Addl. Power Purchase (in MU)	Amount (Rs. Crore)	Average Price (Rs. per unit)	Addl. Burden (Rs.)
2006-07	1433	617	4.31	202.05
2007-08	4075	1991	4.89	810.92
2008-09	7905	6406	8.1	4110.6
Total				5123.57

Source: APERC Common Order, 2009: p. 117.

As the facts stated above point out, the problem with both earlier GAIL and present RIL arrangements is that the contracts are a little more than soft commitments. The 'take or pay' provisions apply only for the buyer and the seller of gas has no reciprocal obligations. There is no 'supply or pay' provision where the gas supplier has to make up for the low supply (PMGER 2011). The reason RIL has continued the trend of GAIL and is also unwilling for such provisions is because they do not have marketing freedom for gas as it is regulated by the Gas Utilization Policy which decides sector-based allocations. And unless there is strong commitment from the supplier of gas, it is obvious that new investments won't come in gas based generation. Gujarat has precisely solved this problem through a dedicated gas supply company which is committed to supply gas and governs it's transactions through secure 'take or pay' contracts.

4.4.2 Investment in Gujarat: Gas Supply and Minimizing Hazards

In 2009 there was a case (GERC 2010) filed by some civil society groups in the Gujarat Electricity Regulatory Commission (GERC) against levying of the fuel price and power purchase adjustment (FPPPA) charges to the consumers by the state power distributor (Gujarat Urja Vikas Nigam Limited (GUVNL). This was a result of the chain of 'take or pay' provisions in the PPA contracts. GUVNL (the single buyer) has a 'take or pay' arrangement with Essar Power and GPEC Paguthan (two major IPPs) where they have to compensate for low off-take of power. The two IPPs in turn have a 'take or pay' contract with the gas supply company Gujarat State Petroleum Corporation Ltd. (GSPCL) which has to be compensated by the IPPs in case of low off-take of gas. As the judgment of the GERC notes, even when the seller of gas fails to deliver the committed amount, it has to compensate the buyer for the losses. This is a more secure 'take or pay' contract with liability on both sides. From July to September, 2009, high monsoon period resulted in lower demand for power. As a result GUVNL bought less power from the IPPs which had to then off-take low gas volumes from GSPCL. Therefore they had to compensate for this loss of GSPCL which was ultimately passed on to the consumers. The nature of the petition is similar as in the case of AP but the difference is that the pass through resulted due to demand uncertainty and not supply uncertainty (as with the GAIL supplies in

AP). However, when there is a supply uncertainty for GSPCL i.e. production from a single seller of gas falls or there is a supply shock, the whole supply chain will be disrupted in spite of the strict 'take or pay' clauses as the cost will be ultimately passed on to the consumers. But the reason why such a situation is unlikely to arise in Gujarat is another key strategy by GSPCL, which is of diversifying its fuel sources.

GSPCL is a state government owned public limited company which has an integrated upstream and downstream sector presence in the gas supply chain of Gujarat. For buyers (like the IPPs) they have Gas Sales Contracts (GSC) and for sellers (of gas) they have Gas Purchase Agreements (GPAs). The GSCs are further of two types: first, on 'take or pay' basis and second, on a 'reasonable endeavors' basis. Under the 'take or pay' basis they are entitled to payment for the contracted volume of the gas regardless of whether the buyer takes the actual delivery or not. Moreover, they have to pay liquidated damages to the buyer in the event of failure to deliver gas. Under the 'reasonable endeavors' basis GSPCL receives payment for only the quantities actually off-taken, without any liabilities for failure of delivery. Under the GSPAs, GSPCL buys gas from sellers on a 'take or pay' basis where they make payments for the contracted volume of the gas irrespective of the actual off-take. And they are compensated by the sellers in case of failure of delivery.

As can be seen from Fig. 4-2,[9] GSPCL actually sources its gas supplies from multiple sources: one is its own exploration and production wing and the rest are different companies[10]. The sources are both national and international because of the close proximity of the LNG terminals at Hazira and Dahej (both in Gujarat). It buys imported gas from three government undertakings - GAIL, Indian Oil Corporation Ltd. (IOCL) and Bharat Petroleum Corporation Ltd. (BPCL) on long term basis using 'take or pay' GPAs. From the Hazira LNG terminal it buys imported gas at spot prices. Besides this, GSPCL has its own offshore fields in Hazira and North Balol. Both of these are governed through 'arm's length' internal arrangements which are non-contractual. It also buys on short term basis from other offshore sources such as the Panna-Mukta-Tapti and ONGC Olpad fields. This has actually enabled GSPCL to delink its gas sales from the purchase contracts and sell the gas sourced from various sources at *blended* rates. The buyers are for most part its own gas distribution companies, the GSPC Gas and Sabarmati Gas. This is again conducted through arm's length arrangements. Additionally they sell to the IPPs on 'take or pay' basis.

---

[9] All information in this section is sourced from the Draft Red Herring Prospectus, 2010 submitted by the GSPCL to the Indian stock market regulator, SEBI (Securities and Exchange Board of India).

[10] The share of GAIL+IOCL+BPCL is 40 % on average and the share of spot purchases are around 52%.

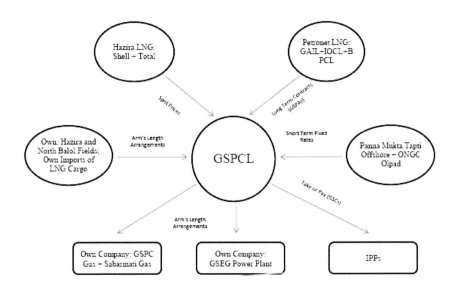

Figure 4-2: Gas supply chain in Gujarat

Source: Red Herring Prospectus, GSPCL, 2010

4.4.3 Summarizing the Two Cases

We see from the situation of IPPs in AP that under uncertainty there is inevitably contractual renegotiation. This renegotiation process is extremely costly in terms of haggling, regulatory time and stranded asset losses. These are the costs of governance which arise invariably due to contractual design never being able to specify all future contingencies. Such uncertainties arising from security-of-supply is a major source of the 'core contracting problem in energy markets' (Helm 2002). According to Helm, there are three forms of this security-of -supply problem:

i) Contracts security: This contracting problem was ignored in earlier waves of deregulation and privatization because security-of-supply was not a concern and hence the stringent 'take or pay' provisions could be passed on to consumers. When there is no security-of-supply concern, contracts actually do not matter, but otherwise there is (what he calls) the contract security problem or (what we call) the contractual hazards problem.

ii)   Networks security: Network infrastructure is crucial for delivery to consumers. Electricity networks for final consumers and fuel distribution networks for delivery to electricity producers. Due to natural monopoly characteristics, however, market alone cannot provide the optimal solution and hence government intervention is required.

iii) Diversity security: Diversity by a mix of fuel sources helps in the face of price, quantity and technology shocks, through the portfolio effect.

The analysis of IPP investments in Gujarat shows how they have been able to manage the supply-of-security problem through smart 'take or pay' provisions, securing networks and diversification of their fuel supply sources. Another reason is that the risks of government reneging (Ramamurti 2003) is reduced due to political stability for the last decade in Gujarat where the same government has been ruling under the same leadership for the last 11 years and will remain the same for the next five years too, having won the latest elections. In Andhra Pradesh, the leadership has changed four times in the last 15 years, with a stable ruler only from the period 1995-2004, when the PPAs were signed and active private investment took place. This does not imply that every change in regime has led to reneging, but sometimes policy reversal under a new regime has an impact. The regime in 2004 which replaced the earlier state government in Andhra Pradesh overturned power sector reforms and offered free electricity to farmers, which impacted the viability of generation plants (Joseph 2010) . In short, the success so far in Gujarat is because they have minimized the risks of contractual hazards and subsequently governance costs, although the tariff structures (incentives) have been similar for IPPs both in Andhra Pradesh and Gujarat.[11] This has an obvious implication for the overall power scenarios in these states. As can be seen in Fig. 4-3, the peak deficit in Gujarat was higher than Andhra Pradesh before 2009-10 but has been falling ever since whereas that of Andhra Pradesh has been on a rise.

---

[11] The tariff guidelines are set by the Central Electricity Regulatory Commission (CERC) and is same for all SERCs. The rate of return (RoR) on the cost of production was 16% on Net Fixed Assets (NFA) before the multi-year tariff (MYT) system was introduced. In Andhra Pradesh the MYT was adopted from FY 2007 and in Gujarat from FY 2009. Under the MYT, in Andhra Pradesh the utilities were allowed a rate of return on capital employed (RoCE) of up to 16% and in Gujarat up to 14% (CRISIL 2010).

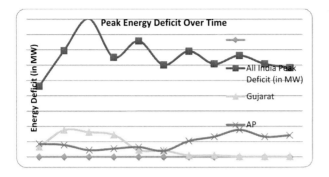

Figure 4-3: Movements in peak deficit over time in AP and Gujarat

Source: Own compilation based on CEA, 2012

4.5 Coal Supply Risks and Vertical Integration

The previous two sections have explained why private investment in gas based generation is not forthcoming and[12] described the *conditions* under which the investment is safe and those under which it is not[13]. A key insight that emerges from the discussion is that the same trends may continue for any fuel based production wherever there are risks of contractual hazards. The implication of this is either investment slows down or generation companies would vertically integrate so as to minimize upstream and downstream risks. The new investment scenario substantiates this logic. Coal based generation has by far the maximum share in IPP projects as 60% of thermal projects run by IPPs are currently coal based (Ghosh et al. 2011). In the 12th plan period (2012-2017), most of the new thermal projects in the state of Andhra Pradesh and Gujarat use coal (CEA, 2012). In fact all over India, 95.7 % of total thermal investment in the next period will be in coal based generation (see Table 4-5). This is an obvious response to the failure of the gas based sector to take-off in a big way. Incidentally, it assumes assurances of secured coal supply. However, there is significant coal supply risk expected till the end of the 12th plan period (*ibid.*).

---

[12] In Gujarat there is 1096 MW of investment forthcoming in gas based generation. But the investors are Gujarat state owned firms, GSECL and GSPCL. http://guj-epd.gov.in/epd_futureplan.htm

[13] This does not necessarily imply that if investments are safe, then more investment has to flow in. One reason for no gas-based private investment in Gujarat could be its highly improved peak deficit situation (as seen in Fig. 3) and the surplus investment already in the pipeline.http://businesstoday.intoday.in/story/gujarats-power-sector-turnaround-story/1/21750.htmln

Table 4-5: Likely capacity addition for 12th plan period, 2012-2017 (in MW)

	Hydro	Thermal Break-up			Total Thermal	Nuclear	Total
		Coal	Lignite	Gas/LNG			
Central	6004	13800	250	827.6	14878	5300	26182
Sector	(6.78)	(15.59)	(0.28)	(0.93)	(16.80)	(5.99)	(29.57)
State	1608	12210	0	1712	13922	0	15530
Sector	(1.82)	(13.79)	(0.00)	(1.93)	(15.72)	(0.00)	(17.54)
Private	3285	43270	270	0	43540	0	46825
Sector	(3.71)	(48.87)	(0.30)	(0.00)	(49.18)	(0.00)	(52.89)
All India	10897	69280	520	2539.6	72340	5300	88537
	(12.31)	(78.25)	(0.59)	(2.87)	(81.71)	(5.99)	(100)

Source: CEA, 2012

The coal based IPPs have two arrangements for coal procurement: either they receive it from Coal India Limited (CIL), a state owned coal supply company based on letter of assurance (LOAs), or through owning captive coal mines (both domestic and abroad). The first arrangement (i.e. LOAs) is the same as the gas based IPPs have with GAIL. LOAs are soft commitments where there is no liability to the supplier (CIL) for failure to deliver the allocated amount of coal. Under a security-of-supply situation this will again become the biggest source of *contractual hazards*. And that such a supply crisis is looming can be seen from the facts: even after accounting for all the plans of CIL to ramp-up production by the end of the 12th plan period there is still a big gap in demand. At the best scenario CIL production will be 120 MMT whereas its supply commitments to power projects (both private and state owned) are 325 MMT (Ghosh et al. 2011). The only option then is to import coal from abroad which is very expensive compared to domestic coal and would raise the cost of production. Many power plants have anticipated this situation of uncertainty and have gone for vertically integrating coal supply through bidding for captive coal blocks. Of the 216 blocks of coal mines allotted by 2009 for an estimated Geological Reserve (GR) capacity of 50,527.42 MT (million tone), almost half of it has gone to private sector power and steel production firms. Twelve blocks with an estimated GR of 4846.26 MT have been specifically allotted to Ultra Mega Power Projects (UMPPs) (CAG 2012)[14].

In short, the risks of contractual hazards persist in the case of coal based generation too and therefore present and future investors face high costs of governing electricity related transactions. Our framework therefore suggests that

---

[14] It is important to note that even the progress in captive coal mine development has been marred with difficulties and the air of uncertainty hasn't disappeared. Twenty four of them were already de-allocated by 2011 for non-performance and more have been recommended for de-allocation post the coal allocation scam of 2012. For details refer, CAG 2012.

in this case the rate of increase in private investment will not be high in future scenarios. The only options are either state-owned generation or large scale power plants reaping advantages of assured fuel supply i.e. the UMPPs. UMPPs are large scale power projects initiated by the central government and offered in competitive bidding to private companies. Four of these UMPPs are in the process of construction and each plant is around 4000 MW capacity. The tariffs at which they will sell power to state distribution utilities will be very low due to the economies of scale. But the crucial element is that all of these UMPPs have secured fuel supply. Some have done it by locating near to pithead mines and owning them for own captive consumption, while others have located themselves on the coastal regions and signed PPAs for imported coal.[15] State owned power plants on the other hand, have 'arm's length' arrangements with fuel suppliers and buyers, both of which are state owned entities and subject to soft budget constraints of the energy department. Both of these, the UMPPs or state-owned firms, though are not traditional vertically integrated regulated firms owning the whole supply chain from generation, transmission up to distribution but are organizational arrangements closer to vertical integration and reduce the costs of governing electricity related transactions.

4.6 Transaction Cost Underpinnings and Lessons Learnt

TCE originated from Coase (1937) indicating transaction costs as a reason for firms to internalize production rather than contracting everything out to the market. However, it did not provide a predictive theory of the conditions under which different transactions would be efficiently carried out either in the market or in the firm. Williamson (1979a, 1985) filled this predictive gap by taking a micro-analytic view of economic organization and looking at it as a contracting problem. Transaction costs, according to Williamson are defined as the costs of writing, monitoring, verifying and enforcing a contract. His main contribution lay in specifying variables which determined whether markets or hierarchies would lower the cost of a particular transaction. The TCE theoretical framework is founded on two key assumptions of *bounded rationality* and *opportunism*. Bounded rationality (as against the complete rationality assumption of neo-classical economics) refers to the fact that people have limited memories and cognitive memories i.e. they are intendedly rational but limitedly so. Opportunism, as Williamson calls it, is the tendency of 'self-interest seeking with guile' where actors could potentially exploit contracting partners under unforeseen favorable circumstances. Under the conditions that these assumptions hold, the interplay of three core variables of *asset specificity*, *uncertainty* and *frequency* determine what kind of transaction costs will be generated and whether a transaction will be carried out in the market or within a

---

[15] Incidentally, the progress of all the UMPPs are not as smooth as expected, however a discussion is beyond the scope of the work.

firm. While it is relatively simple to understand that if frequency of a transaction is high there is increased likelihood that a transaction will be internalized, the critical factors are uncertainty in those transactions and the specificity of assets involved. If an asset is very specific to a particular transaction and has almost zero opportunity costs outside of it, then it is efficient to vertically integrate that asset. According to Williamson, all contracts are eventually incomplete because actors are boundedly rational and can never specify entire future contingencies. So if one party makes a very specific investment, and an *ex-post* situation arises where it generates rents for the other party, then it may behave opportunistically. This is what is known as the 'fundamental transformation' (Williamson 2002), where a contracting party with significant asset-specific investments could face an *ex-post* hold-up situation due to opportunistic behavior or contractual incompleteness. Therefore, according to the discriminating alignment hypothesis (Williamson 1998), governance structures align themselves to minimize these costs (Spanjer 2009). As can be seen from Table 4-6, spot markets are an efficient governance solution when there are low asset specificities and uncertainty involved in the transaction. But as transactions become increasingly complex involving higher degrees of asset specificities for both contracting parties and higher levels of uncertainty, then vertical integration is an efficient governance structure or solution.

Table 4-6: Governance structure, asset specificity and uncertainty

		Asset Specificity		
		Low for both parties	*High for both parties*	*High for one party, low for one party*
Uncertainty	*High*	Contract/Vertical Integration	Vertical Integration	Vertical Integration
	Low	Spot Market	Long-term contract	Vertical Integration

Source: Own matrix based on various other TCE sources

In the case of Andhra Pradesh, the pass through to consumers was difficult not because the distribution utilities had to bear the extra expenses of buying costly power from alternate sources but because they refused to bear the ex-post contractual burden in the form of fixed charge payment to the IPPs in spite of not getting any electric power from them. So the demand rationing had to be done through rolling blackouts. And this situation came to the fore because the gas supplier reneged on its soft commitments. In Gujarat this pass through was possible, enabling demand response, because gas supply was secure and contractually risk-minimizing which meant production of power by the IPPs and its procurement by distribution utilities never got interrupted and there was no demand rationing. This prevented any contractual renegotiations between the IPPs and the utilities. Hence the Gujarat example is of prudent transaction cost management. As can be seen from the case in Andhra Pradesh that the IPPs are caught in a partially deregulated segment in the supply chain where the upstream fuel supply is regulated (has a non-competitive, non-contractual environment) and the downstream pricing is also regulated i.e. does not have a retail component. This uncertainty generates ex-post contractual hazards and imposes transaction costs as the electric equipment investments are highly asset specific. This weakens the demand response abilities of the utilities and hence sends negative signals for future investments. The case shows that under uncertainty contractual renegotiation is inevitable. This renegotiation process is extremely costly in terms of haggling, regulatory time and stranded asset losses.

In Table 4-7, a summary comparison is presented on the key transaction cost variables and drivers in the contexts of Andhra Pradesh, Gujarat and UMPPs. While asset specificities are high for investor utilities in any context, fuel supply uncertainty is high in Andhra Pradesh and lower in Gujarat and the UMPPs. Demand uncertainty is similar among all these and keeps varying, but the presence of supply uncertainties and related contractual hazards makes the net transaction costs for IPPs in Andhra Pradesh very high. Widening the debate on the effect of this on liberalization, and specifically the deregulation program, the table also presents a comparison of the conditions laid down by Joskow (2008) for success[16]. We also discuss this in the context of the investment problem, further narrowing down the listed criterion. Downstream regulation is high in all the three contexts for reasons stated earlier, but upstream regulation is lower in the case of Gujarat and UMPPs. The share of public sector investment is higher in Andhra Pradesh which crowds out or deflates private investment incentives. However, both the states do not operate to sweat out excess capacity as there is enough unfulfilled demand. Given the combination of transaction cost burdens and relative absence of successful liberalization criteria the scenario for future private investment appears to be lower in Andhra Pradesh than in Gujarat. Higher investments are however expected to come more in structures similar to the UMPPs.

4.7 Conclusions

The requirements of investment in power generation are of a completely different nature in developing countries (and specifically India) from that of the matured markets of developed countries. While in developed countries the problem is one of optimal investment in base and peak load equipment, in India it is of secured annual power supply. Theoretically, for electricity markets to evolve, the institutional and regulatory environment has to favor least cost transactions among various actors in the electricity supply chain. These transactions are governed among fuel suppliers, producers and single buyers

---

[16] See Appendix at the end of this chapter for a discussion of Joskow's liberalization conditions.

Table 4-7: Comparative criteria for successful deregulation

	Presence of Attributes	IPPs in Andhra Pradesh	IPPs in Gujarat	UMPPs
Transaction Costs	Asset Specificity	High	High	High
	Fuel Supply Uncertainty	High	Low	Low
	Electricity Demand Uncertainty/Pull	Medium	Medium	Medium
	Net Transaction Costs	High	Low	Low
Joskow's Conditions	Regulation in Upstream Segment	High	Low	Low
	Regulation in Downstream Segment	High	High	High
	Share of Public Sector Investment	Higher	Lower	NA*
	Excess Capacity	No	No	NA
Net Criteria	Future Private Investment Projections	Low	High	High
	Probability of Further Deregulation Succeeding	Low	High	NA

*Not Applicable

(utilities) through contracts and for ultimate consumers through market clearing prices. However, what currently happens in the Indian power sector (and maybe in other similar contexts) is that such contracts are eventually incomplete and in the presence of a security-of-supply situation (of raw material), contractual hazards are very high, raising the costs of governing these transactions. Moreover the electricity prices are regulated by tariffs which do not allow for a pass through of these risks to the consumer (which should ideally happen in a market). We agree with the logic of Helm (2002) which states that when there is less than perfect competition in the upstream fuel supply segment, there cannot be fully fledged competition in the retail markets for electricity. In such a case, less than perfect competition will remain the normal form of industrial organization what becomes fundamental is to maintain tariffs which allow fair recovery of the investments.

The objective of attracting private capital through liberalization and deregulation has not been adequately fulfilled in the context of Indian power generation sector. We explain why this neo-classical prediction has not been fully realized using the landscape of a transaction cost analysis which predicts that in the presence of uncertainty and asset specific investments, contractual hazards will be generated and spot exchange or perfect competition may not be an optimal governance structure for attracting private investment. Through a comparison of gas-based private investments we show how independent power producers (IPPs) face high transaction costs in Andhra Pradesh as compared to that in Gujarat, as their ability for demand response is severely restrained by contractual hazards due to low commitment upstream environment and regulation. Gujarat, on the other hand, has been able to manage transaction costs for IPPs better through a prudent upstream contractual environment through setting up of a gas supply company which hedges its risk through diversified sources. Given that fuel uncertainty and upstream regulation is the prevailing condition for a major part of IPP operation in India, it is therefore no surprise that major private investments currently are coming in the form of UMPPs which are large scale entities having secured or integrated fuel supply sources. We conclude by creating a set of criteria, combining transaction cost variables and Joskow's success conditions, to predict whether private investment will be forthcoming or if deregulation will be an optimal option at this stage of reforms. Our analysis provides a framework for studying liberalization and reforms in settings similar to our cases. This can be used for analyzing reforms and deregulation in other developing countries especially those in South Asia. Future empirical research should identify what kind of transaction costs utility investors face beyond just the generation sector. Unless the regulatory design can be updated to help minimize transaction costs, progress will remain slow. Our analysis will also be helpful for policymakers to understand that less than perfect competition is not always a non-optimal solution. Most importantly it will remind policymakers that the means, deregulation, should not become the end, which is attracting private capital.

Having shown for the case of private utilities how in spite of adequate incentives, transaction costs impede development of a market based system and performance, in the next chapter we look at the case of private non-utilities i.e. firms producing their own electric power primarily for self-consumption. The question of what kinds of costs are imposed on them due to the current state of deregulation and what kind of organizational response they provide in explored in great details.

Appendix

Joskow's criteria for successful liberalization

Joskow (2008) reviews the lessons learnt from electricity reforms in the last three decades and lists some important principles needed for, and concerns raised during, the reform process. The first lesson from liberalization is that significant costs occur if reforms are implemented incompletely or incorrectly. The popular example is of California but Joskow notes that in many countries adequate investment incentives for expanded generation, transmission and distribution have been very slow to emerge. Second, the text-book model of reforms is not a sound guide for all situations. In fact the phrase 'deregulation' used to describe successful electricity reforms is misleading as this cannot be decoupled from related structural, regulatory and market design reforms. And deregulation refers specifically only to competitive wholesale and retail segments. While UK, Argentina and Chile saw significant improvements, it could not be attributed to complete deregulation as Argentina had a partly regulated 'spot market' and Chile also had lot of regulations. Moreover when there is a mix of private and public ownership, investment incentives can be hampered for private owners because public investment can come based on considerations other than market incentives like direct or indirect subsidies i.e. soft budget constraints. In the third lesson Joskow, however, warns that significant deviations from textbook model will lead to performance problems. Mere retail competition will not work in the absence of an appropriate wholesale market, network access and pricing institutions. He cites the example of EU and its member countries which are going back to upstream structural and institutional reforms rather than focus on retail competition at the outset. Fourth, spot markets should be integrated with allocation of scarce transmission capacity and fifth, market power should be dealt with *ex-ante* and not *ex-post*. Sixth, because welfare consequences of electricity sector restructuring depend on both competitive (ex. wholesale) and regulated (ex. transmission) segments, therefore good regulatory institutions which govern networks and the regulated segment is very critical to good performance.

Seventh, creation of a well-functioning transmission investment framework is crucial as congested transmission networks are constraints. Eighth lesson is that system reliability, supply security and resource adequacy are increasingly important for successful liberalization. This was not the case earlier as liberalization in greater part of Europe took place under excess capacity conditions. Therefore, these aspects become more important in those contexts where excess capacity conditions do not exist. Private players then look for stable rules and longer term contractual commitments but are intimidated if there is continuous market redesign, there are regulatory actions that limit wholesale market prices, the actions of system operators are unreliable or there are other market and regulatory imperfections. Ninth, the terms and conditions of the incumbent (or default) retail market design also sway the direction of reforms. Tenth lesson is when there are high transaction costs in practice in the wholesale power market then vertical integration between retail supply and generation could be an efficient response. If there are sufficient number of such vertically integrated players then market power is not much of a concern, otherwise it is. Eleventh lesson is that improving demand response should be given high priority in market design. Electricity, unlike normal goods, can be rationed only through rolling blackouts when there is a spurt is demand beyond capacity constrained supply. Twelfth, although the process of reforms is continuous and involves periodic learning, the benefits of doing so should exceed the costs incurred in deflated investment incentives. Thirteenth, reforms will be successful when political commitment towards wholesale and retail markets is strong; otherwise policymakers may resort to quick fixes.

5. Transaction Specificity and Electricity Self-Generation: A Discrete Choice Analysis[*]

Overview

In the decision problem of self-generation, previous literature concurs on factor demand and marginal cost structure as key determinants. Yet we observe that between firms with similarities in these, some self-generate while others do not. Why do we observe such divergent behavior? Using a contractual perspective and creating a unique quantitative variable to measure the transaction-specificity of electricity use, we test a discrete choice model on firm-level data collected through a primary survey in India. Results are highly responsive to transaction-specificity and the likelihood of self-generation is positively related to it. At the industrial level this explains why food and chemical firms are more likely to make their own electricity. We conclude that, although electricity is a general and non-specific asset, transaction costs economics does explain its vertical integration. We discuss the contextual reasons for this and also posit that this insight may help explain the widely observed vertical organization of energy resources in the developing economies.

5.1 Introduction

Electricity is a critical input in the production process of a firm and is an inevitable factor in the growth of any developing country. However across the developing world, unreliable electricity supply remains an obstacle for economic growth (Fisher-Vanden et al. 2012). Generally, firms enter into agreements with electricity distribution companies for meeting their power requirements. However, in a situation where there is a persistent demand-supply gap in the transmission grid, such agreements are usually not fulfilled[1] and firms are faced with a situation of shortage (De Nooij et al. 2007). Is this a sufficient reason for firms to vertically integrate electricity production?

In this chapter we investigate the reasons for vertical integration of energy resources by analyzing a firm's decision to self-generate electricity. While there have been previous explanations of when (or under what conditions) firms opt for self-generation, they have focused mainly on factor demand and the marginal

---

[*] A preliminary version of this chapter was presented at the 36th Annual Conference of the International Association of Energy Economics (IAEE), June 16-19 in Daegu, South Korea. A previous version of this chapter is available online as USAEE Working Paper No. 13-134. Modified parts of this chapter have been accepted for publication as a journal article in Energy Policy as of 20th October, 2014.

[1] In our industrial survey, we found that approximately 80% of the firms did not receive the full contracted maximum demand (CMD).

cost structure (Rose and McDonald 1991; Lee et al. 1996). But that does not sufficiently explain divergent behavior of similarly oriented firms. By this we mean that although many firms operate under a similar economic environment and have similar firm characteristics in terms of size, marginal cost structure, product profile or location, yet only a few among them opt for self-generation. The remaining, although facing similar situations of power supply uncertainty, do not opt for self-generation i.e. the 'make' option. For this reason we frame it as a 'make or buy' problem rather than a mere marginal cost problem so as to also understand why firms would *not* 'make' electricity and rather prefer buying. Just as an illustration when we compare (in Table 5.5, Appendix) firms sampled in an industrial survey conducted by the authors for one particular location, we find that for firms in a similar range of size (or cost structure) and factor demand (CMD), 43% opted for self-generation whereas 57% did not.

Treating electricity provision to manufacturing firms as a transaction, we hypothesize that the observed vertical integration is a response to the transaction-specific costs imposed on the firms due to unreliable supply. This transaction specificity is generated despite the fact that electric power is a non-specific, standardized asset. Electric power has high alternative uses outside of a particular transaction between any two parties. It can be subverted for use by others. For example, in peak summer seasons in many developing countries the power for use by industries is often diverted to other consumer segments due to shortage. Yet, such a transaction-specificity is generated because there is no substitutability of electricity as an input and any discontinuity in such inputs leads to discontinuity in economic activities dependent on such transactions (Nooteboom 1993). As Masten et al. (1991) note, in certain settings timely performance becomes very critical and 'interruptions at one stage can reverberate throughout the rest of the project' leading to a hold-up situation 'even though the skills and assets necessary to perform the task may be fairly common'. They call it temporal specificity as timing and coordination are of utmost importance. It is precisely this kind of transaction specificity we are referring to, which is determined by the extent to which the production process of the firm critically depends on electricity *supply-continuity*. This implies that only those firms do not 'make' which have either low transaction specificity to electricity or are limited by firm level constraints. To empirically validate this hypothesis we use a binary choice model for selection. The data comes from a representative primary survey of 107 firms (of which nearly 40% have gone for vertical integration). The survey was conducted in the Southern Indian state of Andhra Pradesh over a period of eight months in the year 2012.

In Section 5.2, we give the background and explain the trends in electricity self-generation (captive power production) in India. In Section 5.3, we discuss the existing literature on the relations between power shortages and self-generation, and highlight the gaps. We also discuss the current literature on factors which influence the investment decision to install backyard power plants.

The section then reviews the theoretical basis of vertical integration as per transaction costs economics (TCE) and discusses whether TCE is adequate for explanation. In Section 5.4 we describe our basic model, followed by data, variables and the results of the Probit estimations. The section also discusses how our theoretical claims were met by the estimations and highlights the importance of transaction specificities and contextual factors. In Section 5.5, we conclude as well as lay down some policy concerns and agenda for future research.

5.2 Background of Captive Power Production in India

Self-generation or captive power generation is a situation mostly specific to the developing countries. In developed countries where grid-based electricity is uninterrupted and available at low cost, self-generation is increasingly becoming redundant. By definition, captive power plants (CPPs) are power plants of capacity 1 mega-watt (MW) and above, commissioned by the industries for their self-consumption (Shukla 2004). Between 1995 and 2004 the total CPP generation capacity in the country increased by 68 per cent.[2] In the last decade the installed capacity of CPP has more than doubled. In 2001, the capacity was 16,157 MW whereas by the end of 2011, it became 32,900 MW.[3] Correspondingly, the share of CPP capacity to total installed capacity increased from 13.7% in 2001 to 15.9% in 2011. This phenomenon is mainly attributed to high industrial tariffs, poor service and unreliable grid power (Hansen 2008). Joseph (2010) explains that this has created a dual track economy (Naughton 1995; Qian 2003) as far as the electricity sector goes. It is called a dual track economy as due to the partial reform[4] of allowing open access (post The Electricity Act, 2003), now there is a possibility that industries, facing high cross-subsidizing power and shortages, can exit the grid and set up their own

---

[2] Source: All India Electricity Statistics (General Review), 2005 report by the Central Electricity Authority (CEA) of India.

[3] Source: Energy Statistics, 2012 report by Central Statistics Office, Government, of India, pg.15.

[4] Partial reform is when the electricity sector in somewhere between being regulated and completely deregulated. In India, the generation segment has some private participation but the distribution sector is still mostly state dominated. The Electricity Act, 2003 envisaged a transition towards a market based electricity sector where multiple (state or privately owned) generators and distributors would operate to provide electricity at marginal prices. Any player could set up a generation or distribution utility without seeking state licenses and subject only to regulatory approval and oversight of electricity regulators. Captive power production was also made license free and provided open access to the transmission grid. For details about the reform process refer http://www.powermin.nic.in/acts_ notification/electricity_act2003/pdf/The_Electricity_Act_2003.pdf. However, not all of the features of this Act have materialized, leaving the sector in a state of partial reforms.

CPPs and eventually feed back to the grid. At the same time, this also gives politicians the option where they can continue to cross-subsidize the key political constituencies while not depressing the growth of private power (*ibid.*).

We take a step back and examine closely the assertion that shortages, blackouts or poor quality of power are the key drivers for captive generation. If that is the case, then why all firms facing blackouts do not opt for 'making'? For example in Andhra Pradesh (India) roughly about only 1% of all manufacturing firms have backyard self-generation or CPPs. Why majority of firms still buy power and depend on the grid? How does that impact their performance? Is this divergence a function of firm nature, firm size, location and cost of production or policy uncertainty? Unless this is clear, the whole premise that growth of captives is a true reflection of private growth and hence an assured source of political opportunism[5], as stated by Joseph (2010), is not sound. It could be that firms 'make' for reasons which have nothing to do with quality of supply. Maybe they 'make' simply because it is cheaper than not only for the current tariff but also for future expected tariff.[6] It could be in the anticipation that cross-subsidies will not disappear, so tariffs instead of getting normalized will only become higher in the long run. This could mean that the causality is the other way: policy scenario could influence the decision.

Moreover, factors influencing the extent of generation also need to be understood, so that it is known which firm is more likely to generate enough to be also able to trade surplus electric power and make extra economic gains. But before that, it is useful to review some of the existing literature on electricity shortages, self-generation and its relation to the investment decision on a CPP.

5.3   The Make or Buy Dilemma?

5.3.1 Electricity Shortages and Self-generation

There is some literature on the causes of the growth of captive power production in developing country context, although they mostly hover around macro or meso-level indicators (Lee et al. 1996; Gulyani 1999; Joseph 2010). Lee et al. (1996) using a sample of 179 Nigerian, 290 Indonesian and 300 Thailand firms estimate an econometric model which hypothesizes that *economies of scale* determine self-generation. They find evidence for this in Nigeria and Indonesia,

---

[5]   Political opportunism arises from a dual track economy (Joseph 2010) as due to the partial reform of allowing open access (post The Electricity Act, 2003), there is the possibility that industries, facing high cross-subsidizing power and shortages, can exit the grid and set up their own CPPs and eventually feed the power back to the grid. It gives politicians the option where they can continue to cross-subsidize the key political constituencies while not depressing the growth of private power.

[6]   In our industrial survey, we find that 23.3% of the firms had a per unit generation cost from CPP higher than the grid based tariff.

but not in Thailand. Alby et al. (2010) study the effects of electricity deficiencies and credit constraints on the decision to invest in a generator in a cross country analysis using World Bank Enterprise Survey Data. Although they ask the question of why firms self-generate, they surprisingly take it for given that the two most important reasons for self-generation are uncertainty of power outages and voltage fluctuations. Fisher-Vanden et al. (2012) have studied the impact of input factor reliability on the cost-effectiveness of manufacturing firms for the case of electricity blackouts in China. Using data for the period from 1999-2004 (a period of high electric power shortage in China), they found that manufacturing firms re-organized factor use from energy to other inputs but shortages did not lead to an increase in self-generation.

There is another important, although limited, strand of literature on the *economic costs* of power outages. Wijayatunga and Jayalath (2003) estimate the impact of power outages on the GDP of Sri Lanka. This is done by calculating the cost of un-served power to industrial consumers. They find that not all industries were impacted alike. For example, the planned loss to the industries in Food and Beverages category was as high as 153 US$/hour (US$/h) whereas that of the Tea industry was only 22 US$/h. Similarly the unplanned losses for Food and Beverages industry were 363 US$/h whereas for Tea industry it was only 22 US$/h. In aggregate terms, the costs of outages for industries in Sri Lanka came out to be 0.9 % of the GDP. Pasha et al. (1989) estimate the economic cost of power outage for Pakistan using a method which accounts for the readjustments which firms make in response to the outages. They found that a majority of firms (72% of the sample) responded to outages by adjusting their operations. Twenty seven per cent firms tried to make up for losses by increasing intensity of machine use, 26% stretched working hours and 8% increased the number of shifts. Twelve per cent of the sampled firms went for the option of self-generation where the proportion of chemical and machinery equipment industries were the highest. While the average cost of planned outages for the entire sample was Rs. 6.67/kWh[7], the highest burden was on machinery equipment industries with an average cost of Rs. 25.71/kWh. For some other industries like textiles and non-metallic manufacturing, the average cost was as low as Rs. 4.24/kWh. Moreover, they found that power outages reduced the national GDP by 1.8 % for the year 1984-85. For the case of India, Bose et al. (2006), study the economic impacts of power outages on industries. Through a survey based study in the southern Indian state of Karnataka they find that economic losses due to power outages ranged from 0.09% to 0.17% of the total State Domestic Product (SDP) for High Tension (HT) industries. For the Low Tension (LT) industries it ranged from 0.04% to 0.05 % of the SDP. They also found out that LT industrial consumers had a higher willingness to pay for

---

[7] Where the exchange rate was (Pakistani) Rs. 17.50 per USD at the time these calculations were done.

improved power supply as compared to the IIT consumers indicating that the burden of power outages was higher for them. Moreover, HT consumers have an option to self-generate.

There are a few important insights which come out from the review above. The first is that power outage costs are significant for the industrial sector, impacting its efficiency and the economy in general. The second is that the impacts are not uniform across the cross section of industry and could vary with industry type, firm size, location etc. The insights from India, Pakistan and Sri Lanka point to similar trends which is hardly surprising given that the economic and industrial structure of these sub-continental neighbors are not very different (except on the margin). It means that the results from Sri Lankan and Pakistan case can be a reasonably reliable indicator of what happens in the Indian industrial sector. The third important aspect of outages, as is clear from the discussion above, is that firms have more than a just a single response to such situations. There are short term responses which are more tactical in terms of varying production structures. But there are long term responses which are more strategic in nature and in the expectation that there will not be an improved future scenario. This long term response is what can be called adaptive behavior. The phenomenon of self-generation, as evidence shows above, falls in the category of adaptation. Therefore a more rigorous analysis is needed to throw light on what are the motivators and barriers to this adaptive behavior. This is to emphasize our earlier intuition that: why only some firms adapt and not others? Which factors influence whether to invest in one's own power plant or not?

5.3.2 Investment Decision for Self-generation

Up until the beginning of 20th century, more than half of the total electricity production in the United States came from self-generation by non-utility industrial firms. As utility production increased, cheap and reliable power from large power plants became available and self-generation declined. However, the energy crisis of the 1970s brought back the interest in self-generation, especially cogeneration (Rose and McDonald 1991). The US Public Utility Regulatory Policies Act (PURPA) of 1978 made regulatory provisions for firms generating electricity to get connected to the grid and enabled them to operate alongside the utilities. It also stipulated a buyback rate at which electricity from these firms could be bought by the utilities. Most of the studies (Hess 1983; Barclay et al. 1989; Kim and Byong-Hun 1990) implicitly consider that the level of this buyback rate is a significant determinant for the amount of electric power a firm would supply. However, Rose and McDonald (1991) show that the buyback rate may not be an important factor for producing electricity by a manufacturing firm. They develop a model which shows how a cost-minimizing firm decides to invest in a cogeneration facility based on the interactions of investment costs, fuel prices, electricity prices and rate of buyback. The model predicts that there will be an increase in cogeneration when i) the factor demand for electricity increases, ii) the marginal costs of electricity generation decreases, iii) the higher the ability of the firm to utilize scale economies is, and iv) the higher the price of grid electricity and the buyback rate. Using a sample of 1034 firms in two industries - chemicals and paper industries (representing 50% of all cogeneration capacity) - the authors perform econometric tests to find that plant demand for electric power and price of electricity significantly explain the amount of co-generated electricity, while the buyback rate did not have a very important influence.

This still does not explain some other key contradictions which are especially relevant in the developing context. One obvious difference for the case of India from the US case is that firms in India (and in other similar developing context) operate under a situation of *shortage*, unlike that of US. As a consequence, *supply discontinuity* assumes naturally an important role. The important literature in this regard explains the conditions under which it will be profitable to adopt cogeneration through self-generation (Joskow and Jones 1983; Rose and McDonald 1991; Dismukes and Kleit 1999). However, that is not very useful in understanding why firms would opt for self-generation at the first place, even if cogeneration was not the prime motive. What is also not explained is why plants within homogenous industrial categories and across symmetric plant sizes display divergent behavior in terms of producing own electricity. This question of why similarly oriented firms (i.e. those having same marginal cost structure, abilities to utilize scale economies or facing same factor demand) display divergent behavior would have been redundant if, for example, Rose and McDonald's sample represented the whole manufacturing industry population and not merely the population of cogenerating manufacturing firms. But the sample used by them includes only those firms which have opted for self-generation. If we compare the key characteristics of CPP and non-CPP firms in our sample (see Appendix, Table 5-6) then we can observe that within each sub-category of these characteristics, firm size, location, power intensity and factor demand, there is the presence of both CPP and non-CPP firms. It shows that even if there are two firms of comparable size, one firm opts for CPP whereas another does not. Similarly, it is always a case that for two firms having the same factor demand, power intensities or being located in the same place, if one firm opts for CPP, there is another which does not.

We therefore suspect that there is more to the investment decision for self-generation than mere factor demand and the marginal cost structure. It is here that we introduce the concept of electricity provision as a transaction, rather than merely a matter of resource input, shifting the problem paradigm from cost-effective provision to vertical integration. Electricity provision is a transaction guided through contracts/agreements (either explicit or implicit) between the distribution utility and the buyer. Typically utilities promise a reliable provision of electricity with a certain quality level.[8] But when they fail to provide it as per the promised terms or do so with an element of uncertainty, contractual hazards set in for the buyer. Transaction cost economics suggests that a firm will vertically integrate the production of a very specific asset when there are contractual hazards imposing high transaction costs in procuring that from the market (Masten 1984; Williamson 2002). But electricity is a rather a standardized commodity as far as its physical attributes is concerned. So can transaction cost economics still explain self-generation as an act of vertical integration minimizing transaction costs? We explore this question a little further in the next sub-section.

5.3.3 Vertical Integration

New institutional economics has been applied extensively to the study of power sector deregulation (Crew and Kleindorfer 1986; Dubash and Rajan 2001; Guasch 2004; Finon 2006; Ménard and Ghertman 2009). Transaction cost economics (Williamson 1985) has made significant contributions to the existing debate of whether power is best governed through disintegrated firms engaged in market exchange or through regulated vertically integrated firms (Spiller 2009). However, the focus of these debates have more or less been on the supply side of electricity while often ignoring the fact that electricity is also a vital input in all forms of development activities, especially industrial growth. This directs our attention to the transaction specificity of electricity as an input. Though electricity is not in itself a specific asset, its physical property is such that it requires being simultaneously produced and consumed. It is costly and inefficient (if not entirely impossible) to store electric power unlike other resources or inputs and thereby requires high levels of coordination leading to what some say 'coordination economies' (Meyer 2012). Therefore timing, in electricity provision, is of indispensable importance. Masten et al. (1991) show in the case of shipbuilding how temporal specificity can be an important factor determining organizational form. Similarly Klein et al. (1978) show how because of timing issues, newspapers tend to own their presses more than book publishers. Moreover, the substitutability of electricity as a product is rather limited and ineffective. Discontinuity in such transactions, whether due to

---

[8]   In India, the regulatory commissions have certain guidelines, known as 'General Terms and Conditions of Supply', for electricity supply which are mandatory for distribution utilities. A sample document giving these terms and conditions is available at http://www.apcentralpower.com/tariffs/GTCS.pdf. For example, in Section 3.1.1, it is stated in terms of the fulfillment of Contract Maximum Demand (CMD) that 'The Company shall supply electricity at a frequency of 50 Hz with variation limits as per Rule 55 of the Indian Electricity Rules 1956. The power supply shall be uninterrupted, as far as possible.' There are detailed liabilities listed for both the parties under the breach of this agreement.

coordination or production failures, leads to discontinuity in economic activities dependent on such transactions (Nooteboom 1993). This dependence on the part of the economic actors (in this case industrial producers) creates transaction-specific costs (*ibid.*). Under such situation, the suppliers of electricity may behave opportunistically. Such opportunism, when the supplier is a private utility, could be the raising of prices or when the supplier is a partially deregulated state-owned utility (facing soft budget constraint), just a wave of hand i.e. unscheduled power cuts or supplying power at fluctuating voltages.

This imposes costs on manufacturing firms and could force them to vertically integrate the production of electricity in order to minimize such dependence. We contend that variation in the levels of this dependence among similarly oriented firms could provide an explanation for observing divergent behavior in terms of the 'make or buy' decision. For example, a firm manufacturing a perishable good (like food or beverages) will have a different level of dependence on a continuous supply of electric power than those which are producing comparatively high storage goods. A pharmaceutical firm would risk altering the chemical composition of crucial drugs in the absence of reliable continuous electric power, which may not be the case for a textile manufacturing firm. These examples suggest that although electric power may not be a specific asset in itself, it creates a *chain of specificity* which becomes a crucial determinant in industrial behavior.

However, 'transaction cost explanations are subject to contextual factors'(Coles and Hesterly 1998) and they help explaining vertical integration. These contextual factors may be different for developed and developing country settings. Coles and Hesterly, for example, examine vertical integration in the hospital industry which has a mix of public and private ownership. This makes the context of 'make or buy' decision-making very different from other industries. They find that public-owned hospitals, where pressures for efficiency are less, tend to vertically integrate more than contracting out services and that the decisions were 'less sensitive to transaction costs'. Besides ownership, an important contextual factor which influences the 'make or buy' decision is firm size. Williamson (1985: p. 94) notes that 'larger firms will be more integrated into components than will smaller firms, *ceteris paribus*'. Other contextual factors could be firm location, policy environment and supply uncertainty. Differences in these may have differential effects on firm behavior, even when the assets are comparable or similar. For example, in our case we perceive firm size as not only reflecting the economies of scale but also a factor which determines the ability of the firm to minimize transaction costs. This is only a slight but critical variation of the treatment of firm size (indicated by factor demand) by Rose and McDonald (1991). The next section describes the model specification and data.

5.4 Model, Data and Variables

5.4.1 Binary Choice (Probit) Model

We estimate a binary choice (i.e., *probit*) model where the dependent variable has a binary outcome of 0 when the firm does not install a CPP and 1 when it installs a CPP. This represents the 'make or buy' decision process.[9]
The basic form of a binary dependent outcome variable takes the form[10]

$$y = \begin{cases} 1 \text{ with probability p} \\ 0 \text{ with probability } 1 - p \end{cases} \qquad \text{Eq. 1}$$

With the conditional probability being

$$p_i \equiv \Pr(y_i = 1|x) = F(x_i' \beta) \qquad \text{Eq. 2}$$

x is the regressor vector and β is parameter vector

$F(\cdot)$ is a cumulative distribution function which ensures that the condition $0 \leq p \leq 1$ is satisfied. Specifically when estimating a probit model the distribution function follows the standard normal cumulative distribution function (cdf).

$$\phi(x'\beta) = \int_{-\infty}^{x'\beta} \emptyset(z)dz \qquad \text{Eq. 3}$$

and

$$\emptyset(z) = 2\pi^{-\frac{1}{2}} \exp\left(\frac{-z^2}{2}\right) \qquad \text{Eq. 4}$$

; z being a real number

Based on our discussion in the preceding section, our model for the make-or-buy decision takes the following form:

---

[9] By 'making' we do not mean that the firm does not at all use grid based electric power. The general behavior of India firms producing their own electricity is that they use backyard power plants to partially fulfill their power requirements. According to the Electricity Act, 2003 a firm qualifies as a CPP as long as it uses at least 51% of the self-generated electricity for its production purposes. Any excess production above that is eligible to be sold back to the grid. See page 127, Power Compendium 2011, Ministry of Power, India (http://powermin.nic.in/acts_ notification/pdf/power_compendium.pdf).

[10] Following notations are as per: Microeconometrics Using Stata, Cameron and Trivedi, Stata Press, 2009.

$$\text{Pr}(\text{pwr}_{\text{make}} = 1|x) = F\big(\beta_0 + \beta_i X_{ij} + \beta_k Z_{kj} + \beta_n \text{Dummy}_{nj}\big) \qquad \text{Eq. 5}$$

where, X_{ij} is the vector of i power specificity related variables;

Z_{kj} is the k vector of firm level controls;

and Dummy_{nj} are n dummies for distribution utility environment.

The above equation can be interpreted as giving the direction of change in probability of a firm installing its own backyard CPP. The estimation of the parameters uses a maximum likelihood procedure, also known as the Maximum Likelihood Estimation technique. It gives a value of the parameter vector $\hat{\beta}$, the Maximum Likelihood Estimator (MLE), which maximizes the probability of observing the given sample from the population. For a sample of n independent observations, the MLE maximizes (through iterative methods) the following log-likelihood function:

$$Q(\beta) = \sum_{i=1}^{n} [y_i \ln F(x_i' \beta) + (1 - y_i)\ln\{1 - F(x_i' \beta)\}] \qquad \text{Eq. 6}$$

However, interpreting the parameter values of a probit model is not straight forward (Cameron and Trivedi 2009). The coefficients of the model (as stated in Eq.5), cannot be simply interpreted as giving the percentage change in probability of a firm going for self-generation for a unit change in the variable values. This is because the distribution function is non-linear cdf and the change in probability will vary at different points of the probability function. Therefore, we calculate the marginal effects (at mean) which give the instantaneous rate of change in the probability of observing the non-zero dependent variable, when the explanatory variable changes by a small amount holding all other variables constant at their means. This is, however, only when the explanatory variable is continuous. For categorical explanatory variables the marginal effects show the extent to which probability will be higher of observing the outcome among the categories holding the other variables at their means.

5.4.2 Data

We conduct a primary survey of manufacturing firms in the south Indian state of Andhra Pradesh (AP). This state is a leader in power sector deregulation post liberalization and an industrial state of prominence with one of the fastest growing captive power sectors. However, in recent times the performance of the power sector in this state has not been good, forcing power cuts and holidays on the industries. We initially went for stratified random sampling based on industry type. But the response rate was extremely low owing to various reasons. The most important reason being the general apprehension by firms that sensitive information would be leaked. Additional problems arose because the proportion of self-generating firms (having CPPs) is anyways very low. In AP, firms having CPPs are only 5.28% of the total firms listed in the State Industrial Association directory. If we account for selection bias owing to association membership and take the total number of industries present in AP (including those outside the association), then the proportion is even lower i.e. only 1%. Therefore we went for a complete coverage approach and approached all the CPPs in the major industrial districts of AP. Correspondingly, non-CPP firms in the same location were randomly approached to create a sample representing both. This way the response rate increased. We eventually got filled questionnaires through face-to-face interviews from 107 firms of which 40% have CPP.[11] The pilot phase was conducted exclusively by one of the authors. For the main phase, 8 trained investigators (all electrical engineering graduates) were sent to 13 districts[12] of AP covering a geographical area of 149,446 sq. km. with a population of 53.7 million. It took a period of roughly 8 months from the beginning of the pilot phase to conclude the survey. The main problem, apart from the low response rates, were the geographical spread of the captive industries, which made approaching them very expensive and time consuming. Yet, this has been (at least to our knowledge) a first of its kind of face-to face industrial survey in India where questions about the decision to install CPP was asked directly to the firm level respondents.

Out of the total number of firms, 13 were dropped from the analysis as they were purely power producing firms, incorporated for the sole purpose of selling electricity. Another firm was dropped as it was an outlier in terms of the size. The annual sales figure of this firm was 17.3 times bigger than the next biggest sales figure. The sales figure of the outlier firm was 1217.2 times more than the median firm. Our final sample therefore consists of 93 manufacturing firms, out of which 30 ($\approx$ 35%) have CPPs and 63 do not have CPPs (i.e. depend entirely on the grid for their power requirements). Table 5-1 shows the industry-wise sample stratification and the proportion of CPP and non-CPP firms for each category. As can be seen from the table, Chemicals, Food and Machine Tools have higher proportions in the sample. This is consistent with the fact that these industries have the highest share in the Andhra Pradesh industrial sector. Moreover, Cement and Food are the sectors where the share of firms that have gone for CPPs is very high.

---

[11] The number of CPPs in the sample is 23.95% of the total CPP population in AP.

[12] The colored segments in Fig. 5-1 show the districts covered in the survey namely: Anantapur, Chittoor, East Godavari, Guntur, Hyderabad, Khammam, Krishna, Kurnool, Medak, Nalgonda, Rangareddy, Visakhapatnam and West Godavari.

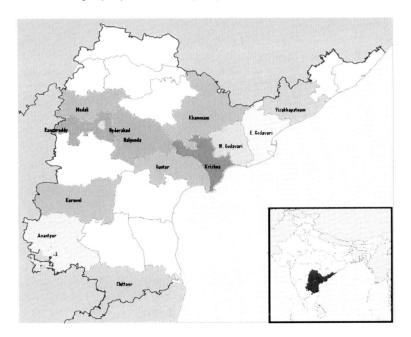

Figure 5-1: Districts of AP state covered in the sample

Source: Own illustration with image from Wikimedia commons

Table 5-1: Industry-wise sample stratification

INDUSTRY	Non-CPP	CPP	Total
Cement	2 (22.2)	7 (77.7)	9 (9.6)
Chemicals	17 (74)	6 (26)	23 (24.7)
Food	7 (36.8)	12 (63.1)	19 (20.4)
Machinery and Tools	15 (88.2)	2 (11.7)	17 (18.2)
Metallic (including Iron and Steel)	12 (92.3)	1 (7.6)	13 (14)
Textiles	10 (83.3)	2 (16.6)	12 (13)
Total	**63 (67.7)**	**30 (32.2)**	**93**

Source: Own calculations from survey data

5.4.3 Variables

The key explanatory variables are: the annual total sales of the firm ($SALE\_2011$) which indicates the size of the firm; power specificity (PWR_SPEC) which measures the specificity i.e. extent of dependence on a critical input (electricity in this case); *land availability* ($LAND\_EX$) which is a proxy for location; and power cuts (*PWR_CUTS*) which reflects power shortages (or supply uncertainty). *PWR_SPEC* is a variable composed of a) power intensity (*PWR_INT*) measured as per unit expense on electricity and b) dependence on continuous supply (*PWR_CONT*) i.e., the costs of discontinuity of the input. The reason is neither the intensity factor nor the dependency factor alone explain the specificity of electricity transaction. Together they explain specificity of electricity transaction. During our pre-survey interviews with a variety of industrial actors we found that there are some firms who have high per unit expense on electric power (for example some machinery manufacturers), but do not critically depend on continuous supply. They can manage and/or adapt their production cycles as per the grid availability. On the other hand, there are firms which have very high dependency on continuous supply but have very less per unit expense ratio for electric power, example being smaller pharmaceutical firms. Therefore, a combination or interplay of these two factors together will give a better perspective on the specificity factor. We hypothesize that this is a key factor which explains the 'make or buy' decision for electricity consumers and test that in our model. The variable *PWR_INT* is an indicator of the relative proportions with which electricity is used by a firm and is therefore another crucial variable which will influence the decision to make own electricity. *PWR_CONT* takes three values depending on the level of dependence. Momentary costs[13] of power outages from Wijayatunga and Jayalath (2004) paper and expert opinion on Indian industries[14] were used to rank the industrial categories. Momentary costs are the closest indicator for the extent of dependency on continuous supply, in the absence of any direct measure. Since such figures for industrial categories in India or AP specifically are not available we have used Sri Lanka figures as proxy. We can expect the engineering behavior between Sri Lanka and India will be quite close. The location variable *LAND_EX* shows whether the firm had extra land available for installing a CPP or had to acquire one for installing a CPP. This is a control variable because those firms who already have extra land available are more likely to install a CPP as they do not have to incur additional costs of finding and buying adjacent land. The variable *PWR_CUTS* is a dummy variable measuring shortages. In the survey, questions were asked about whether firms face no power cuts, scheduled power cuts, unscheduled power cuts or both. *INDS_TYPE* is a dummy for industry type of the firm. Five categories were created based on industrial types from the Indian National Industrial Classification (NIC) 2 digit code system. They were matched with the categories from Wijayatunga and Jayalath (2004) paper for respective industries in Sri Lanka for the sake of consistency and without loss of generality. Andhra Pradesh is divided into four distribution zones with each zone having its own

---

[13] It is defined as the revenue losses due to sudden interruptions.

[14] Experts included firm managers and consultants working for these industries.

state owned distribution company. DISCOM is a dummy for the distribution utility. This is to observe for any operational heterogeneity in the different distribution utilities. Table 5-2 gives a brief description and summary statistics of the key explanatory variables. The firm with the smallest size has annual sales of Rs. 20 million whereas the largest firm has sales of Rs. 763, 64 million with the mean firm earning Rs. 3747 million. The mean transaction specificity to electricity use is 0.19 with the maximum being 1.32.

Table 5-2: Description and summary statistics of independent variables

Variable Name	Description	Obs.	Mean	SD	Min	Max
PWR_INT	Power Intensity = power expense/total expenses	93	0.08	0.09	0.003	0.44
PWR_CONT	Dependency on continuous supply; = 1 if low; = 2 if medium; = 3 if high	93	2.03	0.81	1.0	3
PWR_SPEC	The transaction specificity to electricity use (product of PWR_INT and PWR_CONT)	93	0.19	0.26	0.003	1.32
SALE_2011	Annual Sales in Rs. Million	93	3747	9078	20.0	76364
PWR_CUTS	= 1 if firm faces power cuts; and 0 otherwise	93	0.81	0.40	0.0	1
LAND_EX	= 1 if firm had extra land; and 0 otherwise	93	0.35	0.48	0.0	1
INDS_TYPE	= 0 if Chemicals; = 1 if Food and Beverages; = 2- if Textile; = 3 if Non-metallic; = 4 if Metallic	93	1.90	1.57	0.0	4
DISCOM	Distribution Utility; 1-CPDCL; 2-SPDCL; 3-EPDCL; 4-NPDCL	93	1.68	0.81	1.0	3

Notes: CPDCL - Central Power Distribution Company Limited; SPDCL – Southern Power DCL; EPDCL – Eastern Power DCL; NPDCL – Northern Power DCL
Source: Own calculations from survey data

5.4.4 *Results*

Table 5-3 gives results of the probit model looking into the likelihood of making own power. We explore various specifications of the model and find that the key variables turn out to be significant (see Table 3). In M1[15], we use as regressors the annual sales figure (*LNSALE_2011*), power specificity (*PWR_SPEC*), location (*LAND_EX*), power shortages (*PWR_CUTS*) and a dummy for the industry type (*INDS_TYPE*). In M2 we add the log of sales squared (lnsale2new) to M1. This is to check for the non-linearity for scale economies. While estimating M3 we add to M2 a dummy for the different distribution utilities (*DISCOM*) in the state. This is to account for any differences in utility operation environment. Power specificity (*PWR_SPEC*) is significant and has a positive

---

[15] M1, M2 etc. represent Model 1, Model 2 etc.

co-efficient validating our hypothesis. This shows that when firms have greater intensity for power as well as dependence on continuous supply at the same time, the likelihood for owning one's own backyard CPP will be higher. The variable for firm size is positive and statistically significant. This confirms the hypothesis that bigger the firm size, more likely that it will 'make' its own electricity. Sales-squared is significant and non-linearity is observed. It suggests that beyond a certain level of firm size, the likelihood of a firm opting for the make option will fall. This could be because very large firms have their own substations and receive electric power using very High Tension (HT) transmission lines and hence do not face any power shortage. The location indicator (presence of extra land) is significant and has a positive co-efficient. Once firms start planning to go for a CPP, availability of land may be a concern but not an insurmountable one, especially in semi-urban and rural areas.

Table 5-3: Results of Probit regression on likelihood of 'making' own power

	(1) M1	(2) M2	(3) M3
PWR_MAKE			
LNSALE_2011	0.2681**	1.3055***	1.3536***
	(0.1205)	(0.4401)	(0.4362)
LNSALE_SQR		-0.5160***	-0.5333***
		(0.1966)	(0.1955)
PWR_SPEC	2.9375**	3.7007***	3.7759***
	(1.3507)	(1.3474)	(1.3850)
LAND_EX	1.0042**	1.1903***	1.1912***
	(0.4048)	(0.4215)	(0.4352)
PWR_CUTS	-	-2.0540***	-2.2138***
	2.0066***	(0.6658)	(0.6700)
	(0.6286)		
INDS_TYPE_FOOD	1.1894**	1.4004***	1.6498**
	(0.4900)	(0.5178)	(0.6909)
INDS_TYPE_TEXTILE	-0.7970	-0.7037	-0.3531
	(0.5693)	(0.6058)	(0.7365)
INDS_TYPE_NON-METALLIC	-2.0000*	-2.5770**	-2.4801**
	(1.0717)	(1.0514)	(1.0626)
INDS_TYPE_METALLIC	-0.6683	-0.6057	-0.5758
	(0.5192)	(0.5282)	(0.5104)
DISCOM_SPDCL			-0.4689
			(0.6986)
DISCOM_EPDCL			-0.0205
			(0.5139)
Cons	-1.6177	-1.8227	-1.7779
	(1.2373)	(1.3316)	(1.3204)
N	93	93	93
pseudo R^2	0.529	0.552	0.558
Log lik.	-27.5151	-26.1927	-25.8442
Chi-squared	39.8706	36.0280	38.7148

Standard errors in parentheses
* $p < 0.10$, ** $p < 0.05$, *** $p < 0.01$
INDS_TYPE_0 is Chemicals but does not show in regression results as it is the base category

The result for power shortage variable (*PWR_CUTS*) is interesting. Although it is significant, the co-efficient turns out be negative for all the estimated models. One probable reason for this could be the distinction between how the variable is defined and how it is measured. Since we have clubbed, scheduled power cuts also in the category of power shortage, it is likely that firms may not perceive a power cut a problem if it is scheduled (though we do not have any evidence).[16] Given the available schedule of power cut, they may have already altered their production process or kept a weekly off keeping the scheduled power cut in mind. In fact, our survey also indicates that firms do not have same day as weekly off despite in the same district. Interestingly, all those firms which have indicated unscheduled power cuts as a problem are relatively small in size. The average sales of these firms are at least 50% of those which have reported scheduled power cuts in their region. This implies that these smaller firms may not end up having a CPP due to other constraints like scale economies. This is representative of the entire industrial population trend where the proportion of CPP firms is very low compared to non-CPP firms. However, this points out to a serious policy concern. If with increase in power shortages firms actually are less likely to 'make' (as our results show), then they will be driven out of production eventually. This risk will be higher for those firms which have high transaction specificity for electric power but are limited by their ability to utilize scale economies. In a way such firms will face a 'make or die' situation. Recent trends suggest that indeed a large number of smaller firms have either shut down in many Indian states due to increased power shortages[17] or have located in other states where power is available. M2 appears to be the best among the various specifications as it has all the important controls and yet predicts 70 % of the cases correctly for firms that have gone for CPP and 94% roughly for firms that have not gone for CPP. Therefore, we can look at the marginal effects of M2 for a sense of the proportion.

Table 5-4 gives the marginal effects (at mean) of the explanatory variables on the likelihood of observing self-generation. A unit change in power specificity has a strong effect on the likelihood of self-generation to an extent of more than 100%. Firm size has a positive but not very strong effect. A unit change in firm size (as shown by the variable *LNSALE_2011*) leads to approximately 37% increase in the probability of self-generation. Location also has a mildly strong impact on the likelihood of self-generation. A firm with extra land will have a 28-38% higher likelihood of making own power than a firm which does not

---

[16] When we consider 'scheduled power cuts' as part of no power problem and categorize them accordingly, the variable comes out to be positive but insignificant in all the models. The results are available on request.

[17] http://www.thehindu.com/news/states/tamil-nadu/power-outage-provokes-micro-industries-outrage/article394300.ece; http://www.deccanherald.com/content/273832/power-crisis-takes-toll-andhra.html.

have extra land. When comparing across industries, the marginal effects suggest that a food manufacturing firm will be 48% more likely to opt for a CPP as compared to a chemical firm. On the other hand, a textile, non-metallic or metallic firm will be 15.7 %, 32.4 % and 15.2% respectively less likely to opt for a CPP as compared to a chemical firm. We checked for robustness by restricting the analysis only to the two largest sectors i.e. Food and Chemicals. All the coefficients retain same sign and are still statistically significant with not much change in values from the base model (see Appendix, Table 5-7).

Table 5-4: Marginal Effects for the various probit specifications

	(1) mfx1	(2) mfx2	(3) mfx3
PWR_MAKE			
LNSALE_2011	0.0797*	0.374**	0.393**
	(0.0358)	(0.125)	(0.129)
PWR_SPEC	0.873*	1.060**	1.097**
	(0.409)	(0.402)	(0.418)
_ILAND_EX (d)	0.322*	0.373**	0.378**
	(0.136)	(0.138)	(0.145)
_IPWR_CUTS (d)	-0.679***	-0.687***	-0.728***
	(0.171)	(0.181)	(0.160)
_IINDS_TYPE_FOOD (d)	0.413*	0.480**	0.566*
	(0.180)	(0.182)	(0.225)
_IINDS_TYPE_TEXTILE (d)	-0.180	-0.157	-0.0913
	(0.0972)	(0.104)	(0.168)
_IINDS_TYPE_NON-METALLIC (d)	-0.306***	-0.324***	-0.325***
	(0.0820)	(0.0786)	(0.0812)
_IINDS_TYPE_METALLIC (d)	-0.173	-0.152	-0.148
	(0.110)	(0.110)	(0.112)
LNSALE_SQR		-0.148**	-0.155**
		(0.0562)	(0.0584)
_IDISCOM_SPDCL (d)			-0.123
			(0.166)
_IDISCOM_EPDCL (d)			-0.00592
			(0.148)
N	93	93	93

Marginal effects; Standard errors in parentheses
(d) for discrete change of dummy variable from 0 to 1
$^*p < 0.05, ^{**}p < 0.01, ^{***}p < 0.001$

5.4.5 *Discussion*

We have framed the problem of a firm opting for self-generation of electricity as a case of 'make or buy' because earlier explanations relied on factor demand and marginal cost structure but did not explain why firms with comparable key characteristics show divergent behavior. We obtain a sample of 107 manufacturing firms across key industrial categories through a primary survey in the southern Indian state of Andhra Pradesh. Then several binary choice models are estimated to check for the robustness of the key variables which explain the 'make or buy' decision for electricity. We find that, when the context is of supply shortages, some firms make their own electric power while others buy from the grid depending on their *sensitivity* to transaction specificity (measured by the variable 'power specificity' in our case). According to traditional transaction cost theory, vertical integration is observed or is efficient when there is high asset specificity, *ceteris paribus*. Asset specificity is generated when an asset (or input) has very low opportunity cost outside the particular transaction. This could lead to a potential hold-up situation or opportunistic behavior. In such situations it is often a prudent response by the firm to reduce the related transaction costs by internalizing the production of such a specific asset. However, electricity is not a specific asset with regards to its physical attributes and has a high opportunity cost outside the transaction. Yet, as we show, it generates transaction specificity for the buyer who gets 'locked-in' to non-production. Such specificity is because electricity has high coordination economies which impose high costs on buyers when a *context* of shortages prevails.

As our results show, the power specificity (*PWR_SPEC*) variable comes out significant and matches our hypothesis in terms of the direction of the causality. Higher is the specificity, more likely the firm will opt for self-generation. We observe variation across industrial categories. Food manufacturing firms and chemical firms are more likely to opt for the 'make' option as compared to other industrial categories. This validates the proposition that transaction specificities would be higher for them as their dependence on continuous power supply is higher. Power shortage, firm size and location variables are also significant confirming that contextual factors influence the decision. However, operational environment does not significantly explain this divergent behavior but this could be due to insufficient operational heterogeneity.

5.5 Conclusions

There is a wide scope and need for research on industrial behavior related to energy resources in developing country contexts. This is because the conditions, whether be it policy or operational environment, differ very much from the developed countries. This implies that firms work under constraints that do not often allow marginal cost considerations to be met efficiently. More importantly such contexts are beset with incomplete or uncertain contractual relationships. And when this happens, sensitivity to transaction cost concerns increase. The challenge lies in identifying and dealing with them. Our study demonstrates that there is high responsiveness to transaction-specificity in electricity use by manufacturing firms. This is despite the fact that electricity is a standardized, non-specific asset and in a different context (that of developed countries) would not generate transaction costs or motivate vertical integration at the firm-level. Yet, a mere shift in the context transforms it into a kind of 'transaction-specific' asset leading to vertical integration. We, therefore, contend that transaction cost economics does explain integration of electricity by firms but only when the appropriate type of transaction-specificities are identified, which in turn could vary widely with contexts. More research using the perspective of contractual relationships and contextual factors would be useful in identifying critical transaction-specificities and enhance the understanding of firm behavior in developing economies, especially in relation to energy resources such as electricity, coal or natural gas.

In Chapters 4 and 5, we have shown that in spite of a proper incentive structure neither the private utilities, nor the non-utilities minimize transaction costs in the current structure. It has also been shown that the presence of contractual hazards requires adequate *ex-post* governance structures which can minimize the associated transaction costs. Hence regulatory governance assumes greater importance than regulatory incentives as the question of credible commitments to protect specific investments by electricity producers gain prominence. In the next chapter, therefore, we discuss in greater details the literature on regulatory governance and also try to measure its impact on a concrete indicator of power sector performance.

Appendix

Table 5-5: Firm characteristics in a randomly sampled district

Firm Number	Location (District)	Firm Size (Sales in Rs. Million)	Factor Demand (CMD, Contracted Maximum Demand in MW)	Owns CPP (Captive Power Plant)
1	Guntur	5188.3	4	Yes
2	Guntur	3389.7	8	Yes
3	Guntur	3000	7	Yes
4	Guntur	4800	2.25	No
5	Guntur	3667.3	0.6	No
6	Guntur	5374	3.6	No
7	Guntur	5729	1	No
Average	For Firms Owning CPP	3859	6	
	For Firms Not Owning CPP	4893	2	

Source: Own calculation based on survey data

Table 5-6: Firm characteristics of CPP and Non-CPP firms

S.N.	Firm Characteristic		No. of CPP (as % of total CPP)	No. of Non-CPP (as % of total non-CPP
1	Firm Size (in Rs. Million)	< 500	6 (20)	25 (39.7)
		500-1000	2 (6.7)	12 (19)
		1000-5000	12 (40)	19 (30.2)
		> 500	10 (33.3)	7 (11.1)
2	Location	Industrial Estate	8 (26.7)	36 (57.1)
		Cluster	8 (26.7)	16 (25.4)
		Stand Alone	14 (46.7)	11 (17.5)
3	Power Intensity (ratio of expense on power over total expenses	<0.05	12 (40)	39 (61.9)
		0.05-0.1	2 (6.7)	9 (14.3)
		0.1-0.2	7 (23.3)	12 (19)
		>0.2	9 (30)	3 (4.8)
4	Factor Demand (CMD, Contract Maximum Demand) in Megawatt, MW	< 1	12 (40)	36 (57.1)
		1-2.6	6 (20.0)	16 (25.4)
		>2.6	12 (40)	11 (17.5)

Source: Own calculation based on survey data

Table 5-7: Comparison of restricted model and complete model

Key Variables		M1 (Complete Model) N=93	M1 (Restricted Model) N=36
1.	ANNUAL SALE	.268**	.346*
2.	POWER SPECIFICITY	2.93**	4.02*
3.	INDUSTRIAL TYPE – Food	1.18**	1.30**

$^{*}p < 0.10,\ ^{**}p < 0.05,\ ^{***}p < 0.01$

Source: Own estimations

6. Thermal Efficiency and Regulatory Governance: A Stochastic Frontier Analysis[*]

Overview

The chapter tests the impact of institutional quality on the performance of thermal power sector in India. We estimate a translog inefficiency effects stochastic frontier model using plant age, plant capacity and an index of regulatory governance as determinants of inefficiency. The dataset comprises a panel of 77 coal-based thermal power plants during the period 1994-95 to 2010-11. The mean technical efficiency is 76.7% which means there is wide scope for efficiency improvement in the sector. However, this is 4% points higher than previous estimates which measured productivity up to the year 2001-02. Results are robust to various model specifications and regulatory governance positively impacts plant performance. While technical efficiency is highly sensitive to unbundling of state electricity boards, it is not impacted significantly by the experience of regulators. The policy implication is that the quality of regulatory capacity and experience need to be enhanced for the desired sectoral performance.

6.1 Introduction

Contrary to initial theoretical claims, empirical reality has shown that regulatory structures are critical for effective deregulation. Hence, in recent times there has been an increasing focus on, and acceptance of, the role of institutional quality in determining the performance in the utilities sector (Cubbin and Stern 2006). While the major emphasis of the literature has been on regulatory incentives, new institutional economics is concerned with regulatory governance. While distinguishing between incentives and governance, Levy and Spiller (1994) refer to *incentives* as the rules related to utility pricing, subsidies etc. and *governance* as the ways in which high credible commitments are generated. Unless there is a commitment against expropriation of rents, investments in high asset-specific electricity infrastructure does not take place. In liberalized electricity sectors this role of credible commitments is delegated to an independent regulatory agency. In India a system of independent regulation was set up following power sector liberalization in the late nineties. The chief objectives of setting up such a system was to invite greater private investments, increase efficiency of power plants, improve quality and access to electricity and rationalize tariffs. While

---

[*] A previous version of this chapter is available online as USAEE Working Paper No. 14-155. Modified parts of this chapter are under review as a journal article in Energy Economics as of 20th October, 2014.

there has been some analysis of the effects of regulatory governance on generation capacity (Cubbin and Stern 2006), there is none on utility level efficiency, especially in a country-specific context.

In this chapter, we use a parametric stochastic frontier approach to estimate the effects of regulatory reforms on the dynamic technical efficiency using panel data of 77 coal-based thermal power plants in India from the period 1994-2010. A single stage inefficiency effects model (Battese and Coelli 1995; See and Coelli 2012) is estimated where an index of regulatory governance is used as an explanatory variable for the inefficiency term. The regulatory governance index is an aggregation of sub-indexes of indicators like tariff, transmission and distributions gains, age of regulatory commission, status of unbundling and stability of the regulatory commission composition. The index covers the period 2000-10 and is constructed for 14 Indian states for which information was available.

The rest of the chapter is structured as follows: Section 6.2 gives a background of electricity sector reforms in India and also gives reasons why coal-based thermal production is representative of the generation segment. Section 6.3 extensively reviews the literature on efficiency analysis of Indian thermal power plants and the determinants of technical inefficiency. It also discusses the literature on international comparisons of the role of regulatory governance on utility reforms. There is a very limited set of literature of Indian thermal efficiency with no analysis accounting for the latest years, 2001 to 2010. There is no study which has studied the effect of regulatory reforms on thermal efficiency. In this section we explain how our study makes up for these and other gaps in previous estimations of thermal efficiency. Section 6.4 details the empirical strategy by specifying the translog stochastic frontier model and describing and summarizing the data. The details about how the composite regulatory index is constructed, the data sources for the key indicators is also explained. Section 6.5 discusses the results from the estimation of model parameters and the technical efficiency analysis. It also discusses the potential explanations for the observed results on the determinants of technical inefficiency. Section 6.6 ends with conclusions and potential policy outcomes.

6.2 Background

The process of liberalization and market reforms has been a challenging one in developing countries including India (Singh 2010). In India, repeated efforts to deregulate the power sector modeled on the example of developed countries have not borne expected results. Before 1991, there was hardly any private participation and the electricity sector was highly regulated. There were State Electricity Boards (SEBs) which owned the generation, transmission as well as the distribution segments. The first institutional reform was in 1991 when legislation was passed to allow for private participation in generation. After an initial rush for private capital, the process slowed down as the SEBs defaulted on payments and the policy did not show the expected results (Dubash and Rajan 2002). Then in 1998 another important legislation was passed which led to the establishment of the Central Electricity Regulatory Commission (CERC) and mandated that every federal state have its own State Electricity Regulatory Commissions (SERCs). This was the second most important step in the deregulation process which was meant to ensure a regulatory oversight over state owned as well as privately owned utilities. Finally in 2003 a landmark Electricity Act was passed which lay down clear guidelines for a deregulated market structure (Bhattacharya 2005). There were reforms in every segment with private participation allowed in the distribution segment too. Third party open access was permitted so that generation utilities would be free to trade their electricity. The purpose of these institutional reforms was to provide better incentives for generation and reap dividends from efficient production. In addition to greater investment in the form of private owned utilities, the state owned utilities were expected to improve their productivity in response to induced competition, better incentives and effective regulatory governance.

Our focus is on coal based thermal production as it is the back bone of Indian electricity system comprising nearly 70% of total electricity generated (Malik et al. 2011; Shrivastava et al. 2012). Before efforts of deregulation began in the early 1990s, the state share in thermal generation was also very high and in similar levels as the current but they operated on soft budget constraints due to being entirely owned by SEBs (Malik et al. 2011). Soft budget constraints ensured that any revenue deficit would be compensated from the state budgets and this allowed the losses of the Transmission and Distribution (T&D) segment to be overlooked and weakened the finances of the generation segment. Moreover low tariffs due to the political economy in electricity provision further deflated their budget (Dubash and Rajan 2001). This and the subsequent macroeconomic crisis in early 1990s led to reform measures being instituted. One important measure which has been instituted after the process of deregulation began and which has a direct bearing on the productivity of thermal power plants is the presence of state and central regulatory agencies which designs tariff on the compensation principles based on scheduled generation and operating heat rate. The fixed costs like interest payments on borrowed and working capital, return on equity (ROE), depreciation is based on plant load factor (PLF). There is an availability based tariff (ABT) mechanism which is an incentive to feed electric power so as to balance the grid (Chikkatur et al. 2007). On the fuel supply side, the tariff on imported coal has been reduced and coal washing has been increased so that the heat content is higher and ash content is lower (Malik et al. 2011). Have these reforms brought the desired effect in terms of making the segment more efficient? In order to find this out through an empirical analysis, we first review related literature in the next section.

6.3   Literature Review

6.3.1   Efficiency of Indian Thermal Power Plants

Thermal efficiency of power plants is very low in developing countries as compared to the developed countries (Maruyama and Eckelman 2009). This is not surprising as in most of the developing context the power sector had been under strict governmental control with hardly any competitive pressures or incentives to improve performance. However, with liberalization this has changed and there has been at least a legislative mandate to increase competition. India presents a very interesting case being one of the largest countries to be in this transition phase. Yet, there is a very limited set of studies on the trends in efficiency of thermal power plants in India. Probably the earliest study of Indian thermal power efficiency was conducted by Singh (1991) who uses plant level data for the year 1986-87 to estimate a deterministic frontier production function to calculate technical efficiencies. The analysis finds that the efficiency of a power plant is influenced by its size and capacity utilization but not by its location. Khanna and Zilberman (1999) measure the efficiency of 63 coal-based power plants from the period 1987-1988 to 1990-91. They find that efficiency improves with the use of higher heat content coal, private ownership and improved management practices. The study was important at the time to point out that inefficient operation, lack of coal washing facilities and high imported coal tariffs were barriers to thermal efficiency.

Shanmugam and Kulshreshtha (2005) use a stochastic frontier method to calculate the technical efficiency (TE) of 56 coal-based thermal power plants from the year 1994 to 2001. They used a Cobb-Douglas (CD) function for estimation and calculation of TE. The dependent (output) variable was the quantum of annual power generated in giga-watt hours (GWh) whereas the input variables were capital and fuel inputs like coal consumption, auxiliary consumption and secondary oil consumption. They found out that the mean technical efficiency (inefficiency) of Indian thermal power plants was 73% (27%). The most efficient plant had a TE score of 96% while the lowest plant was at 46%. The western region of India was found to be technically more efficient than the other regions and younger plants performed better than the older ones. Coal input and capital were the most significant determinants of plant productivity. Khanna et al. (1999) estimate a stochastic frontier cost function for 66 thermal power plants in India for the period 1987-88 to 1990-91 and test whether inefficiency is explained by firm-level characteristics. A translog cost function is used where prices are normalized by the price of capital. Total expenditure on inputs i.e. the total cost of generation is the dependent variable and plant age, non-utilized capacity and ownership are the inefficiency terms. Their results indicate that publicly owned power plants are less efficient than private plants and that their capacity utilization explains inefficiency but not plant age. The average inefficiency of plants was 48%, whereas there was a 300 per cent difference between the most efficient and least efficient plants.

Shrivastava et al. (2012) find out the technical efficiency of thermal power plants in India using a non-parametric data envelopment analysis (DEA) method where the output variable is electricity generated and input variables are coal consumption, secondary oil consumption and auxiliary power consumption. Their results suggest that 31.67% of power plants are good performers, 35% are moderate performers, and 23.33% are laggards whereas 10% are poor performers. They also found that the average efficiency of smaller power plants is lesser than medium and large scale power plants whereas state owned power plants have lower performance as compared to central and privately owned power plants. Malik et al. (2011) find out the effects of Indian electricity sector restructuring on the operational efficiency of state-owned thermal power plants using a difference-in-differences (d-i-d) method. The dependent variables they use are specific coal consumption, operating heat rate, deviation of operating heat rate from design heat rate, plant availability, plant load factor and auxiliary consumption. The d-i-d method helps capture the variation in timing of reforms across the different states of India. The unbalanced panel consists of 83 thermal power plants across 17 different states for a long time period from 1988 to 2009. Their key results suggest that while unbundling has improved annual plant availability (PLF) due to a reduction in forced outages there has been no effect on operating heat rate. They also find that the biggest improvements took place in states which unbundled before passing of Electricity Act, 2003.

6.3.2 Determinants of Technical Inefficiency

In determining causes of technical inefficiency, the literature has mostly focused on the question of ownership though there have been inclusion of plant age and capacity utilization as explanatory variables, even if less emphasized (See and Coelli 2012). Other than these, plant size, fuel type, regulatory reform indicators and market share have also been used to explain plant level inefficiency. Although many studies have shown that privately owned utilities have higher efficiency than public owned ones (Bagdadioglu et al. 1996; Hiebert 2002; Berg et al. 2005) there are some studies which have also shown that public ownership has higher efficiency (Färe et al. 1986; Khanna et al. 1999). In fact some have even argued that both private and publicly owned utilities can perform equally (Färe et al. 1985; Pollitt 1995). Generally lower capacity utilization and lower plant age is associated with higher technical inefficiency, although there is no conclusive evidence of that too (Khanna et al. 1999; Hiebert 2002). Similarly there is some literature which suggests that the type of fuel used (i.e. coal or natural gas) and the type of plant (base-load or peak-load) will also have some impact on the efficiency levels, although there are conflicting results about which fuel type or plant type is better (Färe et al. 1986; Pollitt 1995; Diewart and Nakamura 1999). Several studies have also supported a positive relation between bigger plant size and greater efficiency (Joskow and Schmalensee 1987; Meibodi 1998) whereas only some have argued that this relationship may not necessarily hold (Sarica and Or 2007).

There has been very less attention accorded to *regulatory* determinants of technical inefficiency. Lam and Shiu (2004) find for the Chinese electric generation sector that environmental factors and autonomy from state control influence efficiency scores. In a study of US electric generation utilities using the DEA method, Olatubi and Dismukes (2000) find that regulatory expenditures and incentive regulation have a statistically significant influence in reducing generation inefficiency. In a more comprehensive study, Knittel (2002) test the impact of alternative regulatory mechanisms on firm efficiency in the US electric generation plants using a stochastic frontier method. The results suggest that heat rate and plant availability programs have a positive impact on efficiency increases. The study also finds that modified fuel pass through programs[1] have a greater impact on plant efficiency as compared to the traditional pass-through programs.

6.3.3 Role of Regulatory Governance

There are very few studies on the impact of regulation on generation capacity (Pargal 2003; Cubbin and Stern 2006; Zhang et al. 2008). Among these the most significant work is by (Cubbin and Stern 2006) who try to find out the impact of regulatory governance on outcomes in the electricity industry (per-capita generation capacity) of 28 developing countries over the period 1980-2001. Coming from a new institutional perspective which emphasizes that an effective institutional framework is necessary for sustained growth, especially in the utility sector where investments are asset specific, the authors point out that '...(t)he standard institutional solution to handle these infrastructure industry issues is to introduce an independent regulatory agency, operating within a clearly defined legal framework. The agency is intended to provide the high quality institution that permits and fosters sustained growth in capacity and efficiency in the utility service industries, particularly the network elements. So, whether country X has a high- or a low-quality institution is determined primarily by the quality of governance of the regulatory agency (conditional on the quality of governance for the economy as a whole). Developing economies with high-quality regulatory agencies (as measured by regulatory governance) should attract more sustained investment into their utility service industries and at a lower cost of capital. The regulated utilities should also have higher efficiency and growth rates' (Cubbin and Stern 2006: p. 116).

---

[1]   Fuel pass through is when any change in fuel cost is passed on to the consumers through price adjustments. For details of various pass through programs see (Joskow 1974).

This crisply summarizes the core argument of the regulatory governance literature in infrastructure stemming from the seminal work of (Levy and Spiller 1994) and related works (Noll 1989; Levy and Spiller 1994; Stern and Holder 1999; Dubash 2008). This mainly draws from the economics of governance literature of (North 1990) and (Williamson 2005) which refers to the economics of good (private or public) order and workable arrangements. In other words, governance is about those set of devices used to bring order in transactions through well-defined property rights, contracts and other enforcement mechanisms (Dixit 1996). The fundamental problem is about how to bind players into agreements or how to credibly commit to enable complex contracting (North 1993). In the same vein, electricity sector governance is broadly about the rule of law (formal institutions) and the certainty of investment conditions in electricity markets where potential private investors in new generation capacities look for stable market rules and long term contractual commitments. This has also been the reason why the system of independent regulators was set up in liberalized developing countries. However, the total regulatory design consists of both the aspects: regulatory incentives and regulatory governance. While the former basically deal with rules related to utility pricing, subsidies etc., regulatory governance is defined as the mechanism that societies use to constrain regulatory discretion and to resolve conflicts that arise in relation to these constraints (Spiller and Tommasi 2005). It is therefore very critical that the role of regulatory governance in sectoral performance is tested empirically.

Cubbin and Stern (2006) provide some interesting empirical results. They test the hypothesis that a better quality of institutions and high regulatory governance leads to increase in per-capita generation capacity. The sample of 28 countries is drawn from the developing regions of Asia, Africa and Latin America where there has been a lot of unsatisfied demand. The dependent variable was per-capita generation capacity (by country and year) whereas the key independent variables were country wide dummies indicating a) presence of electricity (or energy) regulatory law, b) presence of an autonomous or ministry regulator, c) license fee or government budget regulatory funding, d) civil service pay scales for regulatory staff. Due to lack of data the informal attributes of governance like transparency and quality of regulatory process could not be included in the regulatory governance index. They find that the index of regulatory governance is consistent factor in improved per-capita generation capacity. The results hold for indicators like enacting of a regulatory law, presence of an autonomous regulator and use of license fees. The results are robust to country specific fixed effects and various model specifications including error correction and instrumental regression to overcome endogeneity biases. Privatization and competition also showed significant positive influences. The results matched those of the preceding studies using a similar approach on the impact of regulation on telecommunications reforms (Gutiérrez 2003).

The review of literature in this section has thrown some important gaps. While there are a handful of studies estimating the technical efficiency of thermal power plants in India, there is hardly any analysis of the determinants of technical efficiency, especially in the post Electricity Act (2003) period. Internationally, there are studies which have tried to identify the determinants of technical efficiency but most relate only to plant level characteristics and regulatory incentives. The only study that analyzes the impact of regulatory governance is a cross country comparison of the effect on generation capacity. Therefore, there is no study which tries to estimate the impacts of regulatory governance on the technical efficiency of thermal power plants for an economy that has seen significant changes in electricity deregulation. In our work we therefore try to fill this gap. Our guiding hypothesis is that higher the quality of regulatory institutions (or governance), higher is the efficiency of electric generation utilities.

We also make improvements from the existing literature on thermal efficiency in Indian power plants. While Shanmugam and Kulshreshtha (2005) use a rigid CD function for estimation of the production function, we use a flexible translog function in our present study. We also test for robustness using time variant as well as time invariant, fixed and random effects models. Further, the Shanmugham and Kulshreshtha's study is old because the time period contained only 5 years period from the setting in of liberalization and it could not cover the period from 2001 onwards when regulatory reforms were initiated and regulatory agencies were established. Since India has a federal structure with all the states having some flexibility and individual responsibility for electricity reforms, it is a perfect laboratory for comparative analysis (Sen and Jamasb 2010) . Our present study uses a much longer time period and thus has the advantage of using federal state level regulatory variances to explain technical (in) efficiencies. The time period in Khanna et al. (1999) was merely 4 years and that too before liberalization began. Our present study is not only using the recent data but also for a time period covering 17 years. The Shrivastava et al. (2012) study uses a cross-section data for 60 thermal power plants for the year 2008-09, whereas in our analysis we use a panel dataset which helps us calculate dynamic technical efficiency over a longer time period. They also do not have any input variable for measuring capital stock, a deficiency we overcome in our study. The next section discusses the empirical strategy in detail, our model specification and the data we use.

6.4 Empirical Strategy

6.4.1 Stochastic Frontier Formulation

There are two approaches generally used in the calculation of technical efficiencies: a non-parametric approach known as Data Envelopment Analysis (DEA) and a parametric approach known as Stochastic Frontier Analysis (SFA). Stochastic frontiers have an advantage over deterministic frontiers because they allow for random deviations from the production frontier due to factors beyond the control of producers. It therefore allows for a separation of the error term into a random noise component (unexplained) and an inefficiency component (Seo and Shin 2011). Therefore it gives a clearer idea of how much deviation from the ideal (or maximum possible) output can be explained by random shocks and how much by systematic inefficiencies in plant operation. The foundations of this approach began with three important papers roughly around the same time by Aigner et al. (1977), Meeusen and Broeck (1977), and Battese and Corra. (1977). The first part of the split error term captures the randomness in the production process and can thus take either positive or negative values. The second part specifies plant inefficiency and hence takes only negative values (Kumbhakar and Lovell 2000; Knittel 2002).

A general specification of a stochastic frontier function for panel data following Battese and Coelli (1995) is:

$$Y_{it} = \exp(X_{it}\beta + V_{it} - U_{it}) \qquad \text{Eq. 1}$$

where, Y_{it} is output of the ith plant in t^{th} observation

X_{it} is the vector of values of known functions of production inputs and other explanatory variables of the ith plant in t^{th} year

β is the vector of unknown parameters

V_{it} is the vector of random errors assumed to be independently distributed of U_{it}

U_{it} is the technical inefficiency effect i.e. the vector of non-negative random variables associated with technical inefficiency and assumed to be independently distributed

The technical inefficiency effect U_{it} can be further specified as

$$U_{it} = z_{it}\delta + W_{it} \qquad \text{Eq. 2}$$

where, z_{it} is the set of explanatory variables influencing technical inefficiency

δ is the unknown vector of coefficients

and W_{it} is a truncated random variable of normal distribution with zero mean and variance σ^2

In order to simultaneously estimate the parameters of the stochastic frontier and inefficiency effects, a maximum likelihood method is applied and the resulting technical efficiency takes the form,[2]

$$TE_{it} = \exp(-U_{it}) = \exp(-z_{it}\delta - W_{it}) \qquad\qquad\qquad Eq.\,3$$

6.4.2 Model, Data and Variables

6.4.2.1 Production Inputs and Output

Data for the plant level input and output variables were collected from the annually published Performance Review of Thermal Power Stations by the Central Electricity Authority (CEA) of India. The final dataset, we use, is a balanced panel containing 77 state-owned coal-fired power plants and covering a 17 year time period from 1994-1995 to 2010-2011 across 14 states (see Table 7 for a list of the 14 states) in India. The CEA reports consist of data for nearly 13 more thermal plants (some became operational after 1995 and some ceased to operate in recent years) we could not include them given our objective to observe the change in technical efficiencies of plants which were operational before and after the regulatory reform period. We also did not include power plants from those states which had less than 1 percent of the total share of thermal generation. The plants in our sample constitute roughly 77% of the total coal-fired installed capacity and roughly 60% of the total thermal capacity in India[3]. 89% of the plants in the sample are government (central and state sector) owned whereas 11% are privately owned.

The report gives data on two output variables, first the plant-wise annual power generated (in Gigawatt-Hour, GWh) and the Plant Load Factor (PLF in %). We use annual power generated as the output variable as being followed in the standard literature (Kopp and Smith 1980; Shanmugam and Kulshreshtha 2005; Goto and Tsutsui 2008; Du et al. 2009; See and Coelli 2012). The input variables following previous important studies on Indian thermal power plants (Singh 1991; Shanmugam and Kulshreshtha 2005; Shrivastava et al. 2012) are capital employed in GWh, specific coal consumption per unit of generation in gram/KWh, specific secondary oil consumption per unit of generation in liter/GWh and auxiliary power consumption in percentage (Table 1 gives the descriptive statistics of all the variables). While the other three input variables

---

[2] Following See and Coelli (2012) we estimate a single-step stochastic frontier as it not only allows for estimation of inefficiency determinants but also because a two-step procedure can lead to potential bias. For more discussions on the problems of two-step procedure and applications see (Wang and Schmidt 2002; Kumbhakar and Lovell 2003; Farsi et al. 2006).

[3] Own calculations based on CEA reports.

are straightforward, capital input variable is constructed following previous literature (Dhrymes and Kurz 1964; Singh 1991; Shanmugam and Kulshreshtha 2005) as:

$$CAPITAL = \frac{S*T}{1000} * (1 - PM) \qquad \text{Eq. 4}$$

where, S is the installed plant capacity (in MW)

T is the number of hours in a year

PM is the planned maintenance with (1-PM) term indicating what percentage of time the plant was operational.

6.4.2.2   Regulatory Governance Index

A composite index is developed which approximates performance in terms of state level regulatory governance. The indicators include tariff, transmission and distributions gains, age of regulatory commission, status of unbundling and stability of the regulatory commission composition. First, normalization of parameters is done because they are in different units. This is done using a min-max criterion which is based on the 'distance from the ideal' approach (Klugman et al. 2011). For each state for each year the minimum and maximum values are taken. Using the following identity, the dimension or sub-index is calculated:

$$\theta_{is} = (\beta_{is,actual} - \beta_{is,min})/(\beta_{is,max} - \beta_{is,min}) \qquad \text{Eq. 5}$$

where, β_{is} = value of parameter i for state s
θ_{is} = value of score of each parameter i for state s

This is individually done for all the parameters. Then all the parameter wise sub-indices are aggregated for each state, year wise. Higher weights are assigned to the tariff and T&D sub-index as they are the very important representation of regulatory performance (Berg et al. 2005; Jamasb and Pollitt 2007; Nakhooda et al. 2007), whereas lower weights are attached to other parameters. In alternate models, however, (see the results section) we change the weights of the 'Age of Regulators' and 'Unbundling' and perform a sensitivity analysis. The reason for performing a sensitivity analysis for these two indicators is because there is keen interest in the literature on them (Cubbin and Stern 2006; Sen and Jamasb 2010). It is generally hypothesized that the opening up of the electricity sector through dismantling natural monopoly i.e. unbundling will improve the efficiency of all the segments in the electricity supply chain. It is also believed that with time the experience of regulators will have a positive impact as they will be able to get more information about the utility's production function and perform overall better coordination. This aggregate index is further normalized using the min-max criteria to arrive at the final composite index. The following identity summarizes the steps taken:

$$\delta_{st} = (\sum_{i=1}^{n} \theta_{it,actual} - \sum_{i=1}^{n} \theta_{it,min})/(\sum_{i=1}^{n} \theta_{it,max} - \sum_{i=1}^{n} \theta_{it,min}) \qquad \text{Eq. 6}$$

Where, δ_{st} = value of score of state s for time period t

Data is collected for 14 states in India where thermal power plants are located. The index covers the period from year 2000 to 2010 because the Electricity Regulatory Commissions Act was passed in 1998 and most of the states established their independent regulatory agencies around the year 2000. Sorting indicators of regulatory governance and finding data for them has been challenging. Apart from Cubbin and Stern (2006) there is no study which uses quantitative estimates of regulatory indicators on the electricity sector. However, their indicators were mostly dummies indicating the presence of electricity (or energy) regulatory law, presence of an autonomous or ministry regulator, procedures for license fee or government budget regulatory funding and civil service pay scales for regulatory staff. These are useful for cross country estimation as there can be variation by country. But they are still restricted in terms of temporal variation. For example, once an electricity law is passed or an autonomous regulator is established the dummies will not vary for the subsequent years. For a within-country study like ours, these are not effective as India has an electricity law at federal level (Electricity Act, 2003) and every state has an autonomous regulator. Because the Indian State Electricity Regulatory Commissions (SERCs) were established by legislation, they are funded through government budgets and the staffs being government employees are paid civil service pay scales. Some other India specific studies (Nakhooda et al. 2007; TERI 2007; Sen and Jamasb 2010) throw interesting options but were not possible to include due to data unavailability. Nakhooda et al. (2007), for example come up with qualitative indicators like, a) the institutional structure of regulatory decision-making i.e. whether decisions are made through executive orders or through independent commissions, b) how authorized the regulatory body is in seeking information, investigating, penalizing and enforcing, c) how robust and transparent are the selection criteria for members of regulatory commission, d) appeal mechanisms, e) procedural certainty, f) pro-activeness, g) public participation, h) consumer service, and i) conflict resolution. But there is no available data displaying spatial and temporal variability in these.

Yet if we look carefully, the objective outcomes of regulatory process is a valid indication of how well the regulatory set-up has performed (TERI 2007). If tariff rationalization and reducing Aggregate Technical and Commercial (AT&C) losses were the two most important objectives of regulation, then performance on these two counts would be useful indicators of regulatory governance. Moreover, as time passes, with increase in experiences it is expected that regulatory commissions will mature and function better (Cubbin and Stern 2006). Also stability in regulatory composition will ensure there is higher accountability, learning and autonomy and hence ensure better performance. Moreover, if the state has an unbundled electricity sector (with different generation and distribution companies) or is still under state monopoly will determine competitive pressures, role of private entities and the general regulatory environment. If there is state monopoly it may mean a state agency only regulating another state agency, known as idiosyncratic regulation (Dubash 2008) and hence lower quality regulatory governance. Following this, we have selected five indicators, the key characteristics and data for which are explained as follows (see Table 6-7 in Appendix for descriptive statistics and Table 6-8 in Appendix for their correlations):

- *Annual Power Tariffs (in Rs./KWh)*: Tariff rationalization has been a key objective of regulatory reforms and a key indicator of regulatory effectiveness (TERI 2007). Before the reform period, tariffs were much deflated and any loss made by the generation unit would be financed through fiscal adjustments. Moreover, some segments like households and agriculture were highly subsidized. This meant very high tariffs for industrial (and commercial) users which also caused many of them to set up their own captive power units. This meant even lower revenues for the power plants. With regulatory reforms it is expected that independent regulators will regularize and rationalize the tariff determination process which in turn will incentivize the power plants to increase efficiency in order to gain from higher prices for their power. We therefore collect data for year wise average tariffs of the main consumer categories -domestic, commercial, industry and agriculture - for the 14 states from the year 2000 to 2010. These came primarily from the annual tariff orders[4] of the SERCs and we matched them with other government data sources[5]. Fig. 6-1 (Appendix) gives the average tariffs for each state over the decade of 2000-01 to 2010-11 and also the all-India average. The states of Delhi, Gujarat, Haryana, Maharashtra and West Bengal offered tariff rates higher than the national average. Fig. 6-2 (Appendix) gives the all-India trend of average tariff for the years 2000 to 2010 and Fig. 6-3 (Appendix) plots its relation to the trend in thermal generation.
- *AT&C losses*: These are the losses which take place in the overall system due to lack of investments in system improvement, extensions of distribution lines, overloading of transformers and conductors, low metering efficiency, theft and pilferages. Loss figures have been traditionally very high in India till the reforms began and it reached the peak of 32.86% in the year of 2000-

---

[4] Around 140 tariff orders were analyzed to get the tariff rates where every order ran into hundreds of pages.

[5] http://www.indiastat.com/default.aspx

01[6]. It was expected that with the introduction of independent regulation, there will be reductions in these losses. We collect data on AT&C loss percentages (known earlier as T&D losses) from government data sources[7] and then subtract it from hundred to get AT&C gain figures. Fig 6-4 (Appendix) gives the all-India trend of AT&C loss reductions in the last decade.

- *Age, Unbundling and Regulatory Composition:* The age of regulatory commission was calculated from the year each SERC was established. If an SERC was established after the year 2000, then the previous years were given zero values. Unbundling was given a value of 0 if in that particular year the state had not yet unbundled its electricity board. The change in regulatory composition is indicated by the change in political regime. This is because *de-facto* regulatory commissions are an extended wing of the government (Dubash 2008) and any new state government eventually leads to change in the high ranking regulatory staff. Although this may not always be the case, it is a fair approximation given Indian political conditions. In the absence of any concrete data on the changes in regulatory composition, a dummy value of 0 is given for a year when there was no new government as compared to the previous year and a value of 1 if that year saw a new state government take office.

Table 6-1: Summary statistics of production-function variables

	Obs	Mean	Std. Dev.	Min	Max
POWER (*PGEN_GWH*)	1280	4774.22	4569.7	77.26	27585.85
PLANT LOAD (*PLF*)	1280	65.35	22.07	3.67	102.33
CAPITAL (*PCAPITAL*)	1280	6131.16	4918.38	147.28	27432.43
COAL (*NCOAL_CONS*)	1273	756.85	156.71	110	2000
SECONDARY OIL (*NSECOIL_CONS*)	1278	5395.34	8085.35	50	81890
AUXILIARY (*AUXI_CONS*)	1280	9.77	2.03	0.71	19.72
REG. GOV. (*RGINDEX*)	847	0.44	0.31	0	1

Source: Own compilation

Table 6-1 gives the summary statistics of both the production function variables and the composite regulatory index. Table 6-9 (Appendix) gives the correlation matrix of all the independent variables.

6.4.2.3   *Translog Inefficiency Effects Model*

Given our aim is to find out the effect of regulatory factors on the variation of the inefficiency error term we use stochastic frontier production function which

---

[6]   http://powermin.nic.in/distribution/distribution_overview.htm
[7]   http://www.indiastat.com/default.aspx

models technical inefficiency effects in single stage (Battese and Coelli 1995). It avoids the problem of inconsistency which is possible in the two-stage approach and models both the technical change and time-varying inefficiency effects in a single equation (See and Coelli 2012). The translog specification of the general form of an SFA as given in Eq. 1 above is given as:

$$
\begin{aligned}
\ln \text{POWER}_{it} = {} & \beta_0 + \beta_1 \ln(\text{CAPITAL}_{it}) + \beta_2 \ln(\text{COAL}_{it}) + \\
& \beta_3 \ln(\text{SECONDARY OIL}_{it}) + \beta_4 \ln(\text{AUXILIARY}_{it}) + \\
& 0.5\, \beta_5 \ln(\text{CAPITAL}_{it})^2 + 0.5\, \beta_6 \ln(\text{COAL}_{it})^2 + \\
& 0.5\, \beta_7 \ln(\text{SECONDARY OIL}_{it})^2 + 0.5\, \beta_8 \ln(\text{AUXILIARY}_{it})^2 + \\
& \beta_9 \ln(\text{CAPITAL}_{it}) \ln(\text{COAL}_{it}) + \\
& \beta_{10} \ln(\text{CAPITAL}_{it}) \ln(\text{SECONDARY OIL}_{it}) + \\
& \beta_{11} \ln(\text{CAPITAL}_{it}) \ln(\text{AUXILIARY}_{it}) + \\
& \beta_{12} \ln(\text{COAL}_{it}) \ln(\text{SECONDARY OIL}_{it}) + \\
& \beta_{13} \ln(\text{COAL}_{it}) \ln(\text{AUXILIARY}_{it}) + \\
& \beta_{14} \ln(\text{SECONDARY OIL}_{it}) \ln(\text{AUXILIARY}_{it}) + v_{it} - u_{it} \qquad \text{Eq. 7}
\end{aligned}
$$

where,

v_{it} is the random error term and,

u_{it} is the technical inefficiency effects and can be explained by:

$$u_{it} = \delta_0 + \delta_1 \text{PLANT CAPACITY} + \delta_2 \text{PLANT AGE} + \delta_3 \text{REG. GOV. INDEX} \quad \text{Eq. 8}$$

6.5 Results

6.5.1 Estimated Model Parameters

The results from hypothesis tests (see Table 6-2) performed to find out the relative influence of parameters indicate that the translog production function is more appropriate than the Cobb-Douglas production function. It also confirms that the explanatory variables for inefficiency effects are significantly different from zero.

Table 6-2: Results of hypothesis testing

Test	Null Hypothesis (H_0)	Test Statistic	Critical Value ($\chi^2_{\alpha=0.05}$)	Decision
Cobb-Douglas	$\beta_{5-14} = 0$	215.72	18.31	Reject H_0
Inefficiency Effects	$\delta_{1-3} = 0$	11.02	7.81	Reject H_0

Source: Own compilation

The SFPANEL function in STATA 11 (Belotti et al. 2012) was used to estimate the parameters of the translog production function for Indian thermal power plants. This allowed flexibility in robustness testing as the SFPANEL command allows for estimation of various fixed and random effects, time-varying and time-invariant models (Cornwell et al. 1990; Lee and Schmidt 1993; Battese and Coelli 1995). This also enables to see the robustness of the resulting coefficients. The results from three models we estimated are given in Table 6-10 (Appendix). We finally use a maximum likelihood random-effects time-varying inefficiency effects model, BC95, (Battese and Coelli 1995) as it allows for a single stage estimation of the inefficiency parameters (See and Coelli 2012). Variations of the BC95 model are estimated and the results are shown in Table 6-3. Model 1 has only plant age and installed capacity as determinants of the inefficiency effect and does not include regulatory index. This is the full model used for calculation of the technical inefficiency (TIE) scores.

The inclusion of regulatory index truncates the number of observations to 830 as index is computed for 2000 to 2010 period. CAPITAL and SECONDARY OIL have significant coefficients and positive impact on generation. COAL and AUXILIARY appear not to have significant impact on generation. In Model 2 we introduce RG-INDEX and the coefficients for COAL and AUXILARY come out significant at 5% confidence level.

Table 6-3: Estimated parameters of BC95 inefficiency effect model

IE: Inefficiency Effects	BC95_NORG (Model 1)	BC95_RG (Model 2)	BC95_RG_AHW (Model 3)	BC95_RG_UBHW (Model 4)
	IE: Plant Age + Installed Capacity	IE: Plant Age + Installed Capacity + RG Index	IE: Plant Age + Installed Capacity + RG Index with Higher Weights for *Age of Regulators*	IE: Plant Age + Inst. Cap. + RG Index with Higher Weights for *Unbundling*
LNPCAPITAL	1.645***	1.496***	1.417***	1.500***
	(0.250)	(0.207)	(0.210)	(0.205)
LNNCOAL_CONS	0.498	2.296**	1.581*	1.953**
	(0.960)	(0.895)	(0.927)	(0.897)
LNNSECOIL_CONS	1.414***	0.363	0.466*	0.443*
	(0.185)	(0.244)	(0.245)	(0.242)
LNAUXI_CONS	-0.219	3.763**	2.717*	3.225**
	(1.352)	(1.583)	(1.596)	(1.560)
LNPCAPITAL_SQ	0.002	0.010	0.007	0.004
	(0.007)	(0.006)	(0.006)	(0.006)
LNNCOAL_CONS_SQ	0.061	-0.065*	-0.051	-0.073*
	(0.045)	(0.039)	(0.043)	(0.039)
LNNSECOIL_CONS_SQ	-0.015***	-0.009**	-0.009**	-0.008**
	(0.003)	(0.004)	(0.004)	(0.004)
LNAUXI_CONS_SQ	-0.121***	-0.121***	-0.110***	-0.122***
	(0.025)	(0.023)	(0.023)	(0.022)
CAP_COAL	-0.099**	-0.093**	-0.068*	-0.070*
	(0.042)	(0.039)	(0.040)	(0.040)
CAP_SECOIL	0.007	0.013	0.010	0.005
	(0.007)	(0.008)	(0.008)	(0.008)
CAP_OAUXI	-0.061	-0.084**	-0.086**	-0.081**
	(0.044)	(0.040)	(0.040)	(0.038)
COAL_SECOIL	-0.162***	-0.017	-0.024	-0.014
	(0.027)	(0.036)	(0.036)	(0.035)
COAL_OAUXI	0.312	-0.251	-0.085	-0.159
	(0.203)	(0.230)	(0.232)	(0.226)

SECOIL_OAUXI	-0.141***	-0.145***	-0.155***	-0.158***
	(0.037)	(0.032)	(0.032)	(0.031)
_cons	-8.353*	-14.395***	-10.927**	-12.894***
	(4.567)	(4.355)	(4.444)	(4.285)
LNPLANT_AGE	4.590**	6.796***	13.493	4.857***
	(1.926)	(2.440)	(8.673)	(1.733)
LNCAP_MW	-3.884**	-4.958***	-7.290*	-3.453***
	(1.569)	(1.656)	(4.180)	(1.098)
RGINDEX		-4.692*		
		(2.475)		
RGINDEX_AHW			-7.571	
			(4.981)	
RGINDEX_UBHW				-8.514***
				(2.859)
_cons	-6.716	-8.243	-26.570	-3.533
N	1269	830	830	830
σ_u	1.890	2.120	2.709	1.768
σ_v	0.101	0.051	0.051	0.050
Log lik.	229.135	255.574	256.683	271.403
Chi-squared	31184.051	38365.769	38345.063	40315.822

Standard errors in parentheses: * $p < 0.10$, ** $p < 0.05$, *** $p < 0.01$

The coefficient for RG-INDEX is significant at 10% level and the negative sign shows that an increase in RG-INDEX leads to a reduction in technical inefficiency. In Model 3 we use an RG-INDEX_AHW where there is a higher weight assigned to the indicator 'Age of Regulators'. The coefficient for the regulatory governance index falls in value and is not significant up to 10% confidence level. In Model 4 we give a higher weight to the indicator 'Unbundling'. The coefficient for regulatory governance index becomes highly significant.[8] The result from Model 3 indicates that the experience of regulatory commission has a positive but not significant influence on the performance of power plants. However, the result from Model 4 indicates that if there is unbundling in a state where generation, transmission and distribution are separate functions, then it has a very significant and positive influence on the performance of power plants. PLANT CAPACITY and PLANT AGE also turn out to be significant determinants of inefficiency. Increased plant capacity leads to reductions in inefficiencies indicating that bigger plants are more efficient. There is an inverse relation with plant age which means as power plants become older, their technical efficiency falls. Since Model 2 is our full model with the base regulatory governance index, we look at its coefficients for the interpretations. The coefficients of CAPITAL (1.4963), COAL (2.2963) and AUXILIARY (3.7631) are greater than one showing increasing marginal returns whereas SECONDARY OIL (0.3635) shows diminishing marginal returns. The sum of the four production coefficients (elasticities) is 7.555 which show strong increasing returns to scale in electricity generation. Gamma (γ), the ratio of σ_v^2 and σ_u^2, the variance coefficients of random errors and inefficiency effects is

---

[8]   See Table 6-11 in Appendix for the weights given to different sub-indexes in different models

0.0241 which is greater than zero and indicates the presence of a random component of the technical inefficiency effects.

6.5.2 Technical Efficiency Analysis

As shown in Table 6-4 the Spearman correlations of the inefficiency scores for all the models are very high. The summary statistics of the inefficiency scores is given in Table 6-5. The mean technical efficiency of thermal power plants (Model 2) in India for the period 1994 to 2010 is 0.767 or 76.7%. This is an improvement of approximately 4 percentage points from the mean technical efficiency of 72.66% from the figures of Shanmugam and Kulshreshtha (2005) which were up to the years 2001-02. Because the final model is time-varying for plant level inefficiency scores, the relative technical inefficiencies (RTIE) are calculated where the most inefficient plant for a given year gets a score of 1 and the rest of the scores are normalized accordingly. Table 6-12 (Appendix) gives the plant level technical efficiency scores and also compares with the scores from Shanmugam and Kulshreshtha (2005). The correlation coefficient between the two score cards is 0.4637 and the scatter plot is shown in Fig 6-5 (Appendix). The most efficient plant is at Satpura in the state of Madhya Pradesh whereas the least efficient plant is Santaldih in West Bengal. The distribution of thermal power plants by their technical efficiency values is given in Table 6-13 (Appendix). Around 14% of the total number of plants has efficiency scores higher than 90% whereas a majority 48% plants lie in the range of the score of 80-90%. As can be seen from Table 6-6 the best performing states in terms of thermal power efficiency are Rajasthan, Madhya Pradesh/Chhattisgarh[9] and Maharashtra whereas the plants in states of Uttar Pradesh, West Bengal and Bihar/Jharkhand are the worst performing.

Table 6-4: Spearman rank correlations of TIE scores

	TIE_BC95_NO RG (Model 1)	TIE_BC95_RG (Model 2)	TIE_BC95_R G_AHW (Model 3)	TIE_BC95_RG_UBH W (Model 4)
TIE_BC95_NORG	1.0000			
TIE_BC95_RG	0.9631	1.0000		
TIE_BC95_RG_AHW	0.9632	0.9993	1.0000	
TIE_BC95_RG_UBH W	0.9573	0.9976	0.9980	1.0000

Source: Own compilation

---

[9] We have merged the states of Madhya Pradesh and Chhattisgarh together and Bihar and Jharkhand for our analysis. This is because Chhattisgarh and Jharkhand were carved out of MP and Bihar respectively in 2000.

Table 6-5: Summary statistics of TIE

Variable	Obs	Mean	Std. Dev.	Min	Max
TIE_BC95_NORG (Model 1)	1269	.2112	.2338	.0110	2.3105
TIE_BC95_RG (Model 2)	830	.2330	.2929	.0108	2.3642
TIE_BC95_RG_AHW (Model 3)	830	.2316	.2927	.0106	2.3631
TIE_BC95_RG_UBHW (Model 4)	830	.2331	.2967	.0109	2.3616

Source: Own compilation

Table 6-6: State wise technical inefficiencies

	State-wise TIE	
Rank of Performance	**State Name**	**Mean RTIE**
1	Rajasthan	0.09
2	MP/Chattisgarh	0.14
3	Maharastra	0.14
4	Tamil Nadu	0.14
5	Punjab	0.15
6	Karnataka	0.15
7	Gujarat	0.16
8	Haryana	0.18
9	Andhra Pradesh	0.19
10	Delhi	0.20
11	Orissa	0.20
12	Uttar Pradesh	0.22
13	West Bengal	0.37
14	Bihar/Jharkhand	0.44

Source: Own compilation

6.5.3 Discussion on Regulatory Determinants of Technical Inefficiency

Our analysis of the Indian coal-based thermal power generation sector gives interesting insights on the impacts of regulatory reforms over the last decade. The average technical efficiency is higher by about 4 % points as compared to the earlier estimates by Shanmugam and Kulshreshtha (2005) which shows there has been an improvement between the years 2001 and 2010. This is the period during which independent regulation has been operational. The composite index of regulatory reforms which includes performance and governance indicators like trends in tariff, trends in reduction of losses, age of regulators, unbundling and changes in regulatory composition has a significant and positive influence on plant performance. Better regulation ensures power plants get increased returns on investment through higher tariffs which lead to ramped up technical and managerial abilities. Reduction in losses also ensures higher revenue recovery and affects efficiency through increased marginal returns on machinery and base-load equipment investment. If regulatory composition changes frequently then it is an indicator of poor governance and will adversely affect all the regulatory outcomes like annual tariff determination. The sensitivity analysis with higher weights given to unbundling and age of regulators provide very important insights. Results indicate that with time regulatory experience has not been effective in driving improvements in the generation sector. This may be because there is not enough 'regulatory capacity' as membership of the regulatory commission is part of the governmental civil service limiting 'regulatory culture to a particular set of experiences, one that arguably lacks practical knowledge of business and consumers and favors a public sector mindset' (Dubash and Rao 2008: p. 326). However, dissolution of state electricity boards and separation of generation, transmission and distribution functions appear to be significantly influencing plant efficiency. This is because it reduces the moral hazard of soft budget constraints and allows for competing private power plants to operate.

6.6 Conclusions

A watershed event in recent Indian economic history has been the liberalization program which was introduced in the early 1990s. The power generation sector was one of the key areas where reforms were introduced and a roadmap for deregulation was laid down. Private participation, unbundling of the erstwhile natural monopolies and establishment of an independent regulatory system were the key features aimed towards improved overall efficiency and expansion of the sector. Yet, there has been hardly any study to find out the impacts of regulatory reforms on a concrete indicator of performance. Therefore, in this chapter we employ a stochastic frontier analysis to model the impact of regulatory governance on thermal power efficiency in India. Using a balanced panel of 77 coal-based thermal power plants from the period 1994 to 2010 we estimate a translog production function including determinants of inefficiency in single stage. We find that the average technical efficiency is higher than those estimated by previous studies which considered time period before independent regulation was introduced. We constructed a composite index of regulatory governance and used it as an explanatory variable in the inefficiency effects model. A sensitivity analysis showed that the experience of regulators does not have significant influence but wherever there is unbundling, technical efficiencies are higher. We conclude that regulatory reforms have indeed positively affected the performance of the power sector as indicated by its impact on technical efficiency of coal-based thermal power plants.

The chapter has given empirical insights into how institutional quality, measured here as regulatory governance, is a significant determinant of utility performance. This is especially important in the context of developing and transition countries where the erstwhile state-controlled and inefficient sectors have been reformed in the last few decades. While the results from our analysis are encouraging in spite of all the bottlenecks and poor governance structure of Indian electricity regulation (Nakhooda et al. 2007; Dubash and Rao 2008) as there has been an improvement in performance, yet there is significant gains to be achieved. The result that the experience of regulators has not been effective is a serious concern and pointer towards the fact that the existing 'regulatory capacity' is not adequate and needs changes and reforms. These include greater autonomy and better quality and stable regulatory staff. In the next chapter, therefore, we try to model using a game theoretic approach, under what conditions the quality of regulatory governance (credible commitments) can be high even when there is limited autonomy. We hypothesize that institutions of public information positively impact credibility in the long run and hence is an important component of transaction cost regulation.

Appendix

Table 6-7: Summary statistics of state-level regulatory indicators

Variable	Obs.	Mean	Std. Dev.	Min.	Max.
STATE_TARIFF	154	3.01	0.64	1.54	4.68
TD_GAINS	154	68.49	9.56	42.91	86.53
ERC_AGE	154	5.83	3.36	0	13
UNBUNDLE	154	0.66	0.47	0	1
REG_COMP	154	0.25	0.43	0	1

Source: Own estimations

Table 6-8: Correlations of regulatory indicators

	STATE_TARIFF	TD_GAINS	ERC_AGE	UNBUNDLE	REG_COMP
STATE_TARIFF	1.0000				
TD_GAINS	0.1668	1.0000			
ERC_AGE	0.6087	0.3592	1.0000		
UNBUNDLE	0.2112	-0.1016	0.3840	1.0000	
REG_COMP	-0.1004	0.1156	-0.0834	-0.0773	1.0000

Source: Own estimations

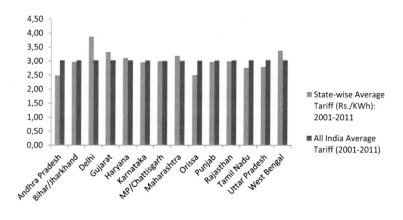

Figure 6-1: State-wise and All-India average tariffs for the last decade

Source: Own compilation based on SERC tariff orders

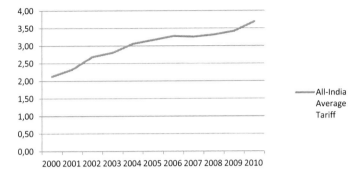

Figure 6-2: All-India trends in average tariff

Source: Own compilation based on SERC tariff orders

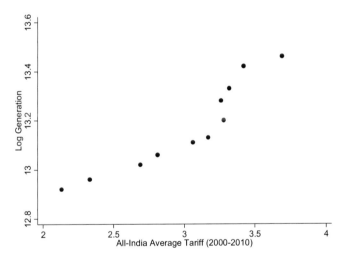

Figure 6-3: Relation between tariff and thermal generation

Source: Own compilation

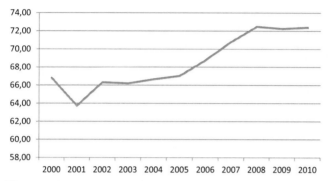

Figure 6-4: All India AT&C gains

Source: Own compilation from government data sources (CEA and Indiastat)

Table 6-9: Correlation matrix of independent variables

	PLANT LOAD	CAPITAL	COAL	SEC. OIL	AUXILIARY	RGINDEX
PLANT LOAD	1.000					
CAPITAL	0.4056	1.000				
COAL	-0.5418	-0.2332	1.000			
SEC. OIL	-0.7061	-0.2976	0.4622	1.000		
AUXILIARY	-0.5424	-0.4880	0.4292	0.4007	1.000	
RGINDEX	0.0893	0.1371	0.1638	0.0005	0.0115	1.000

Source: Own estimations

Table 6-10: Various translog SFA models

TL: Translog; TV: Time Variant; TIV: Time Invariant; FE: Fixed Effects; IE: Inefficiency Effects	TL_FELS_TV (1)	TL_FE_TIV (2)	TL_FECSS_TV (3)	TL_IEBC95_TV (4)
LNPCAPITAL	1.1028	1.2723***	0.2414	1.8091***
	(0.9621)	(0.4286)	(0.4356)	(0.2273)
LNNCOAL_CONS	0.4168	4.4475***	2.0818**	-0.8137
	(1.4916)	(0.9885)	(0.9604)	(0.8597)
LNNSECOIL_CONS	0.2391	0.2946	0.1814	1.5400***
	(0.9340)	(0.2159)	(0.2359)	(0.1884)
LNAUXI_CONS	-1.4410	2.5295*	2.6461**	-0.7996
	(5.1998)	(1.2937)	(1.1603)	(1.3382)
LNPCAPITAL_SQ	0.0047	0.0586***	0.0681***	-0.0137**
	(0.0381)	(0.0130)	(0.0160)	(0.0053)
LNNCOAL_CONS_SQ	-0.0781	-0.1235***	-0.0358	0.0761
	(0.1769)	(0.0473)	(0.0465)	(0.0477)
LNNSECOIL_CONS_SQ	-0.0137	-0.0106***	-0.0159***	-0.0169***
	(0.0160)	(0.0039)	(0.0039)	(0.0035)
LNAUXI_CONS_SQ	-0.0453	-0.0610**	-0.0552***	-0.1093***
	(0.1056)	(0.0249)	(0.0206)	(0.0243)
CAP_COAL	-0.0238	-0.2103***	-0.0975**	-0.0466
	(0.1374)	(0.0501)	(0.0481)	(0.0331)
CAP_SECOIL	-0.0023	0.0036	-0.0025	-0.0009
	(0.0317)	(0.0075)	(0.0088)	(0.0061)
CAP_OAUXI	-0.0323	-0.0167	-0.0464	-0.1318***
	(0.1534)	(0.0352)	(0.0301)	(0.0360)
COAL_SECOIL	-0.0074	-0.0492	-0.0056	-0.1460***
	(0.1320)	(0.0320)	(0.0331)	(0.0283)
COAL_OAUXI	0.3092	-0.3563*	-0.3397**	0.5445***
	(0.6981)	(0.1847)	(0.1689)	(0.1911)
SECOIL_OAUXI	-0.0355	0.0176	0.0209	-0.1985***
	(0.1015)	(0.0251)	(0.0206)	(0.0341)
_cons		-18.6073***		-4.4774
		(5.7412)		(4.1468)
N	1269	1269	1269	1269
pseudo R^2				
σ_u	0.2373	0.3193	0.5530	2.0274
σ_v	0.1786	0.1749	0.1264	0.1035
Log lik.				190.5387
Chi-squared		2605.2383	583.0068	41272.4237

Source: Own estimations

Table 6-11: Different weights of sub-indexes model-wise

			Weights		
	Tariff	Age of Regulators	AT&C Gains	Unbundling	Regulatory Composition
Index in Model 2	0.4	0.1	0.4	0.05	0.05
Index in Model 3	0.3	0.3	0.3	0.05	0.05
Index in Model 4	0.3	0.1	0.3	0.25	0.05

Source: Own compilation

Table 6-12: Comparative technical efficiency (TE) scores

Plant Name	State	Current Study	(Shanmugam and Kulshreshtha 2005)
Satpura	MP/Chattisgarh	92.9	72.32
North Madras	Tamil Nadu	92.6	82.99
Kota	Rajasthan	91.3	87.87
Korba II (E)	MP/Chattisgarh	91.2	60.1
Parli	Maharastra	91.0	76.6
Bhusawal	Maharastra	90.8	76.02
Tuticorin	Tamil Nadu	90.5	95.33
Neyveli	Tamil Nadu	90.4	*
Khaperkheda II	Maharastra	90.4	76.43
Singrauli STPS	UP	90.0	*
Vijaywada	AP	90.0	82.06
Vindhyachal STPS	MP/Chattisgarh	89.9	*
Korba STPS	MP/Chattisgarh	89.8	79.15
Suratgarh	Rajasthan	89.6	*
Nasik	Maharastra	89.3	80.4
Mettur	Tamil Nadu	89.2	80.14
Rajghat	Delhi	89.1	72.28
Wanakbori	Gujarat	88.9	83
Panipat	Haryana	88.9	68.72
Ramagundem STPS	AP	88.7	*
Rayalseema	AP	88.4	77.81
Korba West TPS	MP/Chattisgarh	88.3	78.22
Koradi	Maharastra	88.2	68.43
Kothagudem	AP	88.0	66.29
Rihand STPS	UP	87.8	*
Gandhi Nagar	Gujarat	87.7	86.83
Unchachar	UP	87.6	*
Titagarh	West Bengal	87.3	*
Anpara	UP	87.1	80.12
Sabarmati/Torrent	Gujarat	86.8	*
Ukai Thermal	Gujarat	86.2	75.76
Ropar	Punjab	85.7	80.38
Raichur	Karnataka	85.4	79.34
Lehra Mohabbat (GHTP)	Punjab	85.2	*
Badarpur (NTPC)	Delhi	85.0	*
Southern REPL	West Bengal	84.7	*
Chandarpur	Maharastra	84.7	74.34
Dadri (NCTPP)	UP	83.9	*
Sanjay Gandhi	MP/Chattisgarh	83.7	76.25
Dhanu (BSES)	Maharastra	83.4	96.04
Bhatinda (GNDTP)	Punjab	83.0	76.9
Kolaghat	West Bengal	82.9	74.88
Neyveli (M Cut)	Tamil Nadu	82.7	*

I B Valley	Orissa	82.4	67.03
Korba III (E)	MP/Chattisgarh	81.5	61.95
Kutch Lignite	Gujarat	81.5	*
Mejia	West Bengal	80.7	*
Paricha	UP	80.5	60.94
Sikka REPL	Gujarat	79.9	95.13
Talcher	Orissa	79.6	57.65
Kahalgaon	Bihar/Jharkhand	78.8	*
Durgapur	West Bengal	77.1	84.88
Farakka STPS	West Bengal	77.1	65.03
Talcher STPS	Orissa	76.9	*
OBRA Thermal	UP	74.7	63.85
Faridabad Etxn	Haryana	74.7	64
Ramagundem B	AP	74.5	79.74
A.E.Co.	Gujarat	74.2	*
Budge Budge	West Bengal	73.8	*
Tanda	UP	72.3	*
Ennore	Tamil Nadu	71.7	55.58
Bokaro B	Bihar/Jharkhand	68.1	70.75
Amar Kantak Ext	MP/Chattisgarh	66.2	71.57
Panki	UP	66.1	61.24
IP Station	Delhi	66.1	67.26
Tenughat	Bihar/Jharkhand	63.9	*
Paras	Maharastra	63.3	69.64
Harduaganj B	UP	53.3	47.89
Durgapur DPL	West Bengal	52.4	*
Bandel	West Bengal	52.2	85.82
Patratu	Bihar/Jharkhand	50.7	*
Nellore	AP	43.0	54.51
New Cossipore	West Bengal	35.8	*
Muzaffarpur	Bihar/Jharkhand	30.1	*
Barauni	Bihar/Jharkhand	27.7	46.97
Chandarpura (WB)	West Bengal	25.1	62.39
Santaldih	West Bengal	23.0	75.74

Source: Own compilation

Table 6-13: Distribution of plants by TE (%) values

TE (%)	Number of Plants	Percentage
Above 90	11	14.29
80-90	37	48.05
70-80	13	16.88
60-70	6	7.79
50-60	4	5.19
40-50	1	1.30
30-40	2	2.60
20-30	3	3.90
10-20	0	0.00
Below 10	0	0.00
Total	**77**	**100.00**

Source: Own estimations

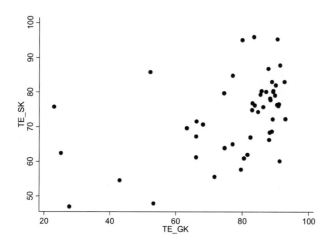

Figure 6-5: Correlation between TE Scores

TE_GK: TE Scores from our analysis
TE_SK: TE Scores from Shanmugam and Kulshreshtha (2005)

7. Regulatory Commitment Revisited[*]

Overview

Can regulatory commitment be credible under *de-facto* non-independent regulation? When state and regulators collude, civil society actors can generate information and try to change voter strategy. Such public interest groups can thus aim at inducing party competition for a change in the regulatory set-up. In this chapter we show using a game theoretical linked action situation approach that in the short run public information produced by public interest groups actually tends to reduce commitment, irrespective of a change in the set-up. This leads to what we call a 'low commitment trap'. We provide some indicative support to this claim through one instance of public monitoring of electricity in India. Yet, as we show, in the long-run this dilemma can be solved under a repeated game situation where state regulators make only public interest moves 'knowing' that a perennial commitment trap would otherwise be created. However, this is possible only when the institutional environment for information production is strong. We conclude that 'institutions of public information' - not independence – is the necessary condition for commitment.

7.1 Introduction

Commitment is the core challenge of independent regulation in recently deregulated economies like India. In this chapter we make a theoretical case for the influence of public information produced by public interest groups on regulatory commitment. In fact the analysis pursues the paradigm problem of institutional change which is all about how to bind players to agreements or how to credibly commit to enable complex contracting (North 1993). The general motivation for delegation by the government of regulatory powers to an independent agency is based on the principal-agent logic of transaction cost economics (Levy and Spiller 1994; Dubash and Rao 2008) which helps the principal, i.e. the government, solve commitment issues, overcome information asymmetries as well as insulate itself from the liabilities of unpopular policies (Thatcher and Stone Sweet 2002). Therefore, unless independent regulation is able to minimize the transaction costs which arise out of the commitment problem, its efficacy will be in doubt. India made its first attempts towards independent electricity regulation in the early 1990s. Some of the federal states went ahead unbundling the State Electricity Boards (the erstwhile monopoly in

---

[*] A preliminary version of this chapter was presented at the 17th Annual Conference of the International Society for New Institutional Economics (ISNIE), June 20-23 in Florence, Italy. A previous version of this chapter is available online as Working Paper 51 of the Jerusalem Papers on Regulation and Governance. I would especially like to thank Christian Kimmich for useful comments in shaping this chapter.

the entire electricity supply chain) and introduced management reforms. The regulators were mandated to take over the tariff policy function of the government and their prime goal was in balancing investor and consumer interests. However, reality turned out to be quite different. Although the government has lost control over tariff setting as a political tool, the regulators have also been unable to raise tariffs to attract investors (Dubash 2008). This is because there is in most occasions a strong government oversight over regulatory decisions. For example in Karnataka, as Dubash explains, the state government used executive orders to change the category applied for tariff rates for IT (information technology) consumers. Similar examples can be found in the instance of Andhra Pradesh (and other) regulators too (see case discussion below). Thus one of the main purposes of setting up regulators, which is to send credible signals for private investment rather than solely protecting consumer interests, is not served. Clearly, in this case, the commitment problem does not seem to have been resolved. How does public information produced by public interest groups impact this?

With a focus to address this, Section 7.2 discusses the problem of regulatory commitment in greater detail and the role of information. The basic elements of a formal stakeholder model of regulation are also discussed. In Section 7.3 we lay down the structure and explain the dilemma situation using ordinal, linked games within a framework known as the Network of Adjacent Action Situations (NAAS) concept. We further discuss the conditions under which this dilemma can be solved in the long run. We show that institutions of public information provisioning strengthen credible commitments. We also show that this condition leads to commitment in the long run, irrespective of regulation being independent. In section 7.4, we present some illustration of our predictions using an example from India. In section 7.5 we link our theoretical formulation with the empirical case and also discuss the necessary institutional conditions for production of public information. Section 7.6 ends with some general conclusions and implications of our research.

7.2   Commitment, Public Information and Stakeholder Models

Whether a regulatory design is adequate or not can be judged by the credibility of its commitments to investors as well as consumers, i.e. voters. Because the interests from either side are in conflict, regulation becomes inherently political. When consumers cannot exit the system in the event of being dissatisfied, they voice their protest through voting and other voice mechanisms, such as public discourse through media (Hirschman 1970). And if the investors are not sure about the safety of their investments, they do not make the required level of investments (Newbery 1999). Therefore the problem of regulatory commitment is central to understanding whether attempts for deregulation and competition will be successful or not in the developing context. The basic idea of having independent regulators can be described with the principal-agent logic, where the state, being a principal, delegates regulatory decision making to an agent, who can even take a politically unfavorable decision without implicating the principal. This helps the elected officials, as the principal, solve commitment issues, but also to overcome information asymmetries through professional regulation, and to allow for unpopular policies (Thatcher and Stone Sweet 2002). Unlike in other principal-agent relations, however, the principal creates an agency that purposely resists interference from the principal (Gilardi 2004). In other words, delegation is meant to reduce certain political transaction costs via solving the commitment problem (Majone 2001).

Majone (2001) develops a positive theory of non-majoritarian institutions using a Coasean logic. The question he concerns himself with is: why do non-majoritarian institutions exist, when they are not directly accountable to voters? The reason is political transaction costs; which can be understood as the cost of reaching and enforcing political agreements. This is an explanation for why independent non-majoritarian agencies exist. But this is no explanation for why the government does not delegate all its policymaking to independent agencies. According to the Coasean explanation, therefore, only that part of policy making which has high political transaction costs, will be delegated. The type of political transaction cost that North (1990) deals with is the lack of instrumental rationality i.e. inability of the participants in the political process to know exactly how their world operates. This is due to insufficient information feedback. So his explanation is that policies fail because the policy makers do not adequately understand the consequences of such policy completely. However, Dixit (1996) identifies another important form of political transaction cost and that is, the problems policymakers face in providing long term credible commitments. This he calls the 'technology of commitment' problem (Majone 2001). In a strategic interaction between the voters and policymakers, there is no incentive for the policymaker to offer a policy which will make the voter better off in the present and the next periods, if that does not guarantee voting by them in the next period. Therefore they try to tie up their policies in a way that voters do not become independent. Similarly, voters knowing this strategy would use their political power to extract short term benefits. Dixit (1996) explains this using the example of labour compensation in declining industries. While the ideal policy would be to make a lump sum compensation and leave the labour to find their best alternative, doing this will not guarantee votes in the next electoral period. Therefore, the policy would be for a stream of payments. However, now the labour is not sure that politicians would not renege on this stream of payments by behaving opportunistically, or due to a change in the government. So there is a double credibility problem from both sides and the outcome would be that labour continues in the declining industry with state help. This is however, a socially inefficient solution.

Dixit (1996) identifies the problem of commitment or time consistency as an important transaction cost. Majone (2001) explains that this time inconsistency problem of policy will happen when there is a disjunction between the long-term and short-term policy objectives of a government, thereby creating an incentive to renege on the long term promises. One way to solve this would be to have independent regulators who are non-political. For example, in the case of utilities, they would allow a fair rate of return along with the credibility that it won't renege over the short run. Delegation, or in other words transfer of political property rights to non-majoritarian institutions, then appears to be a solution to the commitment problem. He further states that due to the growing importance of contractual incompleteness and mutual trust, agency theory is not sufficient to explain delegation. Although the core aspects of hidden action and hidden information between a principal and agent persist, he proposes that the fiduciary principle i.e. a trustee-property-duty relationship provides a better framework to reduce the commitment problem.

In short, commitment through independent regulation has two core components: agency and transaction costs. Both have strong elements of the information problem, though there is a difference in the assumptions about it (Scharpf 1997). The agency view holds that there is hidden information between the principal and the agent thereby reducing the level of effort. The transaction cost view holds that this information problem will eventually lead to incomplete contracting. In the discussion by Scharpf (1997) about hierarchical coordination, he also uses the Hayekian logic that although local information is very important, it is very difficult to transfer it to the central decision makers. Apart from this, he also stresses on the motivation problem. Even if there is adequate information, the benevolent motivation of actors cannot be taken for granted. In transaction cost economics, the owner-manager solves this problem by maximizing economic efficiency of the firm but only as long as the owner and manager do not have separate identities. When this happens the interests of the owner and the manager diverge and lead to lower effort levels. This can theoretically be solved by enforcing the incentive compatibility constraints, or agency contracts. But however mathematically sophisticated such solutions are, they fare poorly in terms of realism and practicability (Jensen 1983). In the sphere of public policy too such principal-agent relations exist, between voters (principals) and elected government (agent) or between the government (principal) and bureaucrats (agent). In the case of regulatory agency, things become more complicated when we see that there are in fact multiple principals (government and the self interest groups) who compete to gain the favour of the regulators (Spiller 1990), where the interests among the principals may not converge. The result is that both would like to control and influence the regulator. In the next paragraph we discuss whether involving the stakeholders more directly in the regulation process, at least theoretically, can reduce the multiple principal dilemma.

Yet when commitment is not successfully achieved through independent regulation, literature suggests that there is a need to move towards more stakeholder-based models of regulation (Dubash 2008) . The 'responsive' and 'stakeholder' models of regulation (Ayres and Braithwaite 1992; Prosser 1999) predict the presence of a third actor apart from the regulator and the regulated who are an equal stakeholder in the decision process. This model is also known as tripartism. It is defined as a polity where active participation of civil society through public interest groups or NGOs is allowed. Ayers and Braithwaite present a game theoretic model of capture and tripartism and show the conditions under which harmful capture can be prevented, efficient capture can be encouraged and regulatory goals through democracy can be furthered. There are three requirements for this model to work: first, the public interest groups have to be given all the information the regulator has; second, the public interest groups have to be given an opportunity to participate directly in the negotiation process; third, they should have the same prosecution powers as the regulators. But these are *institutional* conditions.

The realization of these three theoretical institutional conditions seems to be more unlikely in those environments which *do not* favor regulatory independence. Logically speaking, the institutional environment which facilitates sharing of information, equal opportunity in decision making, and same prosecution powers to third actors, like the public interest groups, may as well not allow capture in the first place. Although an environment where information is no more private to the key decision makers could change the game through informed voters and the mechanism of party competition, these conditions are difficult to be met in most of the developing context. Therefore it is no surprise that the formal stakeholder model hardly exists (Dubash and Rao 2008). Informally, however, a quasi-form of stakeholder engagement exists. Whenever any special interest move is suspected, public interest groups use an institutional mechanism, like filing of RTI (Right to Information) applications (in India), to produce information and amplify this through the media. This way public interest groups try to change the voter strategy (as *de-facto,* regulators are not independent from the government). Their aim is to bring about a regime change and hence a new regulatory set-up which will generate more favorable regulation. But what impact does this process have on regulatory commitment? Do investors feel secure and confident? Regime change is not necessarily indicative of increased commitment as the new elected regulatory set-up could also renege on its pre-electoral promise. And if regime change is the only purported solution, then the whole point of having independent regulation seems redundant.

To answer some of the puzzles above, it is important to understand how regulatory commitment is linked to information production by public interest groups. In this chapter, we try to do that through stylized games using linked action situations. We explain how this form of informal stakeholder engagement leads to a dilemma situation for the investors and creates a 'low commitment trap'. This however, is a short run phenomenon. We provide some tentative empirical illustration by briefly discussing a case of public monitoring of regulation in one region of India. We further argue that in the long run this dilemma can be solved under a repeated game situation where state regulators make public interest moves knowing that *otherwise* a persistent commitment trap will be created. We demonstrate that this is the case even though regulation is de facto not independent.

7.3   An Actor-Centered Game Based Illustration

Arguably, the most well-known form of the regulatory game tries to capture the conflict which arises over the sharing of rents between the investor and the regulator (Newbery 1999). There are two players in the game, the utility and the regulator, whose payoffs are affected by each other's strategies. The advantage of using a game structure to study interactions between rational agents is that their behavior can be observed under a situation when they know each other's strategies. However, the approach is limited by the difficulty to define the possibility set of the agents' actions and to include all the important aspects of interactions between the agents. For example, Newbery (1999) contends that there are a number of players whose actions may affect the investor's return (payoff), like the fuel suppliers, worker union, politicians, consumers, environmental groups, etc. But he includes only two players, the utility and the regulator as players in the game for the purposes of simplification and understanding a particular phenomenon, which in this case is commitment.

   In Newbery's model the utility's payoff is given by the profit it earns $\pi_t = R_t - bQ_t - rK_t$, where R_t is the revenue, Q_t is the quantity sold and K_t is the tariff. The regulator's payoff is given by $U_t + \theta \pi_t$, where U_t is the consumer surplus, π_t is the investor profit, and θ is the weight on profits relative to consumer benefits. It is also assumed that $\theta < 1$ implies the regulators will serve the interests of the local consumers first, as compared to the investors, who may not serve as local voters. This also means that the regulator can behave opportunistically with respect to sunk investments. The sequence of the game is such that first the utility chooses capital, i.e. the amount of investment; then the demand is realized; then the regulator chooses a reward or tariff to be offered, and finally, the payoffs are realized. For this one shot game, assuming regulators have no legal restrictions on their freedom to decide whether to pay or not, Newbery finds out that in the Nash equilibrium regulators set price equal to the variable cost and the utility does not invest. However, when the game is repeated and the concept of sub game Nash equilibrium is used, the condition under which the utility has the best outcome of making positive investment is derived as $(1 - P)(c - b) > r$, where $(1 - P)$ is the probability of high demand, $(c - b)$ is the extra cost of losing out on the utility's investment and r is the level of investment. This condition means that a certain rate-of-return needs to be offered for the utility to be able to invest and this rate acts as a restraint on regulatory discretion and prevents opportunistic behavior. Such restraints are good for regulatory commitment, and the regulatory governance literature (Levy and Spiller 1994) too maintains that it is a critical aspect of the total regulatory design.

There are some limitations to the basic regulatory game explained above. Firstly, the number of agents is limited to only two, thereby restricting the scope of strategic interactions. While θ shows that the actions of the regulators are guided by its implication on the voting behavior, the voter is not considered to be an active player. The fact that electricity is very political in nature, being provided to all voters in a state, and especially in the developing context where satisfying basic needs and demand is still an unfulfilled objective, suggests that voting behavior cannot be overlooked to understand how regulation works. Similarly the government is not included as an active player, thereby overlooking the role of party competition. Secondly, there is an assumption of information completeness. That is a direct fallout of the fact that the regulatory process is not the basis of setting up the game. The purpose of this game is to find out when restraints on regulatory discretion are needed so as to increase commitment.

We try to extend the basic regulatory game with an actor-centered approach. The nature, structure, resources and interests of the actors do have an influence on the design and the outcomes of games (Klijn and Koppenjan 2000). Institutions determine how the game is played and may vary from one game to the other (Scharpf 1997). In short, games differ when actors and institutions differ. Therefore, the actor-centered institutional approach offers a more detailed possibility to study the strategic interactions between players in a regulatory game. This is so because the core assumption of actor-centered institutionalism is that any analysis of structures independent of the reference to the actors involved is incomplete and vice versa (Mayntz and Scharpf 1995). By maintaining a sharp distinction between institutions and observable action by actors, this approach combines methodological individualism and institutionalism (Scharpf 1997).

We use a linked action situation approach (Kimmich 2013) because we study the interactions between two games. Such an approach has been proposed with the concept of Networks of Adjacent Action Situations (NAAS), where "an action situation X_i is *adjacent* to Y if the outcome of X_i directly influences the value of one or more of the working components of Y" (McGinnis 2011: p. 53). McGinnis built the concept as an extension of the Institutional Analysis and Development framework, based on the links between the seven sets of rules (Ostrom 2010) to identify related types of adjacent action situations. The NAAS concept has been demonstrated with several empirical cases (Lubell et al. 2010; McGinnis 2011; Dutton et al. 2012). The approach can be extended to physical, informational, and actor linkages, and take into consideration causation and boundary conditions (Kimmich 2013). The network of linked action situations reveals the complexity of games that condition each other. The researcher has to analyze different types of outcome. While the outcome of the focal situation in our context is a certain level of regulatory commitment, the outcome of an adjacent situation is a working component of the focal situation (McGinnis 2011). This outcome can be both physical in nature, or as in most cases, an institution. The underlying situation creating an institution can be the singular legislation of a law or a highly repetitive and long-lasting situation of reproducing habits and norms of behavior. Especially in the case of the latter, the outcome is part of an underlying and persistent institutional structure that shapes the focal situation.

7.3.1 The Model

In this section we explain our game model using simple ordinal payoffs with three different actors in the regulatory process; the regulator (which includes both the regulatory agency and government, given our assumption of regulatory non-independence in a developing context), the generation utility (investor), and the voter. It is based on the party competition model of Scharpf (1997). In the first game, information about special interests is private and not known to voters. In the second game we introduce public information produced by public interest groups (PIGS) about the suspected special interest motives of the regulator.

We start with the regulator deciding to increase the production capacity in electricity generation. It expresses an interest that private investors should come and set up their own power plants (utilities) and produce electric energy which they should sell to distribution utilities on a long-term basis for a rate of return decided by it. Through this the government-cum-regulator aims to satisfy the median voter who will be happy to see that the peak demand is met. However, the government has two choices. Either it gives concessions (examples are captive coal mines or generous take-or-pay fuel contracts), which have an opportunity cost in terms of budgetary adjustments, or it does not give any special concession. Accordingly the utility decides whether and how much to invest. However, the key concern for the utility will be whether the regulator sticks to its commitments about concessions and a rate of return so that their investments are secure and they can appropriate rents. The voter plays another game with the utility where it observes the move of the utility and decides to vote in or vote out the incumbent government based on whether it perceives reliable electricity at affordable prices. These two games are linked via the utility being present in both games and hence have important feedback and causation effects. With this background we explain the game structure below:

Set of players
SR: State Regulator; includes combined decision making by state government and the regulatory agency
U: Utility; in this case the independent power producer (IPP) or the investor
V: Voters (consumers)
Set of actions and choices
SR: Invites private investment and either offers a Concession (*C*) or No-Concession (*NC*)
U: Decides to make high investment (*Inv^h*) or low investment (*Inv^l*)
V: Vote for (*V^y*) or Vote against (*V^n*) the incumbent government based on levels of investment by U

Stage 1: Private Information

State Regulator (SR) and Utility (U) Game
There is a set of legislated formal institutions where the government has to invite private investments through an open tender (competitive bidding) procedure. And the government can change the composition of the regulatory agency. This justifies our strong assumption that both government and regulatory agency have a common strategy. Therefore, SR represents the entire set of regulatory decision makers, including the government. In this game information is only shared between the players: regulator (SR) and utility (U), i.e. a privately owned electric company involved only in generation. SR and U also have common knowledge that V is unaware of any special interest motives, whereas their game plan has special interests. The preferences of both the players are written in an extensive form as shown in Fig. 7-1 along with the attached payoffs, which are ordinal preferences. U prefers making high investment with concessions over high investment without concession: p (i_{high}; c) > p (i_{high}; ~c). Higher investment means higher revenues: p (i) = e^{x*i}. It prefers lower investments with some concessions than lower investments without any concession: p (i_{low}; c) > p (i_{low}; ~c). It always prefers high investment over low investment p (i_{high}) > p (i_{low}).

Utility (U) and Voter (V) Game
In parallel, utility (U) and voter (V) also play a game. This is because the only way V can observe the actions of the regulator (SR) is through the level of investments U makes. V believes that the higher the level of investment, the higher will be the availability of electricity and the lower the prices. This game is illustrated in Fig. 7-2 where U prefers making high investment and government being voted in to being voted out. However, when it makes low investment it prefers the government being voted out so that there is new government and new SR. V clearly prefers high investment over low but cannot

decide in either case whether to vote in or out. The payoff structures reflect this set of preferences.

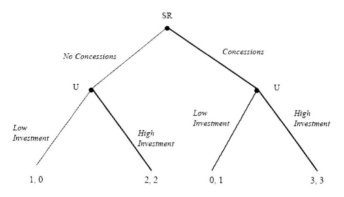

Figure 7-1: Investment game: regulators and utility

We solve both games through backward induction, deriving the Sub-game Perfect Nash Equilibria (SPNE) and the game equilibrium. The equilibrium in the 'investment game' (see Fig. 1) is where the regulator offers concessions and the utilities make high investment. There is no single pure strategy equilibrium in the 'voting game' (see Fig. 7-2). The outcome could be both where utilities invest highly and the voters vote in or out the incumbent or utilities make low investment and voters voting in or out the incumbent. This is because the voter cannot observe the reasons for the low or high investment and her payoff from voting for (or against) the incumbent is the same. In addition, U receives the same payoff for his decision, as $p\ (i_{high};\ c) + p\ (i_{low};\ c) = p\ (i_{high};\ \sim c) + p\ (i_{low};\ \sim c)$, or $1+2 = 0+3$. Therefore, we see this indeterminate solution.

Stage 2: Information about special interests available to voters

The voter has now more public information about the regulatory process of private investment due to the presence of public interest groups. Its strategies are now informed by the fact that there could be special interests in awarding concessions, so it is cautious. V receives information of the move taken by SR, although this information is imperfect and also incomplete, because the payoffs are not known to V. It is very important to remember that the assumptions we have on the information public interest groups produce will decide the outcome of the game. We assume that the information is primarily biased against SR and V now thinks that, a) there is rent seeking by utilities, through favored concessions from the government, b) tariffs will ultimately increase as generated electric energy will be sold outside their own regions.

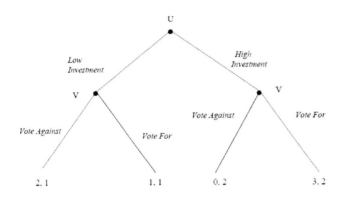

Figure 7-2: Incomplete information voting game: utility and voter

In game theory, complete information refers to common knowledge of the game structure, including the payoff functions. Common knowledge itself can be defined even broader as a meta-axiom, where the axioms of logic and game theory, including the behavioral assumptions, are known by each player (Gilboa and Schmeidler 1988). In our case we are especially concerned with knowledge of the payoff functions. The game-theoretic literature has dealt with information concerning payoffs in different ways: The classical approach is Bayesian updating of priors (Heap and Varoufakis 2004). Gilboa and Schmeidler (1988) first proposed the concept of information-dependent games which states that information can change players' payoffs in non-cooperative games. An example given by the authors is gossip, where the information told to a player may change his utility of a certain move. We take a similar approach, where public information is the information known to all players involved. We simplify the role of information in the sense that the information made available to the public is "objective". An extension could also include social information, where information is not neutral, but can be *biased* in different ways and also used strategically. This would require modeling the bias of information, however. Public or social information can concern both the payoff of the player who the information is addressed to, as well as the payoff of other players involved in the same game.

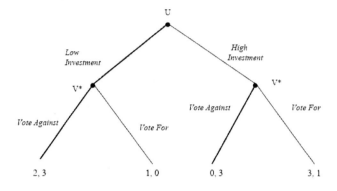

Figure 7-3: Complete information voting game: utility and voter

New game in the next electoral cycle

The preferences of U remain the same but the preference ordering of V changes in the game between them for votes. This is due to the media-amplified information V receives from public interest groups. As V observes that U acquires some rents, V realizes that its own payoffs could be potentially better with putting the government under pressure. So V feels that voting against will give it a higher reward. If U makes high investment V wants to vote against the incumbent government as it sees concessions as a form of special interest. If U makes low investment, V does not get improved electricity provision and also wants to vote the incumbent out. The new payoffs of the voter V* can be seen in Fig. 7-3. In the next time period, but within a short run context, the preference ordering of U will change, irrespective of regime change. U is a common player in both the games and has to make its decisions according to the potential outcomes of both games in which it is involved. The preference ordering of the new regulator, SR*, will remain same as it will employ the same strategy to invite investment[1]. But U* will now clearly prefer low investment over high investment as it is not sure if the concessions will be overturned by a regime change. This will affect the viability of its investment project. The new payoffs of utility U* can be seen in Fig. 4. Applying the pure strategy Nash algorithm, we see that for the complete information voting game (see Fig. 3), the equilibrium is where the utility does not want to invest and the voters still want to vote out the incumbent. The result can be explained as follows: the voter does not vote for the incumbent under low investment as this translates into reduced power availability. It also does not vote for the incumbent when the investment

---

[1]   This is of course a short run phenomenon.

is high as it, even though not observing, at least believes that it is a special interest move. *This leads to a dilemma and is the source of the commitment problem.* Because of this dilemma, in the next period the preference ordering of U changes (see Fig. 7-4). It now values low investment more than high investment as it is in a dilemma that V will always vote against the incumbent if it believes the public information it receives from public interest groups. The equilibrium now is (see Fig. 7-4) where regulators do not offer any concessions and there is low investment by utilities. This, we call the *'low commitment trap'* arising out of the investment problem. In the next section we will illustrate our arguments through the example of People's Monitoring Group on Electricity Reforms (PMGER), an influential public interest group in Hyderabad, India. We will discuss the case of their active public scrutiny of power purchase contracts between the private generation utilities and buyers.

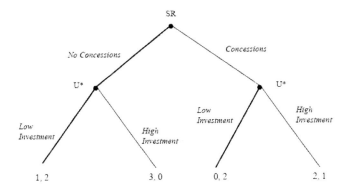

Figure 7-4: New period investment game: regulators and utility

7.4 The Case of Private Investment in Andhra Pradesh, India[2]

The Andhra Pradesh electricity sector has some resemblance to a form of quasi-stakeholder engagement because civil society activity is strong. This is due to

---

[2] We only present an indicative case of electricity regulation and investment in Andhra Pradesh, but recently there have been two other cases of private investment which suffered on similar counts. One is the 2G spectrum bandwidth auction failure (http://www.bbc.co.uk/news/business-20335147); and other, the allocation and subsequent de-allocation of private licenses of captive coal mines (http://businesstoday.intoday.in/story/coal-scam-coalgate-caganalysis/1/187782.html). A common thread in all of these cases is the revoking of government (or regulator) awarded contracts ex-post the investment.

the presence of PMGER[3], a public interest body which monitors the activities of the electricity regulator. PMGER also has a formal representation on the advisory board of the electricity regulator, but that is only formal in nature and has no significant policy influence. That is why we refer to it as quasi-stakeholder engagement. The main strategy of PMGER is filing of litigations against any moves by the utilities or the regulators to increase the tariff burden on the consumers. PMGER actively scrutinizes the power purchase agreements (PPAs) between private investor-backed independent power producers (IPPs) and the distribution utilities. These power purchase contracts have strict 'take or pay' clauses which mean that any fuel risk is ultimately passed on to the consumers. This is a potential contractual hazard and indeed has led to multiple instances of renegotiations and amendments to the contract, as can be seen from the case of four major IPPs in Andhra Pradesh (see Table 7-1). This was because natural gas, which is the primary fuel for these private generation plants, was not available for the first eight years after the power contracts were signed (Ghosh and Kathuria 2011).

Table 7-1: Features of current power purchase agreements (PPAs)

S.N	Name of the IPP	Entry Route	Capacity (MW)	Year of First PPA	Year of Final PPA	Year of COD#	Initial Allotment of Gas (MCMD)	Nr. of Rene-gotia-tions
1	GVK Ltd.	MoU	220	1998	2003	2006	1.1	2
2	Gouthami Ltd.	Bidding	464	1997	2003	2006	1.96	2
3	Konaseema Ltd.	Bidding	445	1997	2005	2007	1.60	3
4	Vemagiri Ltd.	Bidding	370	1997	2007	2006	1.64	3

Notes: # COD - Commercial Operation Date; MCMD: million cubic meters per day; MoU – Memorandum of Understanding
Source: Ghosh and Kathuria (2013); various PPAs and APERC reports

Usually the IPPs enter into power purchase agreements, long term contracts ranging from 15-23 years with the state distribution utilities. Table 1 summarizes the important features and contractual evolution of 4 such IPPs[4], which faced huge delays in operation and have had to face contractual renegotiations several times even before operations began. These four IPPs were almost ready to generate electricity by 2005-06, but could not do so because there was no gas available from Gas Authority of India Ltd. (GAIL)[5] to them.

---

[3] http://www.pmger.org/
[4] The detailed contractual and related information presented in this section is sourced from the individual Power Purchase Agreements (PPAs) and other records availed from the regulatory commission (Common-Order 2009).
[5] GAIL is the state-owned gas supplying agency in India.

Upon analyzing the whole negotiation process we observe that some of the key reasons why the contracts between the IPPs and the distribution utilities ran into rough weather are transactional in nature. The shortfall of natural gas meant that the existing contracts were rendered incomplete and ineffective. To deal with this 'perceived' uncertainty, an 'alternate fuel' clause was introduced in the initial contract as it was known even during the drafting phase that there would be uncertainties about fuel supply in the future. But as per the 'take or pay' contract once the plant operation date is declared, the distribution utility gets locked in and has to buy the higher cost electricity generated by high cost alternate fuel or pay at least the fixed charges in the absence of any generation. But once gas became unavailable for generation purposes and there was indeed a need for alternative fuel, the distribution utilities objected to the alternative fuel clause and moved the regulators for ex-post amendments. The IPPs agreed to delete this clause on the condition that they would be allowed to sell 20% of their contracted capacity in the open market. This would enable them to recover the losses due to non-generation and earn net positive returns. However this meant that the already deprived distribution utilities would have to buy a portion of their own legitimate share from the open market at higher rates. These negotiations went through the regulatory process and the regulators, being the 'independent' authorities, decided on the final outcome. The next sub-section describes this briefly.

7.4.1 The Role of Civil Society Actors and Regulatory Decision

The PPAs, with the proposed amendments, along with the report of a state government appointed committee to look into the amendments, were submitted to the Andhra Pradesh Electricity Regulatory Commission (APERC) for approval on the 02.02.2009. The APERC then conducted - in the spirit of the 'law and philosophy' of electricity reforms - a series of public hearings, where all stakeholders, including public interest groups, discussed and debated the proposed amendments. In multiple hearings ranging over 10 months, all the parties presented their cases and debated over issues related to consumer welfare, contractual cost benefits and micro mathematics of the incentives. The public interest groups raised tough questions on the intent of the IPPs in trying to maximize their profits at the cost of loss to the consumers whereas the IPPs defended themselves on the basis of their stranded costs and high risks of future gas unavailability. In the meantime, gas supplies improved from April 2009 due to increased availability from the KG Basin and Reliance Industries Limited (RIL) committing regular supply of gas to the IPPs. Finally, in a gas order dated 05.12.2009, the APERC overturned the appeals for amended agreements keeping in view the *'public interest at large'*.

The regulators further recommended some options to be reworked, which would allow the IPPs to cover up their losses without hampering consumer welfare. But as stated in Section 3, these PPAs are different from the privately ordered relational contracts. These are more of the nature of public contracts and hence subject to scrutiny by the third party public or private interest groups. In this case the regulatory process was constantly tracked and monitored by civil bodies, like PMGER and some other independent energy auditors and journalists. At every stage of the amendments and fresh PPA proposals, there were objections filed by PMGER during the last 10 years. Moreover, the public hearings which covered the whole span of the year 2009[6] went back and forth with PMGER raising objections and the IPPs, distribution utilities and the regulators responding (Common-Order 2009). This whole process of public hearing of the case filed by PMGER was covered by the media. In the meantime, the Government of Andhra Pradesh appointed an independent committee to look into the amendments and it passed an order G.O. 135 (Government Order). This order overruled most of the objections raised by the PIGS and ruled in favor of the IPPs and distribution utilities. While 'respect(ing) and hold(ing) the observations of APERC in the highest esteem', the order claimed to supersede the authority of the regulatory commission in having the final word. In the public hearing subsequent to the passing of G.O. 135, the PIGS raised this issue and reminded the regulatory commission of its independent powers that "the APERC is a quasi-judicial authority and it cannot be directed to decide the matter in a particular manner" (Common-Order 2009: p. 162).

In its final order, the regulatory commission '(in) view… (of) the legitimate interests of the various stakeholders, including the IPPs, DISCOMs (distribution companies, *added by the authors*), electricity consumers and general public interest at large' and having well taken the content of the objectors, overruled the G.O 135 and agreed to the amendments as proposed by PMGER. The regulators also cited various references from previous court orders (some brought to their notice by PMGER) to prove that the government order was not binding and that they were independent in framing their own regulations and stated that 'APERC being an independent regulator cannot be influenced by any authority including the Government in the matter of balancing the interest of all the stakeholders by issuing directions by invoking section 108 of the Electricity Act, 2003' (Common-Order 2009: p. 193). Finally, the regulatory commission *rejected* all those amendments which were *not* in tune with the *public interest* at large and accepted only those which matched the interests of the IPPs, the distribution as well as the electricity consumers at large.

We contend that this uncertainty surrounding the commitment of the regulator to protect their investment could well explain the current lack of enthusiasm in the levels of gas-based private investment in Andhra Pradesh. During the period

---

[6] Between 04.03.2009 and 17.11.2009, 13 public hearings were conducted by the APERC (APERC Common Order, 2009).

from 2007-2012, there was private investment to the tune of 1275 Megawatt (MW) installed capacity in gas-based power plants in Andhra Pradesh, but for the period from 2012-2019, there is not even a single forthcoming private investment in Andhra Pradesh[7]. This is despite the fact that there have been huge discoveries of gas in the Krishna-Godavari basin off the coast of Andhra Pradesh. In fact the share of non-gas based private investment has also slumped in Andhra Pradesh. This is in sharp contrast to another Indian state, Gujarat, where the growth of IPPs has been quite high.

7.5 Discussion: Institutions for Information Production

7.5.1 Long Run Equilibrium

The case above shows how in Andhra Pradesh IPPs moved initially with high investments in response to concessions, like a generous 'take or pay' contract from the state regulators, in this case offered by the government of Andhra Pradesh and the regulatory agency APERC. This is consistent with our modeling in the first game. Eventually public information set in, which led to increased scrutiny of the regulators in the minds of the general public or the voters. In fact in 2004, the ruling regime in Andhra Pradesh was replaced by a new government which came into power on the promise of free electricity to farmers (Shah 2009). This eroded the credibility of the regulatory agency as far the investors and the urban consumers were concerned. This is consistent with our complete information voting game which has, in the current short term, now changed the way investors perceive regulatory intervention. This has changed the payoffs of the utilities which now are not sure if their high investments based on earlier concessional contracts are secure. The regulatory process in the presence of third party actors like the PMGER, which produce information, has been inclined towards the *'public interest at large'* and has led to regulators reneging on their commitments, as in the case of 'alternate fuel' clause. The current state of investment in Andhra Pradesh is partly reflective of this 'low commitment trap' and follows the modeling pattern in our complete information, new period investment game.

To sum up, so far we have shown using a linked action situation approach that information produced by public interest groups changes the payoffs of the key actors in the investment and voting games and in fact leads to a fall in regulatory commitment, at least in the short run. This is because investors perceive that the incumbent regulatory regime will be voted out and concessions may be reneged upon. This means that *in the presence of public information, special interest moves by the regulatory regime will not be successful in attracting sustained investment.* We have given at least one instance of this through the example of

---

[7] The information is based on the official report 'Power Scenario at a Glance, 2012' published by the Central Electricity Authority of India (CEA).

private investment in power plants in Andhra Pradesh and its public monitoring. Albeit without much elaboration, we have also guided the readers (in an earlier footnote) to the problems of 2G spectrum auctions and captive coal mine allocation. However, greater empirical research is needed to substantiate or negate this prediction in other settings. But what does it mean for commitment in the long run? Precisely because special interest moves will *not* be effective in the presence of public information, the only long run solution to overcome the commitment trap will be when, under a repeated game situation, the regulator's payoff changes in a way that it places higher values on public interest moves. But how will this happen? This outcome will result as long as *public information is produced* and helps voters know their payoffs better. With every special interest move being detected and regulatory regime being voted out repeatedly, the regulator's pay-off will change. It can be illustrated using the game structure as shown in Fig. 7-5. The regulator now attaches a lower value to concessions. The long run equilibrium in that case will be where utilities make high investment without special concessions but with assured stable and flexible contracts or vertical integration.

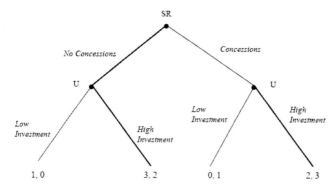

Figure 7-5: Long run equilibrium with public information

Fig. 7-6 summarizes the relationship between commitment over time and public information. From the curve AB we can see that in the short (T_0) and medium term (T_M) regulatory commitment falls over time for a certain constant rate of information production. But in the medium term the commitment trap is broken and it starts to slope upwards in the longer term (T_L). The definition of medium term and long term is arbitrary for the moment (and actually needs to be empirically determined), ranging from one or two electoral cycles to even more. When the rate of information production increases the curve would become steeper as shown by the dashed line MN. The commitment trap would be overcome earlier and a higher commitment level will be reached quickly.

However, when the institutional environment for information production is weak and information is generated at a slower rate, then the curve takes the shape of the dashed line CD, where the commitment trap is never broken and with time commitment keeps on falling.

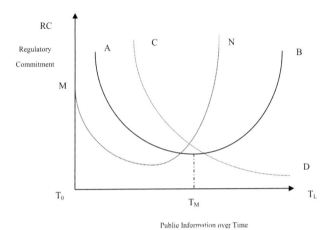

Figure 7-6: Relationship of commitment with public information over time

7.5.2 Conditions for Long Run Equilibrium: Public Information

This brings us to the key insight of the chapter, which is that this long term equilibrium can be achieved only when the institutional environment is favorable for production of public information. So there needs to be laws which facilitate public interest groups to gather information from state agencies, and there needs to be a judiciary which protects those rights. In India, such an environment exists ever since the Right to Information Act (2005)[8] was enacted. Information produced through such a process is generally high quality (i.e. backed by data) and credible to the voters. Having said that more research on the impacts of information producing institutions like the 'right to information' on the levels of rent seeking, concessions and investment in public and private infrastructure provision like energy and telecommunications or on the way natural resources are managed or exploited like forestry, sand mining, coal mining and water bodies, could substantiate the claim that public information could lead to stable public interest outcomes in the long run.

---

[8]   Under the provisions of the Act, any citizen may request information from a "public authority" (a body of Government or "instrumentality of State") which is required to reply expeditiously or within thirty days. (http://rti.gov.in/)

7.6 Conclusions

In pursuit of the bigger problem of how to generate credible commitments to bind players into agreements (posed by Douglass North and others) we have made an attempt to show what role institutions of public information can play in that. Using a linked action situation approach through a network of adjacent action situations (NAAS) we show a way in which public information could affect regulatory commitment by creating a 'low commitment trap' in the short run. This, however, can be solved in the long run under a repeated game situation where state regulators make public interest moves being aware that otherwise a trap will be created. We have thus demonstrated that even under de facto dependent regulation where the government and regulator act in collusion, regulatory commitment can evolve. This result counters the principal-agent logic that is often provoked when analyzing the role of independent regulation.

Our game models and the corroborative example of the public monitoring of electricity in Andhra Pradesh are indications that in the presence of public information, the state policy of offering special interest concessions does not necessarily lead to sustained higher investment. Active public interest actors help the voter know its own payoff better through increased public information. Therefore, the long run best response for state regulators will be to always make credible public interest moves. This is somewhat similar to the prediction by earlier literature that 'by choosing public interest oriented policies, the government will assure itself a moderately good outcome' (Scharpf 1997, p. 186). But such prediction hangs on the stringent condition that political opposition opposes the moves by the incumbent and voters react each time. What we have shown is that even when this condition of active political opposition does not apply, the long run strategy of state regulators (the incumbent) would be to make public interest moves. However, the necessary condition for this is the presence of an institutional environment which facilitates the production of public information. We showed that in India this has been made possible by the RTI Act which allows public interest groups to access credible information on administrative and policy processes. However, follow up research is needed to empirically establish this relationship in various settings, especially historical. A wider implication of this reasoning is that institutions of public information lead to strengthening of credible commitments.

Appendix

Genesis of the Investment Problem in Andhra Pradesh

Usually the Independent Power Producers (IPPs) enter into power purchase agreements, long term contracts ranging from 15-23 years (PPAs), with the state distribution utilities. We discuss the important features and contractual evolution of 4 such IPPs[9], which faced huge delays in operation and have had to face contractual renegotiations several times even before operations began. These four IPPs were almost ready to generate electricity by 2005-06, but could not do so because there was no gas available from Gas Authority of India Ltd. (GAIL)[10] to them. The first IPP, GVK Industries Pvt. Ltd. entered into a MoU with the Andhra Pradesh state government for installing a power plant with 400 MW capacities on 14.02.92. The allotted gas base was for 1.5 MCMD.[11] But after the agreement was entered into, the Ministry of Petroleum and Natural Gas, Government of India (MoPNG) reduced the allotment to 0.75 MCMD. In India the MoPNG is the highest authority related to all activities of exploration, refining as well as marketing and distribution of petroleum and natural gas. It is a central government ministry and regulates the allocation and pricing of natural gas.[12] Based on the allotment by the MoPNG, the Gas Authority of India Limited (GAIL), a central government owned enterprise, supplies natural gas to the different thermal power plants. However this supply, guided by the Gas Supply Agreements (GSAs), is dependent on the actual production of natural gas by the two major public sector companies Oil & Natural Gas Corporation Ltd., (ONGC) and Oil India Limited (OIL). While the allocations are based on projected demand and supply, the net supplies are based on the actual production levels. Thus the contract (PPA) with Andhra Pradesh State Electricity Board (APSEB) was renegotiated and GVK went ahead with a capacity of 216 MW to be set up as Phase 1 of the project based on the actual gas allotment and the remaining capacity 184 MW to be installed as Phase 2 based on future availability of gas. In 1998, GVK proposed approval for commencement of the Phase 2 with an increased capacity of 360 MW to be installed. This capacity expansion was done to bring the terms on par with the new PPAs entered with short gestation projects, selected through competitive bidding, like Gouthami, Vemagiri and Konaseema EPS Oakwell. The MoPNG allotted 1.1 MCMD gas for this Phase 2 project. But again on 01.09.2000 the

---

[9] The detailed contractual and related information presented in this section is sourced from the individual Power Purchase Agreements (PPAs) and other records availed from the regulatory commission: (Common-Order 2009)

[10] GAIL is the state-owned gas supplying agency in India.

[11] Million Cubic Meters per Day

[12] http://expenditurereforms.nic.in/petroleum.pdf
http://petroleum.nic.in/ng.htm

MoPNG informed that unless more supply from KG (Krishna Godavari) Basin was available, no additional gas could be allotted. Thus Phase 2 was again split into two stages with Stage I (220 MW) based on 1.1 MCMD and Stage II (220 MW) based on further availability of gas. The final amended PPA was consented after public hearings by the newly established APERC, dated 18.06.2003.

Another IPP, Gouthami Power Private Limited entered a PPA on 31.03.97 with APSEB for setting up 300 MW gas based (either on naptha or natural gas) power plant at Peddapuram, through the route of competitive bidding. Subsequently, two years later, they obtained an expansion order for the plant to be of 358.9 MW capacity. During the same time another company, Nagarjuna Construction Company (NCC) entered into a separate PPA for setting up a 227 MW liquid fuel based power plant at Ammanabrolu, which was later shifted to Peddapuram. In the year 2000, Government of Andhra Pradesh (GoAP) decided to convert the Gouthami project to be run only on natural gas based on 'least cost' considerations. Upon request for gas allotment, only 1.22 MCMD gas was allotted to Gouthami and 0.74 MCMD to NCC Power. This gas was not sufficient for either of them for the given installed capacity and the two firms decided to merge. The new entity, by the name of Gouthami, agreed to proceed with the project in two stages. The first stage would be of 464 MW capacity based on gas supply of 1.96 MCMD and the second stage would be of 133.9 MW based on further availability of gas. The final amended PPA was signed on 18.06.2003. The third IPP, Konaseema EPS Oakwell Power Limited originally entered into a PPA with the APSEB on 31.03.1997 for setting up a 445 MW gas based power plant at Deverapalli, also through the bid route. There were some amendments later on and it finally entered into a new PPA with APTRANSCO on 21.11.2003. However, beginning 2003 there were concerns about availability of natural gas for new projects and hence a new agreement was reached 12.01.2005 with clauses which restricted the use of alternate fuel before 2007. The fourth IPP, Vemagiri Power Generation Ltd. (earlier Ispat Power) entered into a PPA with the APSEB on 31.03.1997 for setting up a 468 MW gas based plant at Vemagiri. In the year 2000, the MoPNG allotted it 1.64 MCMD gas from the Krishna Godavari (KG) Basin. Thus the project was decided to be implemented in two stages. Stage I would be with 370 MW capacity with the existing gas allotment and Stage II would be with 150 MW capacity based on future availability of gas. The amended agreement was entered into on 18.06.2003 (later on we will see how Vemagiri is a special case as it renegotiated again on 02.05.2007).

These four IPPs were almost ready to generate electricity by 2005-06, but could not do so because there was no gas available from GAIL to these. Actually, GAIL could not supply the complete allocation even to the existing power plants in Andhra Pradesh. As per the terms of the PPA, due to the "alternate fuel" clause, the burden of this unavailability lay on the distributors who would still have to pay the full fixed charges in the event of non-generation. This commitment towards fixed charges, in the presence of the alternate fuel clause, would have cost the distributors an additional Rs. 1020 crores[13] per annum (Common-Order 2009). Thus the distributors (APTRANSCO at that time) filed for the deletion of the "alternate fuel" clause (in July 2004) from the contract. However, only one firm, Vemagiri, accepted the deletion of this clause and entered an amended contract. In return the PPA term was extended from 15 to 23 years to be able to recover the losses. Upon this they were provided the interconnection facilities and they declared their commercial operation date (COD) of the project on 16.09.2006 (Common-Order 2009). But there was yet no gas available and hence the plant remained in 'preservation mode' till gas supply was restored around mid of 2009. The other three plants landed in similar fate and could not produce any power either. This not only caused stranded losses to the firms but also placed an additional burden on the distributors in the form of buying higher cost power to meet the shortfall due to delay in production by these IPPs. Following the example of Vemagiri, the other three IPPs agreed to delete the "alternate fuel" clause. While this request was pending with the regulatory commission, one of them, Gouthami, obtained interim orders for gas supply from the AP High Court in year 2007. Learning from this, the other IPPs also withdrew their 'deletion proposals' and prepared for commissioning their plants by 'first' testing. But this High Court order was challenged by the distribution companies and a division bench of the High Court overturned the previous 'Order' and disallowed the supply of gas to the new IPPs. In September 2007, the IPPs proposed again to delete the 'alternate fuel' clause under the condition that they would be allowed to sell '20% of the PPA capacity plus any tested capacity over and above the PPA capacity to third parties' in order to recover their losses from non-operation. The Vemagiri project, for example, was built at a cost of Rs. 1100 crores and did not see any returns for the first 5 years. Through this renegotiation, the IPPs would be able to easily make up for their past losses and hence Vemagiri too proposed a renegotiation in line with the proposed amendments of the other three IPPs.

Upon analyzing the whole negotiation process we observe that some of the key reasons why the contracts between the IPPs and the distribution utilities ran into rough weather are transactional in nature. The shortfall of natural gas means that the existing contracts were rendered incomplete and ineffective. To deal with this 'perceived' uncertainty, the 'alternate fuel' clause was introduced in the initial contract as it was known even during the drafting phase that there may be uncertainties about fuel supply in the future. Since generation utilities make asset specific investments, such adaptive elements are important. But this clause also creates scope for opportunistic behavior by them. Once the COD is declared, the distribution utility gets locked in and has to buy the higher cost

---

[13] 1 Crore = 10 Million

electricity generated by high cost alternate fuel or pay at least the fixed charges in the absence of any generation.

The IPPs agreed to delete this clause on the condition that they are allowed to sell 20% of their contracted capacity in the open market. This would enable them to recover the losses due to non-generation and earn net positive returns. However this meant that the already deprived distribution utilities would have to buy a portion of their own legitimate share from the open market at higher rates. This again was considered as opportunistic behavior of the IPPs by the distributors and hence objected to. Another adaptive response by the IPPs would be to extend he period of the contract. This follows the TCE prediction that long term contracts are safeguards against ex post contractual hazards. So while one of the IPPs did initially agree to this amendment, it later reversed on its decision in favor of open market sale. However these negotiations went through the regulatory process and the regulators being the 'independent' authorities decided on the final outcome. The next sub-section describes it briefly.

8. Conclusions and the Way Forward

Synopsis of Research Findings

The aim of power sector reforms in India was to invite private participation, normalize tariffs and increase efficiency. In pursuance of this a system of independent regulation was set up which would manage the various actors through assurance and credible commitments. In essence, commitment was clearly the ultimate aim. The means adopted to achieve this were market oriented liberalization and partial deregulation. This thesis has re-evaluated the claim that the *means* meet the *end* adequately. Through analysis of the three key segments in the generation side - public utilities, private utilities and private non-utilities – it has been shown that there are inefficiencies and high transaction costs in the current environment. It has been argued, using a comparative institutional analysis framework, that when the neo-classical assumption of zero transaction costs is violated, power markets may not be an efficient or a feasible solution. Therefore, a regulatory structure which minimizes transaction costs and increases commitment is a priority, even if this means moving away from the benchmark solution of perfect competition.

8.1 Summary

The thesis began by explaining how the early 1990s was a watershed period in Indian economic history. Following a break-away from the earlier mixed model of economic growth, which characterized Indian economy for the four decades after independence in 1947, the country made a paradigm shift through opening up all the major sectors to international competitive forces. India embarked on an ambitious power sector reform program, as a part of the broader set of nationwide economic reforms and liberalization policy. The aim was to basically improve the performance of the power sector in terms of better quality provision of electricity which includes longer hours of (and reliable) supply, improved prices for consumers, efficiency gains in terms of lesser T&D losses, less theft etc. As has been discussed in an earlier section (Section 1.2) of the thesis, although there is some progress, it has not matched the expectations of economists or policy-makers alike. The key question which is investigated is: why have electricity reforms not been able to achieve its stated objectives? A key insight from the present analysis is that somewhere down the line, the *means* got mixed with the *aims* and policy-makers lost sight of the actual objective of breeding credible regulatory commitments. The entire focus was confined to the development of a market-based system, which is a *means* to arrive at credible commitments through appropriate contracting. The thesis has shown that a key reason for this fallacious approach was the lack of a *comparative institutional analysis*. While the previous literature on Indian power sector reforms has given due attention to the incentive structure, it has simply assumed that markets are the most efficient governance structure. However, a governance structure is efficient or not can be known only when compared to the other alternative structures. In Chapter 2, therefore, the foundation for such a comparative analysis using the strand of literature from transaction cost economics (TCE) (Williamson 1979b, 1985) and 'institutions of regulation' (Stern and Holder 1999; Spiller and Tommasi 2005; Dubash 2008) was laid down.

The basic proposition from TCE is that an efficient governance structure (markets, hierarchies or hybrids) minimizes transaction costs. The neo-classical prediction that electricity markets are efficient is only valid under the assumptions of zero transaction costs. In the world of positive transaction costs, however, efficiency is essentially relative and alternative governance structures need to be subjected to a comparative analysis (Coase 1964). In Chapter 4 an empirical application of this was presented for the case of private utilities. The question of why the aim of inviting private capital has not been successful was examined through a transaction cost comparison of gas-based private investments in two coastal Indian states - Andhra Pradesh and Gujarat. These states have a similar regulatory set-up, similar incentive structures and have seen bulk of the initial gas-based private investment being made. Yet they have differed greatly in terms of actual generation. Andhra Pradesh's lack of success owes to upstream regulation and arm's length contractual design. This has created a weak demand response giving rise to high transaction costs. Whereas in Gujarat, upstream contractual design has ensured that demand response is strong enough that minimizes transaction costs for utilities downstream. With some evidence from the upcoming ultra-mega power projects, it was shown that as long as contractual hazards are high, organizational forms closer to vertical integration is a more economical option than deregulation to solve the investment problem.

In Chapter 5 another empirical application is presented where it is shown that non-utilities minimize transaction costs through vertically integrating electricity production. In Andhra Pradesh, as in many other industrialized states of India, industries are often plagued with power shortages. In response, some firms make their own electric power but most of the others do not. The question of why there is a divergent behavior in the decision to self-generate was explored. While previous literature focused on factor demand and marginal cost structure as key determinants for the decision to self-generate, it did not explain divergent behavior in firms with similar characteristics. Therefore, a perspective of contractual relationships was introduced and electricity provision was treated as a transaction. A discrete choice 'make or buy' model was applied on a primary and disaggregated dataset of Indian manufacturing firms. Results confirmed that 'transaction-specificity' in electricity use primarily drove the decision to self-generation. This was added by contextual factors like firm size, land availability and operational environment. The analysis showed that even a standardized and physically non-specific asset could generate 'transaction-specific' costs. It also revealed that the burden of poor grid supply is highest on those firms which are smaller but manufacture high transaction-specific cost generating products (like food and chemicals). In that case the only options left for such firms would be either to downsize their production, or run losses or shut down. Therefore, policies of open access to the grid aimed at incentivizing greater self-generation may be ineffective unless it accounts for transaction cost variability and firm level characteristics.

These two carefully designed and detailed empirical analyses (Chapters 4 and 5) have shown that in the world of positive transaction costs adequate incentives may be a *necessary* but not a *sufficient* condition. The case of investor owned utilities in Andhra Pradesh has shown that high contractual hazards impede the path towards a market mechanism in spite of an appropriate incentive design. The case of captive non-utilities in Andhra Pradesh has also shown that a market for captive power has failed in spite of the incentives for grid access. In both the cases organizational forms closer to vertical integration appear to be the appropriate governance structure minimizing transaction costs. The bottom line is that the *governance* aspect of electricity and regulatory reforms (stemming from comparative institutional analysis) is non-trivial and needs further attention. The 'institutions of regulation' approach provides an avenue for precisely that kind of an analysis.

The core concern of the 'institutions of regulation' approach is credible commitments. Commitments from regulators are credible when there are adequate restraints on their abilities to renege on promises, thereby protecting the asset-specific investments. This, according to literature, is the *governance* aspect of regulation which focuses on the *ex-post* component of regulatory design. Its other component emphasizes on the *ex-ante* aspect of incentives, which we have shown through the empirical work in Chapters 4 and 5 to be inadequate. Therefore, the next two chapters of the thesis study the impact of regulatory governance and the strength of commitments. In Chapter 6, the impact of regulatory governance is measured through a parametric method on a concrete indicator of Indian power sector performance: the efficiency of thermal power plants (mostly state-owned generation utilities). A unique index of regulatory governance is created which is composed of sub-indexes reflecting electricity tariffs, reductions in aggregate technical losses, the age of regulators, status of electricity unbundling and stability of the regulatory composition. A stochastic frontier analysis showed that thermal efficiency increased by nearly 4 percentage points from the time independent regulators were commissioned. Because an inefficiency effects model was used, it could also be tested if regulatory governance had any impact on performance. Results indicated that it did have a significant impact on plant level performance. A further sensitivity analysis showed that the plant performance improved significantly in those states where the electricity boards were unbundled. However, the age (or experience) of regulators did not significantly impact plant performance. This is an indicator of low commitment by independent regulators. The prime reason for this being *de-facto* non-independence of the regulatory commission from the government.

In Chapter 7, regulatory commitment is revisited with a normative view to model if commitments could be high even under the conditions of *de-facto* non-independence. Using actor-centered institutionalism (Scharpf 1997), the basic regulatory game (Newbery 1999) is extended to include other key actors like the government, the voter and third party public interest groups. The basic form of the regulatory game considered only 2 players, the utility and the regulator, and hence ignored complexities of the regulatory process which lead to a certain regulatory outcome. Therefore, the earlier prediction of Newbery was that a minimum rate-of-return would be sufficient to generate credible commitments. Experience from world-wide implementation of deregulation and the empirical cases from India in the Chapter 4 have shown that a mere rate-of-return is not sufficient to generate credible commitments, especially when the regulators are not independent of the government. Hence a linked action situation approach through stylized games is developed. It is shown that in the short run, information produced by public interest groups tend to reduce regulatory commitment. This leads to a 'low commitment trap'. Some indicative support to this claim is also presented through one instance of public monitoring of electricity in India. But it is shown in a repeated game situation that in the long run regulators make only public interest moves 'knowing' that a perennial commitment trap will be created. However, the necessary condition for this is the presence of an institutional environment which facilitates the production of public information. The conclusion is that 'institutions of public information' strengthen commitments and increase the effectiveness of regulatory governance even in the absence of pure independence.

8.2   Policy Implications

An important policy implication which emerges from the present analysis is that the focus of electricity reforms should be on increasing generation capacity rather than creation of market based incentives for electricity trade. Under conditions of excess demand, where quantity rationing (through power cuts) is prevalent, achieving efficient contracting and price mechanism is difficult. As has been shown in the contractual hazards frame of investor owned utilities (refer Chapter 4) the situation gets more complicated when there is upstream regulation and prices cannot adjust to reflect input scarcity. With natural gas and coal supply scenarios not particularly optimistic, this problem is more likely to further aggravate leading to potentially greater contractual hazards and related transaction costs. Either fuel supply contracts need to have two way take-or-pay liabilities where suppliers too will be sanctioned for non-provision or downstream segment needs to witness greater public investment. The situation of partial deregulation where access to fuel inputs is based on soft governmental commitments but recovery of production related investments is left to rigid regulated tariffs is clearly unsustainable. A prudent alternative solution is greater vertical integration where generation utilities secure their fuel supply through reliable private contracts (especially for gas procurement) or through ownership of fuel sources like captive mines (in the case of coal).

Similarly in the case of industrial electricity self-generation, the policy of incentivizing production through third-party open access will remain ineffective unless there is greater attention on firm-level characteristics. As shown in chapter 5, the decision of a firm to self-generate is primarily driven by the transaction-specific costs imposed due to disruptions. These in turn depend on the kind of industrial processes it is involved in. The ability to respond to such costs is severely influenced in most cases by firm-level constraints like its size, location and access to other resources. Hence policy-makers need to devise different strategies for small and medium size firms as compared to bigger stand-alone firms. One such strategy could be separate electric feeders where quantity rationing can be eliminated. Another strategy could be to install community captive power systems based on a common-pool withdrawal mechanism. This would cut investments costs for captive units drastically for each firm while allowing them to reap benefits from a reliable back-up

The detailed study of regulatory governance aspect has also given some crucial policy insights. While technical efficiency of thermal production in India has improved, the analysis points to the fact that regulatory commitment is not high. This is primarily because of inadequate regulatory autonomy, staffing and expertise. Hence regulatory capacity needs to be increased and while there is no exogenous handle over increasing their autonomy, information institutions can be very helpful in augmenting credibility. Hence public interest groups should be made a part of the regulatory process to the extent possible and as much information as feasible should be shared with them. In fact this can be done with limited state intervention and/or restriction.

8.3 Summum Bonum: Transaction Cost Regulation

North (1993: p.1) has tersely noted the essence of economic analysis of institutions: "(h)ow have economies in the past developed institutions that have provided the credible commitment that has enabled more complex contracting to be realized; and what lessons can we derive from that experience that will be of value today in the ongoing process of building or rebuilding economies? The issue is straightforward: how to bind the players to agreements across space and time." The thesis has made an attempt to marginally further this objective by looking into the case of electricity sector reforms in India. It has reinforced the claim made by North further in his essay that while game theorists have shown that players credibly commit themselves to agreements only as long as the gains from doing so exceed the costs of defecting under favorable conditions, they have not been able to effectively 'answer the key question of how to realize those conditions' (*ibid. p. 2*). As discussed earlier, Newbery's basic regulatory game showed that the condition for regulators to credibly commit to their promises was a certain minimum rate of return. Yet, it did not throw enough light on how this condition would be met, especially in diverse institutional set-ups? In order to improve upon this constricted approach the present study combines insights from transaction cost economics and institutions of regulation. The taxonomy of transaction cost regulation (TCR) provided by (Spiller 2013) is followed. As Spiller notes (*ibid. p. 232*) notes, "(TCR) consists of the study of the governance features of the interaction between governments and investors…. (and) the nature of contracting hazards is what determines the fundamental features of the governance of these interactions. Spiller goes on to state that "(A)s emphasized by Coase (1964) and subsequently by Williamson (1979b), the analysis of regulation must be done within the proper institutional comparison, and with a heavy micro-analytic dose. Thus, the supposed inefficiency of regulatory contracts, and of regulatory outcomes, must be assessed in reference to all relevant alternatives (*ibid. p. 233*)." The essence of TCR is that regulatory commitment can be maximized only when the associated contractual hazards from the interactions between the key players in the sector will be minimized. As shown through empirical and theoretical discussions in the thesis, this will be possible either through organizational forms closer to vertical integration or through increased public information which will bind regulators to their promises. In short, these are the institutional conditions under which rate-of-return regulation will be successful. And the absence of these conditions answers our original puzzle of why deregulation has not shown the expected results in Indian electricity generation sector? TCR reverses the conventional wisdom that a certain rate-of-return on investments is an adequate framework to launch sweeping regulatory reforms in developing countries. The present study empirically shows that unless institutional conditions support such a framework, results will be disappointing. However, TCR also presents an encouraging normative alternative with its focus on governance structures which help maximize commitments and hence take the sector towards self-sufficiency.

8.4 Limitations and Future Scope

The thesis hopes to have made some contribution to the growing literature in this field which engages in greater institutional analysis of conditions under which reforms will be successful. It cautions against generalizations and does not detach theoretical insights from empirical realities. Yet, there are ways in which the TCR framework can be enriched. A current limitation of this approach is that it does not delve into the concept of regulatory space and hence does not specify in great empirical details the rules that guide the behavior of specific actors. A useful additional would be to look at regulation as an action situation which is an outcome of several adjacent action situations. This will help identify determinants of the rules which occupy regulatory space and gain greater insights into how the institutional conditions evolve over time. There are some other missing dimensions in the current literature which needs to be addressed. Firstly, following the spirit of Spiller (2010) of assessing real behavior in real environments requires not only looking at regulation as a product of the complex interactions between the elements of a country's institutional endowments, but also the actors involved in the regulatory process and the outcomes of their transactions. To fill this gap approaches which emphasize the role of actors transacting with each other in different action arenas (Hagedorn 2008) and creating a need for regularizing transactions through institutions and governance structures, need to explored. However, it is hoped that this thesis will serve as a useful stepping stone in research towards that direction and help in the critical mission of an energy secure developing world.

References

Aigner, D., Lovell, C.A.L., Schmidt, P. (1977). Formulation and Estimation of Stochastic Frontier Production Function Models. Journal of Econometrics 6.1, 21-37.

Alby, P., Dethier, J.-J., Straub, S. (2010). Firms Operating under Infrastructure and Credit Constraints in Developing Countries: The Case of Power Generators. World Bank Policy Research Working Paper 5497.

Anderson, D.D. (1981). Regulatory Politics and Electric Utilities. Auburn House, Boston.

Aoki, M. (2001). Toward a Comparative Institutional Analysis. MIT Press.

APERC, C.O. (2009). O.P.No.9-12 dated 05-12-2009, Andhra Pradesh Electricity Regulatory Commission (APERC), Hyderabad.

Arrow, K.J. (1951). Little's Critique of Welfare Economics. American Economic Review 41.5, 923-34.

Audinet, P., Verneyre, F. (2002). Electricity in India: Providing Power for the Millions. International Energy Agency, OECD Publishing.

Averch, H., Johnson, L. (1962). Behavior of the Firm under Regulatory Constraint. American Economic Review 52.5, 1052-69.

Ayres, I., Braithwaite, J. (1992). Responsive Regulation: Transcending the Deregulation Debate, Oxford.

Bagdadioglu, N., Price, C.M.W., Weyman-Jones, T.G. (1996). Efficiency and Ownership in Electricity Distribution: A Non-Parametric Model of the Turkish Experience. Energy Economics 18.1, 1-23.

Bailey, E. (1973). Economic Theory of Regulatory Constraint. Lexington Books, Lexington, Mass.

Bailey, E., Malone, J.C. (1970). Resource Allocation and the Regulated Firm. Bell Journal of Economics and Management Science 1.1, 129-42.

Barclay, P., Douglas, G., Tschirhart, J. (1989). Industrial Cogeneration and Regulatory Policy. Journal of Regulatory Economics 1.3, 225-40.

Baron, D.P. (2000). Business and its Environment. Prentice Hall, New Jersey.

Battese, G.E., Coelli, T.J. (1995). A Model for Technical Inefficiency Effects in a Stochastic Frontier Production Function for Panel Data. Empirical Economics 20.2, 325-32.

Battese, G.E., Corra., G.S. (1977). Estimation of a Production Frontier Model: With Application to the Pastoral Zone of Eastern Australia. Australian Journal of Agricultural and Resource Economics 21.3, 169-79.

Becker, G.S. (1976). The Economic Approach to Human Behavior. University of Chicago Press.

Becker, G.S. (1983). A Theory of Competition Among Pressure Groups for Political Influence. The Quarterly Journal of Economics 98.3, 371-400.

Becker, G.S. (1985a). Pressure Groups and Political Behavior, in: Coe, R.D., Wilber, C.K. (Eds.), Capitalism and Democracy: Schumpeter Revisited. University of Notre Dame Press, Indiana, pp. 120-46.

Becker, G.S. (1985b). Public Policies, Pressure Groups, and Dead Weight Costs. Journal of Public Economics 28.3, 329-47.

Belotti, F., Daidone, S., Ilardi, G. (2012). Stochastic Frontier Analysis Using Stata. The Stata Journal 15.2, 1-39.

Bentley, A.F. (1908). The Process of Government. University of Chicago Press, Chicago.

Berg, S., Lin, C., Tsaplin, V. (2005). Regulation of State-Owned and Privatized Utilities: Ukraine Electricity Distribution Company Performance. Journal of Regulatory Economics 28.3, 259-87.

Bernstein, M. (1955). Regulating Business by Independent Commission. Princeton University Press, Princeton.

Bertrand, E. (2006). The Coasean Analysis of Lighthouse Financing: Myths and Realities. Cambridge Journal of Economics 30, 389-402.

Bertrand, M., Mullainathan, S. (2001). Do People Mean What They Say? Implications for Subjective Survey Data. American Economic Review 91.2, 67-72.

Bhattacharya, S.C. (2005). The Electricity Act 2003: Will It Transform the Indian Power Sector? Utilities Policy 13.3, 260-72.

Bhattacharyya, S.C. (2007). Power Sector Reform in South Asia: Why Slow and Limited So Far? Energy Policy 35.1, 317-32.

Black, D. (1958). The Theory of Committees and Elections Cambridge University Press, Cambridge.

Blaug, M. (1992). The Methodology of Economics: Or, How Economists Explain. Cambridge University Press.

Boiteux, M. (1960). Peak-Load Pricing. Journal of Business 33.2, 157-79.

Bose, R.K., Shukla, M., Srivastava, L., Yaron, G. (2006). Cost of Unserved Power in Karnataka, India. Energy Policy 34.12, 1434-47.

Boyer, K.D. (1977). Minimum Rate Regulation, Modal Split Sensitivities and the Railroad Problem. Journal of Political Economy 85.3, 493-512.

Bromley, D.W. (2006). Sufficient Reason: Volitional Pragmatism and the Meaning of Economic Institutions. Princeton University Press.

Bromley, D.W. (2008). Volitional Pragmatism. Ecological Economics 68.1, 1-13.

Buchanan, J.M., Tollison, R.D., Tullock, G. (1980). Toward a Theory of the Rent-Seeking Society. Texas A&M University Press, College Station.

CAG (2012). Comptroller and Auditor General of India Report No. 6 of 2012-2013 on Ultra Mega Power Projects under Special Purpose Vehicles.

Caldwell, B.J. (1993). The Philosophy and Methodology of Economics. Edward Elgar.

Cameron, A.C., Trivedi, P.K. (2009). Microeconometrics Using Stata. Stata Press, College Station, TX.

Çetin, T. (2009). Toward a New Institutional Economics Theory of Regulation, ESNIE, 18-22 May 2009, Corsica-France.

Cheung, S.N.S. (1978). The Myth of Social Costs: A Critique of Welfare Economics and Public Policy. The Institute of Economic Affairs, London.

Chikkatur, A.P., Sagar, A.D., Abhyankar, N., Sreekumar, N. (2007). Tariff-Based Incentives for Improving Coal-Power-Plant Efficiencies in India. Energy Policy 35.7, 3744-58.

Coase, R.H. (1937). The Nature of the Firm. Economica N.S. 4.16, 386-405.

Coase, R.H. (1960). The Problem of Social Cost. Journal of Law and Economics 3, 1-44.

Coase, R.H. (1964). The Regulated Industries: A Discussion. American Economic Review 54, 194-7.

Coase, R.H. (1974a). The Lighthouse in Economics. Journal of Law and Economics 17.2, 357-76.

Coase, R.H. (1974b). The Lighthouse in Economics. Journal of Law and Economics 23, 357-76.

Coase, R.H. (1975). Marshall on Method. Journal of Law and Economics 18.1, 25-31.

Coase, R.H. (1982). How Should Economists Choose? The G. Warren Nutter Lectures in Political Economy, American Enterprise Institute for Public Policy Research, Washington, DC.

Coase, R.H. (1984). The New Institutional Economics. Journal of Institutional and Theoretical Economics 140, 229-331.

Coase, R.H. (1988). The Nature of the Firm: Origin. Journal of Law, Economics and Organization 4.1, 3-17.

Coase, R.H. (2006). The Conduct of Economics: The Example of Fisher Body and General Motors. Journal of Economics and Management Strategy 15.2, 255-78.

Coase, R.H. (2012). Saving Economics from Economists. Harvard Business Review December.

Coles, J.W., Hesterly, W.S. (1998). The Impact of Firm-specific Assets and the Interaction of Uncertainty: An Examination of Make or Buy Decisions in Public and Private Hospitals. Journal of Economic Behavior & Organization 36.3, 383-409.

Common-Order (2009). O.P.No.9-12 dated 05-12-2009, Andhra Pradesh Electricity Regulatory Commission (APERC), Hyderabad.

Commons, J.R. (1932). The Problem of Correlating Law, Economics, and Ethics. Wisconsin Law Review 8, 3-26.

Commons, J.R. (1934). Myself. Macmillan, New York.

Cooter, R., Rappoport, P. (1984). Were the Ordinalists Wrong About Welfare Economics? Journal of Economic Literature 22.2, 507–30.

Corbeau, A.S. (2010). Natural Gas in India, International Energy Agency.

Cornwell, C., Schmidt, P., Sickles, R.C. (1990). Production Frontiers with Cross-Sectional and Time-Series Variation in Efficiency Levels. Journal of Econometrics 46.1, 185-200.

Crew, M.A., Kleindorfer, P.R. (1986). The Economics of Public Utility Regulation. MacMillan Press, London.

CRISIL (2010). Study on Analysis of Tariff Orders and Other Orders of State Electricity Regulatory Commissions: Submitted to FORUM OF REGULATORS.

Cubbin, J., Stern, J. (2006). The Impact of Regulatory Governance and Privatization on Electricity Industry Generation Capacity in Developing Economies. The World Bank Economic Review 20.1, 115-41.

Dahlman, C.J. (1979). The Problem of Externality. Journal of Law and Economics 22, 141-62.

Dasgupta, S. (2013). The Open Access Consumer: Deemed or Damned. Economic and Political Weekly XLVIII.

De Nooij, M., Koopmans, C., Bijvoet, C. (2007). The Value of Supply Security: The Costs of Power Interruptions: Economic Input for Damage Reduction and Investment in Networks. Energy Economics 29.2, 277-95.

Demsetz, H. (1968). Why Regulate Utilities? Journal of Law and Economics 11.1, 55-65.

den Hertog, J.A. (2010). Review of Economic Theories of Regulation, Discussion paper series - Tjalling C. Koopmans Research Institute, pp. 1-59.

Dhrymes, P.J., Kurz, M. (1964). Technology and Scale in Electricity Generation. Econometrica: Journal of the Econometric Society 32.3, 287-315.

Diewart, W.E., Nakamura, A.O. (1999). Benchmarking and the Measurement of Best Practice Efficiency: An Electricity Generation Application. Canadian Journal of Economics 32.2, 570-88.

Dismukes, D.E., Kleit, A.N. (1999). Cogeneration and Electric Power Industry Restructuring. Resource and Energy Economics 21.2, 153-66.

Dixit, A.K. (1996). The Making of Economic Policy. MIT Press, Cambridge, MA.

Douglas, G., Miller, J.I. (1974). Economic Regulation of Domestic Air Transport. Brookings Institution, Washington, D.C.

Downs, A. (1957). An Economic Theory of Democracy. Harper and Row, New York.

Driscoll, D.L. (2011). Introduction to Primary Research: Observations, Surveys, and Interviews, Writing Spaces: Readings on Writing 2, pp. 153-74.

Du, L., Mao, J., Shi, J. (2009). Assessing the Impact of Regulatory Reforms on China's Electricity Generation Industry. Energy Policy 37.2, 712-20.

Dubash, N.K. (2002). The Changing Global Context for Electricity Reform, in: Dubash, N.K. (Ed.), Power Politics: Equity and Environment in Electricity Reform. World Resources Institute, Washington, DC.

Dubash, N.K. (2008). Independent Regulatory Agencies: A Theoretical Review with Reference to Electricity and Water in India. Economic and Political Weekly 43.40, 46-54.

Dubash, N.K., Rajan, S.C. (2001). Power Politics: Process of Power Sector Reform in India. Economic and Political Weekly 36.35, 3367-90.

Dubash, N.K., Rajan, S.C. (2002). India: Electricity Reform Under Political Constraints, in: Dubash, N.K. (Ed.), Power Politics: Equity and Environment in Electricity Reform. World Resources Institute, Washington DC.

Dubash, N.K., Rao, D.N. (2008). Regulatory Practice and Politics: Lessons from Independent Regulation in Indian Electricity. Utilities Policy 16.4, 321-31.

Dutton, W.H., Schneider, V., Vedel, T. (2012). Ecologies of Games Shaping Large Technical Systems: Cases from Telecommunications to the Internet, in: BAUER, J., LANG, A., SCHNEIDER, V. (Eds.), Innovation Policy and Governance in High-Tech Industries: The Complexity of Coordination. Springer, Berlin, Heidelberg.

Färe, R., Grosskopf, S., Logan, J. (1985). The Relative Performance of Publicly-Owned and Privately-Owned Electric Utilities. Journal of Public Economics 26.1, 89-106.

Färe, R., Grosskopf, S., Pasurka, C. (1986). Effects on Relative Efficiency in Electric Power Generation due to Environmental Controls. Resources and Energy 8.2, 167-84.

Farrell, K., Luzzati, T., van den Hove, S., eds. (2013). Beyond Reductionism: A Passion for Interdisciplinarity. Routledge.

Farsi, M., Filippini, M., Kuenzle, M. (2006). Cost Efficiency in Regional Bus Companies: An Application of Alternative Stochastic Frontier Models. Journal of Transport Economics and Policy 40.1, 95-118.

Faulhaber, G.R. (1975). Cross-Subsidization: Pricing in Public Enterprise. American Economic Review 65.5, 966-77.

Feldstein, M. (2000). Preface: The NBER-Sloan Project on Productivity Change." Industrial Technology and Productivity: Incorporating Learningfrom Plant Visits and Interviews into Economic Research", National Bureau of Economic Research (NBER), Cambridge, MA.

Finon, D. (2006). Incentives to Invest in Liberalised Electricity Industries in the North and South. Differences in the Need for Suitable Institutional Arrangements. Energy Policy 34.5, 601-18.

Fisher-Vanden, K., Mansur, E.T., Wang, Q.J. (2012). Costly Blackouts? Measuring Productivity and Environmental Effects of Electricity Shortages, No. w17741, National Bureau of Economic Research.

Friedman, M. (1966). The Methodology of Positive Economics, Essays in Positive Economics. University of Chicago Press, pp. 3-43.

Gallagher, R., Appenzeller, T. (1999). Beyond Reductionism. Science 284.5411, 79.

GERC (2010). Judgement on PPA and Gas Purchase Agreements, Gujarat Electricity Regulatory Commission, Ahmedabad.

Ghosh, A., Majumdar, S., Kadam, G. (2011). Private Sector IPPs: Trends & Outlook, ICRA Rating Feature.

Ghosh, R., Kathuria, V. (2011). Barriers to Governance in Evolving Power Generation Markets. Conference Papers and Proceedings IAEE International Conference on 'Institutions, Efficiency and Evolving Energy Technologies, Stockholm, June 19-23.

Ghosh, R.K., Kathuria, V. (2013). Do Governance Costs Explain the Problem of Private Investment in the Indian Power Generation Sector?, USAEE Working Paper No. 13-110.

Gilardi, F. (2004). Institutional Change in Regulatory Policies: Regulation through Independent Agencies and the Three New Institutionalisms, in: Jordana, J., Levi-Faur, D. (Eds.), The Politics of Regulation: Institutions and Regulatory Reforms for the Age of Governance, pp. 67-90.

Gilboa, I., Schmeidler, D. (1988). Information Dependent Games: Can Common Sense be Common Knowledge? Economics Letters 27.3, 215–21.

Glachant, J.M., Hallack, M. (2009). Take-or-Pay Contract Robustness: A Three Step Story Told by the Brazil–Bolivia Gas Case? Energy Policy 37.2, 651-7.

Goldberg, V.P. (1976). Regulation and Administered Contracts. The Bell Journal of Economics 7.2, 426-48.

Goldenfeld, N., Kadanoff, L.P. (1999). Simple Lessons from Complexity. Science 284.5411, 87-9.

Goto, M., Tsutsui, M. (2008). Technical Efficiency and Impacts of Deregulation: An Analysis of Three Functions in US Electric Power Utilities during the Period from 1992 through 2000. Energy Economics 30.1, 15-38.

Gould, J.A., Winters, M.S. (2007). An Obsolescing Bargain in Chad: Shifts in Leverage Between the Government and the World Bank. Business and Politics 9.2, 1-34.

Grossman, P.Z., Cole, D.H. (2003). The End of a Natural Monopoly: Deregulation and Competition in the Electric Power Industry. Routledge.

Grover, R.B., Chandra, S. (2006). Scenario for Growth of Electricity in India. Energy Policy 34.17, 2834-47.

Guasch, J.L. (2004). Granting and Renegotiating Infrastructure Concessions: Doing it Right. World Bank Publications.

Gulyani, S. (1999). Innovating with Infrastructure: How India's Largest Carmaker Copes with Poor Electricity Supply. World Development 27.10, 1749–68.

Gutiérrez, L.H. (2003). The Effect of Endogenous Regulation on Telecommunications Expansion and Efficiency in Latin America. Journal of Regulatory Economics 23.3, 257-86.

Hagedorn, K. (2008). Particular Requirements for Institutional Analysis in Nature-related Sectors. European Review of Agricultural Economics 35.3, 357-84.

Hägg, P.G. (1997). Theories on the Economics of Regulation: A Survey of the Literature from a European Perspective. European Journal of Law and Economics 4.4, 337-70.

Hansen, C.J. (2008). Bottom-up Electricity Reform Using Industrial Captive Generation: A Case Study of Gujarat, India, Oxford Institute for Energy Studies.

Hausman, D.M. (1989). Economic Methodology in a Nutshell. The Journal of Economic Perspectives 3.2, 115-27.

Hausman, W.J., Neufeld, J.L. (2002). The Market for Capital and the Origins of State Regulation of Electric Utilities in the United States. The Journal of Economic History 62.4, 1050-73.

Heap, S.H., Varoufakis, Y. (2004). Game theory: A Critical Text. London, New York: Routledge.

Helm, D. (2002). Energy policy: Security of Supply, Sustainability and Competition. Energy Policy 30.3, 173-84.

Helper, S. (2000). "Economists and Field Research:" You Can Observe a Lot Just by Watching. American Economic Review 90.2, 228-32.

Hess, R.W.e.a. (1983). Factors Affecting Industry's Decision to Cogenerate, Rand Corporation Report R-2950-DOE, Santa Monica, CA.

Hiebert, L.D. (2002). The Determinants of the Cost Efficiency of Electric Generating Plants: A Stochastic Frontier Approach. Southern Economic Journal 68.4, 935-46.

Hirschman, A.O. (1970). Exit, Voice and Loyalty: Responses to Decline in Firms, Organizations, and States. Harvard University Press, Cambridge, Mass.

Houthakker, H.S. (1957). Electricity Tariffs in Theory and Practice. Economic Journal 61.241, 1-25.

Hsiung, B. (2001). A Methodological Comparison of Ronald Coase and Gary Becker. American Law and Economics Review 3.1, 186-98.

Hunt, S. (2002). Making Competition Work in Electricity. Wiley, New York.

Huntington, S.P. (1966). The Marasmus of the ICC: The Commission, the Railroads, and the Public Interest, in: Woll, P. (Ed.), Public Administration and Policy: Selected Essays. Harper & Row, New York.

Ichniowski, C., Shaw, K., Prennushi, G. (1997). The Effects of Human Resource Management Practices on Productivity: A Study of Steel Finishing Lines. American Economic Review 87.3, 291-313.

Jain, A., Sen, A. (2011). Natural Gas in India: An Analysis of Policy WP 50, April, Oxford Institute for Energy Studies.

Jamasb, T., Pollitt, M. (2007). Incentive Regulation of Electricity Distribution Networks: Lessons of Experience from Britain. Energy Policy 35.12, 6163-87.

Jean-Luc, M. (1977). Controls versus Subsidies in the Economic Theory of Regulation. Journal of Law and Economics 20.1, 213-21.

Jensen, M.C. (1983). Organization Theory and Methodology. Accounting Review 58.2, 319-39.

Joseph, K.L. (2010). The Politics of Power: Electricity Reform in India. Energy Policy 38.1, 503-11.

Joskow, P. (1973). Cartels, Competition and Regulation in the Property and Liability Insurance Industry. Bell Journal of Economics and Management Science 4.2, 375-427.

Joskow, P. (1979a). Electric Utility Rate Structures in the United States: Some Recent Developments, in: Sichel, W. (Ed.), Public Utility Ratemaking in An Energy Conscious Environment. Westview, Boulder, Colorado.

Joskow, P. (1979b). Public Utility Regulatory Policy Act of 1978: Electric Utility Rate Reform. Natural Resources Journal 19, 787-809.

Joskow, P. (1998). Electricity Sectors in Transition. The Energy Journal 19.2, 25-52.

Joskow, P.L. (1974). Inflation and Environmental Concern: Structural Change in the Process of Public Utility Price Regulation. Journal of Law and Economics 17, 291-327.

Joskow, P.L. (2008). Lessons Learned from Electricity Market Liberalization. The Energy Journal 29.2, 9-42.

Joskow, P.L., Jones, D.R. (1983). The Simple Economics of Industrial Cogeneration. The Energy Journal 4.1, 1-22.

Joskow, P.L., Noll, R.G. (1981). Regulation in Theory and Practice: An Overview, Studies in Public Regulation. MIT Press, pp. 1-78.

Joskow, P.L., Schmalensee, R. (1987). The Performance of Coal Burning Electric Generating Units in the United States: 1960–1980. Journal of Applied Econometrics 2.2, 85-109.

Kahn, A. (1970). The Economics of Regulation. Wiley, New York.

Kalton, G., Anderson, D.W. (1986). Sampling Rare Populations. Journal of the Royal Statistical Society. Series A (General), 65-82.

Kanbur, R., Shaffer, P. (2007). Epistemology, Normative Theory and Poverty Analysis: Implications for Q-squared in practice. World Development 35.2, 183-96.

Kannan, K.P., Pillai, N.V. (2001). The Political Economy of Public Utilities: A Study of the Indian Power Sector, Working Paper No. 316. Centre for Development Studies, Thiruvananthapuram.

Kay, J.A., Vickers, J.S. (1990). Regulatory Reform: An Appraisal, in: Majone, G. (Ed.), Deregulation or Re-regulation. Pinter Publishers, London, pp. 223-51.

Keeler, T.E. (1984). Theories of Regulation and the Deregulation Movement. Public Choice 44.1, 103-45.

Kennedy, R.D., Jr. (1991). The Statist Evolution of Rail Governance in the United States, 1830-1860, in: John L. Campbell, J.R.H., and Leon N. Lindberg (Ed.), Governance of the American Economy. Cambridge University Press, Cambridge, MA, pp. 138-81.

Khanna, M., Mundra, K., Ullah, A. (1999). Parametric and Semi-Parametric Estimation of the Effect of Firm Attributes on Efficiency: The Electricity Generating Industry in India. Journal of International Trade & Economic Development: An International and Comparative Review 8.4.

Khanna, M., Zilberman, D. (1999). Barriers to Energy-Efficiency in Electricity Generation in India. The Energy Journal 20.1, 25-41.

Kim, B., Prescott, J.E. (2005). Deregulatory Forms, Variations in the Speed of Governance, Adaptation and Firm Performance. Academy of Management Review 30.2, 414-25.

Kim, J.-C., Byong-Hun, A. (1990). On the Economics of Cogeneration: Pricing and Efficiency in Government Owned Utilities. The Energy Journal 11.1, 87-99.

Kimmich, C. (2013). Linking Action Situations: Coordination, Conflicts, and Evolution in Electricity Provision for Irrigation in Andhra Pradesh, India. Ecological Economics 90, 150-8.

Klein, B., Crawford, R.G., Alchian, A.A. (1978). Vertical Integration, Appropriable Rents, and the Competitive Contracting Process. Journal of Law and Economics 21.1, 297-326.

Klevorick, A. (1971). The Optimal Fair Rate of Return. Bell Journal of Economics and Management Science 2.1, 122-53.

Klijn, E.H., Koppenjan, J.F.M. (2000). Public Management and Policy Network: Foundations of a Network Approach to Governance. Public Management Review 2.2, 135-8.

Klugman, J., Rodríguez, F., Choi, H.-J. (2011). The HDI 2010: New Controversies, Old Critiques. The Journal of Economic Inequality 9.2, 249-88.

Knittel, C.R. (2002). Alternative Regulatory Methods and Firm Efficiency: Stochastic Frontier Evidence from the US Electricity Industry. Review of Economics and Statistics 84.3, 530-40.

Kolko, G. (1965). Railroads and Regulation, 1877–1916. Princeton University Press, Princeton.

Kopp, R.J., Smith, V.K. (1980). Frontier Production Function Estimates for Steam Electric Generation: A Comparative Analysis. Southern Economic Journal 46.4, 1049-59.

Kumbhakar, S.C., Lovell, C.A.K. (2000). Stochastic Frontier Analysis. Cambridge University Press.

Kumbhakar, S.C., Lovell, C.A.K. (2003). Stochastic Frontier Analysis. Cambridge University Press.

Laffont, J.J., Tirole, J. (1993). A Theory of Incentives in Procurement and Regulation. MIT Press, Cambridge, MA.

Lal, S. (2006). Can Good Economics Ever Be Good Politics? Case Study of India's Power Sector, World Bank Working Paper No. 83, Washington DC.

Lam, P.-L., Shiu, A. (2004). Efficiency and Productivity of China's Thermal Power Generation. Review of Industrial Organization 24.1, 73-93.

Landers, R.M., Rebitzer, J.B., Taylor, L.J. (1996). Rat Race Redux: Adverse Selection in the Determination of Work Hours in Law Firms. The American Economic Review 86.3, 329-48.

Lazear, E.P. (1996). Performance Pay and Productivity, National Bureau of Economic Research (NBER), Cambridge, MA, pp. 1346-61.

Lee, K.S., Anas, A., Verma, S., Murray, M. (1996). Why Manufacturing Firms Produce Some Electricity Internally, Policy Research Working Paper Series 1605. World Bank, Washington DC.

Lee, Y.H., Schmidt, P. (1993). A Production Frontier Model with Flexible Temporal Variation in Technical Efficiency, The Measurement of Productive Efficiency: Techniques and Applications. Oxford University Press, pp. 237-55.

Leiserson, A. (1946). Interest Groups in Administration, in: Marx, F.M. (Ed.). Prentice-Hall, New York.

Levin, R.C. (1978). Allocation in Surface Freight Transportation: Does Rate Regulation Matter? Bell Journal of Economics and Management Science 9.1, 18-45.

Levy, B., Spiller, P.T. (1994). The Institutional Foundations of Regulatory Commitment: A Comparative Analysis of Telecommunications Regulation. Journal of Law, Economics, and Organization 10.2, 201–46.

Lubell, M., Henry, A.D., McCoy, M. (2010). Collaborative Institutions in an Ecology of Games. American Journal of Political Science 54.2, 287-300.

MacAvoy, P., Noll, R.G. (1973). Relative Prices on Regulated Transactions of the Natural Gas Pipelines. Bell Journal of Economics and Management Science 4, 212-34.

MacAvoy, P., Sloss, J. (1967). Regulation of Transport Innovation: The ICC and Unit Coal Trains to the East Coast. Random House, New York.

Madhok, A. (2002). Reassessing the Fundamentals and Beyond: Ronald Coase, The Transaction Cost and Resource Based Theories of the Firm and the Institutional Structure of Production. Strategic Management Journal 23.6, 535-50.

Majone, G. (2001). Nonmajoritarian Institutions and the Limits of Democratic Governance: A Political Transaction-Cost Approach. Journal of Institutional and Theoretical Economics 157.1, 57-78.

Mäki, U. (1998). Against Posner Against Coase Against Theory. Cambridge Journal of Economics 22.5, 587-95.

Mäki, U., Gustafsson, B., Knudsen, C. (1993). Rationality, Institutions and Economic Methodology. Routledge, London.

Malik, K., Cropper, M.L., Limonov, A., Singh, A. (2011). Estimating the Impact of Restructuring on Electricity Generation Efficiency: The Case of the Indian Thermal Power Sector. National Bureau of Economic Research (NBER) Working Paper No. 17383.

Martimort, D. (1999). The Life Cycle of Regulatory Agencies: Dynamic Capture and Transaction Costs. The Review of Economic Studies, 929-47.

Maruyama, N., Eckelman, M.J. (2009). Long-Term Trends of Electric Efficiencies in Electricity Generation in Developing Countries. Energy Policy 37.5, 1678-86.

Masten, S.E. (1984). The Organization of Production: Evidence from the Aerospace Industry. Journal of Law and Economics 27.2, 403-17.

Masten, S.E., Meehan, J.W., Snyder, E.A. (1991). The Costs of Organization. Journal of Law, Economics, & Organization 7.1, 1-25.

Mayntz, R., Scharpf, F.W. (1995). Der Ansatz des akteurzentrierten Institutionalismus, in: Scharpf, R.M.F.W. (Ed.), Steuerung und Selbstorganisation in staatsnahen Sektoren, Frankfurt am Main: Campus, pp. 39-72.

McChesney, F.S. (1991). Rent Extraction and Interest-Group Organization in a Coasean Model of Regulation. Journal of Legal Studies 20.1, 73-90.

McDonald, F. (1962). Insull. University of Chicago Press, Chicago.

McGinnis, M.D. (2011). Networks of Adjacent Action Situations in Polycentric Governance. Policy Studies Journal 39.1, 51-78.

McKay, D. (1976). Has the A-J Effect Been Empirically Verified?, Social Science Working Paper 132, California Institute of Technology.

McKelvey, R.D. (1976). Intransitivities in Multidimensional Voting Models and Some Implications for Agenda Control. Journal of Economic Theory 12.3, 472-82.

Meeusen, W., Broeck, J.V.d. (1977). Efficiency Estimation from Cobb-Douglas Production Functions with Composed Error. International Economic Review 18.2, 435-44.

Meibodi, A.E. (1998). Efficiency Considerations in the Electricity Supply Industry: The Case of Iran. Surrey Energy Economics Centre (SEEC) Discussion Paper 95, School of Economics, University of Surrey.

Ménard, C., Ghertman, M. (2009). Regulation, Deregulation, Reregulation: Institutional Perspectives. Edward Elgar.

Meyer, R. (2012). Vertical Economies and the Costs of Separating Electricity Supply - A Review of Theoretical and Empirical Literature. The Energy Journal 33.4, 161-85.

Nair, S.K.N. (2008). Electricity Regulation in India: Recent Reforms and their Impact. Margin-The Journal of Applied Economic Research 2.1, 87-144.

Nakhooda, S., Dixit, S., Dubash, N.K. (2007). Empowering People: A Governance Analysis of Electricity – India, Indonesia, Philippines, Thailand. World Resources Institute & Prayas Energy Group, Washington, D.C

Naughton, B. (1995). Growing Out of the Plan: Chinese Economic Reform, 1978-1993. Cambridge University Press.

Nelson, P. (1974). Advertising as Information. Journal of Political Economy 82.4, 729-54.

Newbery, D.M. (1999). Privatization, Restructuring and Regulation of Network Utilities. MIT Press, Cambridge, Mass.

Ng, Y.K. (1990). Welfare Economics. Macmillan, London.

Noll, R.G. (1989). Economic Perspectives on the Politics of Regulation, in: Schmalensee, R.a.W., Robert D. (Ed.), Handbook of Industrial Organization II. North Holland, Amsterdam, pp. 1253-87.

Nooteboom, B. (1993). An Analysis of Specificity in Transaction Cost Economics. Organization Studies 14.3, 443-51.

North, D.C. (1990). Institutions, Institutional Change and Economic Performance. Cambridge University Press.

North, D.C. (1993). Institutions and Credible Commitment. Journal of Institutional and Theoretical Economics 149.1, 11-23.

Ogus, A. (2004). W (h) ither the Economic Theory of Regulation? What Economic Theory of Regulation?, in: Jordana, J., Levi-Faur, D. (Eds.), The Politics of Regulation: Institutions and Regulatory Reforms for the Age of Governance. Edward Elgar, pp. 31-44.

Olatubi, W.O., Dismukes, D.E. (2000). A Data Envelopment Analysis of the Levels and Determinants of Coal-Fired Electric Power Generation Performance. Utilities Policy 9.2, 47-59.

Olson, M. (1965). The Logic of Collective Action. Harvard University Press, Cambridge, Massachusetts.

Ordover, J.A., Pittman, R.W., Clyde, P. (1994). Competition Policy for Natural Monopolies in a Developing Market Economy. Economics of Transition 2.3, 317-43.

Ostrom, E. (2007). A Diagnostic Approach for Going Beyond Panaceas. Proceedings of the National Academy of Sciences 104.39, 15181-7.

Ostrom, E. (2010). Beyond Markets and States: Polycentric Governance of Complex Economic Systems. American Economic Review 100.3, 641-72.

Panzar, J.C., Willig, R.D. (1977). Free Entry and the Sustainability of Natural Monopoly. Bell Journal of Economics and Management Science 8, 1-22.

Pargal, S. (2003). Regulation and Private Sector Investment in Infrastructure: Evidence from Latin America. Policy Research Working Paper 3037, World Bank, Washington DC.

Pasha, H.A., Ghaus, A., Malik., S. (1989). The Economic Cost of Power Outages in the Industrial Sector of Pakistan. Energy Economics 11.4, 301-18.

Peltzman, S. (1976). Towards a More General Theory of Regulation. Journal of Law and Economics 19.2, 211-40.

Peltzman, S. (1993). George Stigler's Contribution to the Economics of Regulation. Journal of Political Economy 101.5, 818-32.

Pittman, R. (2007). Make or Buy on the Russian Railway? Coase, Williamson, and Tsar Nicholas II. Economic Change and Restructuring 40.3 207-21.

Plott, C.R. (1967). A Notion of Equilibrium and Its Possibility under Majority Rule. American Economic Review 57.4, 787-806.

PMGER (2007). Andhra Pradesh Power Sector Status and Issues. People's Monitoring Group on Electricity Regulation, Hyderabad.

PMGER (2011). Submission Made on Take or Pay Provisions in Gas. People's Monitoring Group on Electricity Regulation, Hyderabad.

Pollitt, M.G. (1995). Ownership and Performance in Electric Utilities: The International Evidence on Privatization and Efficiency. Oxford: Oxford University Press.

Popper, K.R. (1959). The Logic of Scientific Discovery. London: Hutchinson.

Posner, R.A. (1971). Taxation by Regulation. The Bell Journal of Economics and Management Science 2.1, 22-50.

Posner, R.A. (1974). Theories of Economic Regulation. Bell Journal of Economics and Management Science 5.2, 335-58.

Posner, R.A. (1993). Nobel laureate: Ronald Coase and methodology. The Journal of Economic Perspectives 7.4, 195-210.

Potters, J., Sloof, R. (1996). Interest Groups: A Survey of Empirical Models That Try to Assess their Influence. European Journal of Political Economy 12.3, 403-42.

Priest, G.L. (1993). The Origins of Utility Regulation and the "Theories of Regulation" Debate. Journal of Law and Economics 36.1, 289-323.

Prosser, T. (1999). Theorizing Utility Regulation. The Modern Law Review 62 (2 March).

Purkayastha, P. (2001). Power Sector Policies and New Electricity Bill: from Crisis to Disaster. Economic and Political Weekly 36.25, 2257-62.

Qian, Y. (2003). How Reform Worked in China, in: Rodrik, D. (Ed.), In Search of Prosperity: Analytic Narratives on Economic Growth. Princeton University Press, Princeton.

Rallapalli, S.R., Ghosh, S. (2012). Forecasting Monthly Peak Demand of Electricity in India—A Critique. Energy Policy 45 (June, 2012), 516-20.

Ramamurti, R. (2003). Can Governments Make Credible Promises? Insights from Infrastructure Projects in Emerging Economies. Journal of International Management 9.3, 253-69.

Ranganathan, V. (2004). Electricity Act 2003: Moving to a Competitive Environment. Economic and Political Weekly 39.20, 2001-5.

Rao, S.L. (2004). Governing Power. TERI Press, New Delhi.

Rawls, J. (1971). A Theory of Justice. Harvard University Press, Cambridge, MA.

Rose, K., McDonald, J.F. (1991). Economics of Electricity Self-generation by Industrial Firms. The Energy Journal 12.2, 47-66.

Rosser Jr, J.B., Rosser, M.V. (2004). Comparative Economics in a Transforming World Economy. MIT Press.

Samuels, W.G., Mercuro, N. (1984). A Critique of Rent-Seeking Theory, in: Collander, D.C. (Ed.), Neoclassical Political Economy, reprinted in Samuels, Warren J. (ed.) Essays on the Economic Role of Government, Volume 2. Ballinger Publishing, Boston, pp. 55-70.

Sarica, K., Or, I. (2007). Efficiency Assessment of Turkish Power Plants using Data Envelopment Analysis. Energy Policy 32.8, 1484-99.

Scharpf, F. (1997). Games Real Actors Play: Actor-centered Institutionalism in Policy Research. Boulder/Cumnor Hill: Westview Press.

Schofield, N. (1978). Instability of Simple Dynamic Games. The Review of Economic Studies 45.3, 575-94.

Schwab, S. (1989). Coase Defends Coase: Why Lawyers Listen and Economists Do Not. Michigan Law Review 87, 1171-98.

See, K.F., Coelli, T. (2012). An Analysis of Factors that Influence the Technical Efficiency of Malaysian Thermal Power Plants. Energy Economics 34.3, 677-85.

Sen, A., Jamasb, T. (2010). Diversity in Unity: An Empirical Analysis of Electricity Deregulation in Indian States. The Energy Journal 33.1, 83-130.

Seo, D., Shin, J. (2011). The Impact of Incentive Regulation on Productivity in the US Telecommunications Industry: A Stochastic Frontier Approach. Information Economics and Policy 23.1, 3-11.

Shah, T. (2009). Taming the Anarchy: Groundwater Governance in South Asia, Resources for the Future, Washington, D.C.; International Water Management Institute, Colombo, Sri Lanka.

Shanmugam, K.R., Kulshreshtha, P. (2005). Efficiency Analysis of Coal-Based Thermal Power Generation in India During Post-Reform Era. International Journal of Global Energy Issues 23.1, 15-28.

Sharma, D.P., Nair, P.S., Balasubramanian, R. (2005). Performance of Indian Power Sector During a Decade under Restructuring: A Critique. Energy Policy 33.4, 563-76.

Sheshinski, E. (1971). Welfare Aspects of Regulatory Constraint: Note. American Economic Review 61, 175-8.

Shrivastava, N., Sharma, S., Chauhan, K. (2012). Efficiency Assessment and Benchmarking of Thermal Power Plants in India. Energy Policy 40 (January 2012), 159-76.

Shukla, P.R., et al. (2004). Captive Power Plants: Case Study of Gujarat India, Working Paper 22, Program for Sustainable Energy Development (PESD), Stanford University.

Singh, A. (2005). Policy and Regulatory Environment for Private Investment in the Power Sector. Asian Development Bank Institute (ADBI) Research Policy Brief No. 23.

Singh, A. (2010). Towards a Competitive Market for Electricity and Consumer Choice in the Indian Power Sector. Energy Policy 38.8, 4196-208.

Singh, J. (1991). Plant Size and Technical Efficiency in the Thermal Power Industry. Indian Economic Review 26.2, 239-52.

Sinha, S. (2005). Introducing Competition in the Power Sector: Open Access and Cross Subsidies. Economic and Political Weekly 40.7, 631-7.

Snitzler, J.R., Byrne, R.J. (1958). Interstate Trucking of Fresh and Frozen Poultry Under Agricultural Exemption, Marketing Research Report 244.

Snowdon, B., Vane, H. (1997). Modern Macroeconomics and its Evolution From a Monetarist Perspective: An Interview With Professor Milton Friedman. Journal of Economic Studies 24.4, 192-222.

Spanjer, A.R. (2009). Regulatory Intervention on the Dynamic European Gas Market–Neoclassical Economics or Transaction Cost Economics? Energy Policy 37.8, 3250 - 8.

Spann, R., Erickson, E.W. (1970). The Economics of Railroading: The Beginning of Cartelization and Regulation. Bell Journal of Economics and Management Science 1, 227-44.

Spiller, P. (2010). Transaction Cost Regulation, Working paper 16735, National Bureau of Economic Research, Cambridge, MA.

Spiller, P. (2013). Transaction Cost Regulation. Journal of Economic Behavior & Organization 89, 232-42.

Spiller, P., Tommasi, M. (2005). The Institutions of Regulation: An Application to Public Utilities, in: Menard, C., Shirley, M.M. (Eds.), Handbook of New Institutional Economics. Springer, Netherlands, pp. 515-43.

Spiller, P.T. (1990). Politicians, Interest Groups, and Regulators: A Multiple-Principals Agency Theory of Regulation, or "Let Them Be Bribed". Journal of Law and Economics 33.1, 65-101.

Spiller, P.T. (2009). An Institutional Theory of Public Contracts: Regulatory Implications, in: Ghertman, C.M.a.M. (Ed.), Regulation, Deregulation and Reregulation: Institutional Perspectives. Edward Elgar, UK, pp. 45-66.

Spiller, P.T., Urbiztondo, S. (1994). Political Appointees vs. Career Civil Servants: A Multiple Principals Theory of Political Bureaucracies. European Journal of Political Economy 10.3, 465-97.

Starr, M.A. (2012). Qualitative and Mixed-Methods Research in Economics: Surprising Growth, Promising Future. Journal of Economic Surveys Early View.

Stern, J., Holder, S. (1999). Regulatory Governance: Criteria for Assessing the Performance of Regulatory Systems. An Application to Infrastructure Industries in the Developing Countries of Asia. Utilities Policy 8.1, 33–50.

Stigler, G.J. (1971). The Theory of Economic Regulation. Bell Journal of Economics and Management Science 2, 3–21.

Stigler, G.J., Friedland, C. (1962). What Can Regulators Regulate? The Case of Electricity. Journal of Law and Economics 5, 1-16.

Sweeny, J.L. (2002). The California Electricity Crisis. Hoover Institution Press.

TERI (2007). Analysis and Compilation of Tariff Orders, Project Report No. 2006 RP23, TERI and Ministry of Power, Government of India.

Thatcher, M., Stone Sweet, A. (2002). Theory and Practice of Delegation to Non-Majoritarian Institutions. West European Politics 25.1, 1-22.

Thomas, S. (2005). British Experience of Electricity Liberalisation: A Model for India? Economic and Political Weekly 40.50 (Dec. 10-16), 5260-8.

Toumanoff, P.G. (1984). A Positive Analysis of the Theory of Market Failure. Kyklos 37, 529-41.

Truman, D.B. (1951). The Government Process: Political Interests and Public Opinion. Knopf, New York.

Tullock, G. (1993). Rent Seeking. Edward Elgar, Aldershot.

Vernon, R. (1971). Sovereignty at Bay: The Multinational Spread of U.S. Enterprises. Basic Books, New York.

Viscusi, W.K., Vernon, J.M., Harrington, J.E., Jr (2005). Economics of Regulation and Antitrust. MIT Press, Cambridge, MA.

Wang, H.-J., Schmidt, P. (2002). One-step and Two-step Estimation of the Effects of Exogenous Variables on Technical Efficiency Levels. Journal of Productivity Analysis 18.2, 129-44.

Wang, N. (2003). Coase on the Nature of Economics. Cambridge Journal of Economics 27.6, 807-29.

Weingast, B. (1981). Regulation, Reregulation, and Deregulation: The Political Foundations of Agency Clientele Relationships. Law and Contemporary Problems 44.1, 147-77.

Wijayatunga, P.D., Jayalath, M.S. (2003). Assessment of Economic Impact of Electricity Supply Interruptions in the Sri Lanka Industrial Sector. Energy Conversion and Management 45.2, 235-47.

Williamson, O.E. (1976). Franchise Bidding for Natural Monopolies-In General and with Respect to CATV. The Bell Journal of Economics 7.1, 73-104.

Williamson, O.E. (1979a). Transaction Cost Economics: The Governance of Contractual Relations. Journal of Law and Economics, 233 - 61.

Williamson, O.E. (1979b). Transaction Cost Economics: The Governance of Contractual Relations. Journal of Law and Economics 22.2, 233 - 61.

Williamson, O.E. (1985). The Economic Institutions of Capitalism. Free Press, New York.

Williamson, O.E. (1991). Comparative Economic Organization: The Analysis of Discrete Structural Alternatives. Administrative Science Quarterly 36, 269-96.

Williamson, O.E. (1994). Correspondence: Evaluating Coase. The Journal of Economic Perspectives 8.2, 201-9.

Williamson, O.E. (1996). Transaction Cost Economics and the Carnegie Connection. Journal of Economic Behavior & Organization 31.2, 149-55.

Williamson, O.E. (1998). The Institutions of Governance. American Economic Review 88.2, 75-9.

Williamson, O.E. (2002). The Theory of the Firm as Governance Structure: From Choice to Contract. The Journal of Economic Perspectives 16.3 171-95.

Williamson, O.E. (2005). The Economics of Governance. American Economic Review 95.2, 1-18.

Williamson, O.E. (2009). Pragmatic Methodology: A Sketch, With Applications to Transaction Cost Economics. Journal of Economic Methodology 16.2, 145-57.

Wilson, J.Q. (1974). The Politics of Regulation, in: McKie, J.W. (Ed.), Social Responsibility and the Business Predicament. The Brookings Institution, Washington, pp. 135-68.

Wilson, J.Q. (1980). The Politics of Regulation, in: Wilson, J.Q. (Ed.), The Politics of Regulation. Basic Books, New York, pp. 357-94.

Winston, C. (1993). Economic Deregulation: Days of Reckoning for Microeconomists. Journal of Economic Literature 31.3, 1263-89.

Wong, S. (1973). The "F-Twist" and the Methodology of Paul Samuelson. The American Economic Review 63.3, 312-25.

Zerbe, R.O., Jr., Urban, N. (1988). Including the Public Interest in Theories of Regulation. Research in Law and Economics 11, 1-23.

Zhang, Y.-F., Parker, D., Kirkpatrick, C. (2008). Electricity Sector Reform in Developing Countries: An Econometric Assessment of the Effects of Privatization, Competition and Regulation. Journal of Regulatory Economics 33.2, 159-78.

Ziegler, H. (1964). Interest Groups in American Society. Prentice-Hall, Englewood Cliffs, N.J.

Annexure

A. Descriptive Statistics and Information on Primary Data

Table A 1: Sample distribution of CPP

S.N.	Diesel Gen-sets (DG) and Captive Power Plant (CPP) in Sample	Number	Proportion of Total Sample
1	Firms having DG sets	83	89.25
2	Firms having DG sets 1 MW and above	41	44.09
3	Firms having DG sets 2 MW and above	13	13.98
4	Firms having DG sets 3 MW and above	8	8.60
5	Firms having no CPP but DG greater than 1 MW	27	29.03
6	Firms having CPP	30	32.26
	Total Sample	93	

Source: Own calculation based on survey data

Table A 2: CPP and relation to key attributes

S.N.	Key Attribute	Relation of CPP with Key Variables	Number	Proportion
1	Location	CPP firms in Industrial Estate	8	26.67
		CPP firms in Cluster	8	26.67
		CPP firms Stand Alone	14	46.67
2	Excess Land	CPP with Excess Land Available	17	56.67
		CPP without Excess Land	13	43.33
3	Power Dependency	CPPs needing minimum 24 hours supply	16	50
		CPPs needing minimum 18 hours supply	15	46.88
		CPPs needing minimum 12 hours supply	1	3.13
4	Firm Size	Firms with annual income between 0-500 Million INR having CPP	8	24.24
		Firms with annual income between 500-1000 Million INR having CPP	2	14.29
		Firms with annual income between 1000-5000 Million INR having CPP	12	38.71
		Firms with annual income above 5000 Million INR having CPP	10	58.82

Source: Own calculation based on survey data

B. Captive Power Survey: Step-by-Step Explanation

There are three main methods of conducting primary research: observations, interviews and surveys (Driscoll 2011). When mere observations do not give enough information, investigators need to interact with the involved stakeholders through interviews. This could be for the dual purpose of extracting a closely approximating working hypothesis, or to track the root of the research problem or to find out explanations. Yet, interviews are not always sufficient to find out repeated trends and patterns of interaction on economic actor's behaviour and choices. Surveys are then useful to generate 'self-reported' data (*ibid.*). This research has used all the three methods of primary research to arrive at comprehensive estimations of observed phenomena, in this case, the 'make or buy' decision of the firm for electricity.

Observations

As has been already mentioned in the main text, our observations led to the understanding of divergent behaviour in similarly oriented firms (Table A.1, A.2). For example, there are two big firms in the same location of Peddapuram in Anantapur district of Andhra Pradesh: Sudha Agro Oil Limited and RAK Ceramics Limited. Whereas Sudha Agro Oil makes its own power by installing a backyard CPP, RAK Ceramics continues to depend only on the grid. In the same district in the sub-district called Samalkot, there are two other big firms: Sri Venkatarama Oil Limited and Navabharat Ventures Limited. While Navabharat Ventures has its own CPP, Sri Venkatarama Oil does not have one. If we now compare two oil manufacturing plants in more or less the same location: Sudha Oil and Venkatarama Oil, one has a CPP whereas the other does not, even if the firm size is roughly same. Such anomalies are present in the entire observation set i.e. the industrial sector of Andhra Pradesh. The above description is just an example. Yet, this observation was not enough to answer the question: why some firms make their own electricity while others buy?

Interviews

So we moved to the next stage of primary research: interviews. Preliminary interaction was conducted with some experts in the industry, regulation and civil society to arrive at a list the factors which explained firm behaviour. This process also gave deeper insights into the problems faced by industries in general. Due caution was exercised so as to eliminate bias and bring clarity to the conversation with experts. Driscoll (2011) surveys the literature on important interview cautions which we list below and also explain the actual conduct of the interview process in response to these:

a. **Ask about one thing at a time**: The questions were kept short and precise. For example: Do you have captive power facility in your plant?

b. **Avoid leading questions**: The questions were straight and avoided any subjective connotations

c. **Proper use of open and closed questions**: While precise questions were asked, it was take due care that the respondent is not interrupted in the process of answering. This often led to hidden and subtle information not being blocked

d. **Clarity in questioning**: The interviewee (in this case the author) employed suitable communication clarity

e. **Choosing the right respondents**: Experts were chosen based on their involvement with the various aspects of the industry, both manufacturing and electricity

f. **Choosing a proper method to conduct the interview**: Mostly face-to-face interviews were conducted although, one or two were contacted on telephone as the physical distance was too expensive to overcome

g. **Finding a suitable location**: Interviews were mostly conducted in the office premises of the interviewee, with some exceptions being at a place of social gathering like a restaurant.

h. **Recording interviews**: According to the ethics of interview recording, due permission has to be first sought from the interviewee. However, given the sensitive nature of the sector and corporate details being discussed, none of the interviewee agreed upon recording. Moreover, several respondents spoke off-record and asked anonymity to be maintained.

The table below gives some details of those interviews which did not have the conditions of anonymity applied. Annex A.1at the end of the thesis gives sample excerpts from the interviews.

Survey

Once the interview stage got over, it became increasingly clear that the reasons for firm's decision-making towards making own electricity were not as linear or simple as projected in the literature or policy circles. While some firms said power supply discontinuity was their main driver, other said cost minimization was the key driver for them. Some said that nature of their manufacturing process was what made them opt for self-generation, while others cited co-generation or firm-size. Therefore, the observations and interview stages of investigation although did throw up interesting possibilities, it did not give a clear causality or estimations of the extent to which the possible variables were influencing this decision making.

Table B 1: Sample List of Expert Interviews

S.N.	Respondent Name	Designation	Category	Date	Interview Mode	Interviewer
1	KVSS Murthy	Vice President (Power Projects), Sree Rayalseema Alkalies and Allied Chemicals Ltd.	Industry Actor/Expert	14.12.11	Face-to-Face	Ranjan Ghosh
2	J. Dwarkanath	GM (BD & Projects), Renewable Energy Group, HBL Power Systems Ltd.	Industry Actor/Expert	13.12.11	Face-to-Face	Ranjan Ghosh
3	S.N. Keshri	MD, Andhra Cements	Industry Actor	08.12.11	Telephonic	Ranjan Ghosh
4	M. Sreeram Murthy	Chairman, Industrial Development Committee, FAPCCI	Expert	08.11.11	Face-to-Face	Ranjan Ghosh
5	B. Ravishankar	CMD, Fleming Labs. (P) Ltd.	Industry Actor/Expert	15.12.11	Face-to-Face	Ranjan Ghosh
6	PVV Satyanarayancharulu	Purchase Manager, Kakatiya Cements Ltd.	Industry Actor	14.12.11	Face-to-Face	Ranjan Ghosh
7	P. Solomon Herme	Deputy Director, APERC	Regulator/Expert	10.12.11	Face-to-Face	Ranjan Ghosh
8	K. Raghu	APTRANSCO and PMGER	Civil Society Expert	06.12.11	Face-to-Face	Ranjan Ghosh

In order to arrive at a reasonably generalizable conclusion, a survey was designed which would elicit responses from decision makers directly. Following Driscoll 2011, the important steps of primary survey were conducted:

a. **Questionnaire Creation**: The questionnaire schedules were kept prudently short and precise. The aim was to cover all the important aspects of a firm's basic characteristics, yet to keep the core questioning restricted only to the 'make or buy' decision making. Part A contained the contact details of the respondent; Part B contained general information about the company/firm; Part C asked electricity use and production related information. In total there were 48 questions and the average interview time was 15-20 minutes. Some questions were Yes/No binary type, while others had larger categories while maintaining a discrete variable structure. Rest of the questions asked for quantitative information. The basic form questionnaire is in Annex A.2 at the end of the thesis.

b. **Pilot Testing**: Before going for a full survey, it is useful to do pilot testing of the survey questionnaires. The author conducted pilot testing in 10 manufacturing firms in parts of Andhra Pradesh (mostly in and around Hyderabad) during the months of December-January, 2011-12. This lead to several iterations and revisions of the questionnaire and significantly improved the effectiveness of the whole survey design.

c. **Sampling**: Sampling is a very critical aspect of the survey design, as this has direct influence on the interpretation of statistical results. It provides the platform to collect relevant information needed to conduct research (Kalton and Anderson 1986). The core idea of using statistical methods is to be able to provide a reasonably accurate account of a particular phenomenon taking place in a defined population. However, generally the population sizes are so big that it is practically impossible to cover every unit, due to obvious time and space constraints. The second best approach then is to draw a subset comprising limited number of units and conduct the study on that subset in a way that it brings the insights as close as possible to those that would have been if the whole population were to be studied instead. Such a subset is called a 'sample' and the choice of units which make up the sample have an obvious bearing on the representativeness for the whole population, thereby compelling the process of selecting those units to be a very sensitive and scientific endeavor. This also means that sample selection has to be as randomized as possible. In the real world however, sampling is always a challenging procedure and though there is never an ideal sample, the guiding force for researchers is to make it as representative as possible.

Best attempts were made to follow sampling strategy as carefully as possible. Difficulties arose because of the very small proportion of the target population in the share of the total universal population. The total number of industrial units listed in Federation of Andhra Pradesh Chambers of Commerce and Industry (FAPCCI) were 3165. If we expand the list to include all industrial units (ranging from very small to big sizes) irrespective of their listing in FAPCCI directory the number reaches 16741 units. But the total number of CPP firms in AP is only 167, making it only 1% of the total number of industrial units (see Table A. 9). Because we wanted industry-wise representation the total set of CPP firms was stratified into the major industrial categories of Cement, Chemicals, Engineering, Metals & Minerals, Paper and Sugar. The aim was to create a sample of 75 CPP firms with proportional representation from each stratum. So a random number series was generated in EXCEL and assigned to each firm. Then they were sorted in increasing order and every third firm was picked. A parallel exercise was done for non-CPP firms and the combined samples from both were merged to generate the final sample.

This strategy was, however, not entirely successful at the execution stage of the survey for the following reasons:

i)   The response rate was very low, specifically for CPP firms. CPP firms generally tend to be public limited companies and treat their production information and strategies with caution and secrecy.
ii) The 75 CPP firms in the sample were all located across the state of Andhra Pradesh and interspersed with huge distances among them. This made approaching them very costly and time-taking. And if the investigator was turned away from entering the firm premises, then it led it huge sunk costs.

Table B 2: Sample proportions

S.No.	Description	Number of Firms
1	Total Industrial Firms in Andhra Pradesh (members of FAPCCI)	3165
2	Total Industrial Firms in Andhra Pradesh (ASI, 2007-2008; also non-members of FAPCCI)	16741
3	Total CPP in Andhra Pradesh	167
4	CPP in Sample	40
5	% of CPP in Andhra Pradesh to total ASI based industry figures	1
6	% of CPP in Andhra Pradesh to total FAPCCI based industry figures	5.28
7	% of sample CPP to total CPP	23.95

Source: Own survey data and FAPCCI Report, 2011

To overcome this, therefore, the research strategy had to be slightly modified. A complete coverage approach was adopted and all the CPPs in the major industrial districts of AP were approached. Correspondingly, non-CPP firms in the same location were randomly approached to create a sample representing both. This way the response rate increased. We eventually got filled questionnaires through face-to-face interviews from 107 firms of which 40% have CPP. The number of CPPs in the final survey sample is 23.95% of the total CPP population in AP.

d. Survey Mode and Execution: The entire final survey was conducted in the face-to-face mode where trained investigators travelled across the thirteen major industrial districts of Andhra Pradesh. All the investigators, eight of them were electrical engineers by profession and underwent several rounds of familiarization and training in the survey design and the research objective. Investigator training lasted for 8 – 10 sessions spread over 3 days in the initial period and several other sessions conducted by Philip N. Kumar, consultant and trainer.

Table B 3: Members of Survey Team

S.N.	Name of the Investigator	Qualification	Trainer
1.	P. Anwesh	B.Tech. Electrical and Electronics Engineering, JNTU	Philip Kumar
2.	Gautam Kaveti	B.Tech. Electrical and Electronics Engineering, JNTU	Philip Kumar
3.	K. Kaushik Reddy	B.Tech. Electrical and Electronics Engineering, JNTU	Philip Kumar
4.	B. Maheeza	B.Tech. Electrical and Electronics Engineering, JNTU	Philip Kumar
5.	D. Rahul	B.Tech. Electrical and Electronics Engineering, JNTU	Philip Kumar
6.	T. Srinath	B.Tech. Electrical and Electronics Engineering, JNTU	Philip Kumar
7.	Suresh Reddy	B.Tech. Electrical and Electronics Engineering, JNTU	Philip Kumar
8.	P. Swaroop	B.Tech. Electrical and Electronics Engineering, JNTU	Philip Kumar

Sample Excerpts from Interviews

Interviewee Name: Mr. B. Ravishankar
Details: CMD, Fleming Laboratories, 6th Floor (B), Ashoka Janardhan Chambers, Begumpet, Hyderabad
Role: Industry Actor/Expert
Date: 15.12.11
Mode: Face to Face
Venue: Residence, Vikram Puri, Secunderabad. Andhra Pradesh
Interviewer Name: Ranjan Kumar Ghosh

Q: Do you have a captive facility?
A: No.

Q: Why? Do you not face power shortages and holidays?
A: Our contracted load is of 1MW. Earlier we had lesser requirement and used diesel gensets for backup. Yes, we face power problems. But now we are migrating to HT connection where there will not be any power shortage or voltage fluctuation.

Q: Why do you need to move to an HT connection?
A: Firstly, we are a chemical process unit where nonstop supply of electricity is essential. We cannot stop chemical processes mid-way as that will be very loss making and also dangerous. So we need continuous power supply. Now we have a 11kV LT connection where power holidays are enforced, voltage levels fluctuate and there are scheduled and unscheduled power cuts. Till now we used 2 DG sets as the requirement was below 900kW. So it was not cost effective or viable to make investments for an HT connection. But now it does.

Q: What investments do you need to migrate to HT line?
A: We had to make an investment of around Rs. 1 crore because our plant is about a kilometre away from the grid. The cost is proportional to the distance from the grid as *we have to bear all the costs* of setting up the transformers etc.

Q: Why do you not produce your own power i.e. have a captive facility?
A: Firstly, captive is beneficial or viable only beyond 2.5-3 MW capacity requirement as the costs of setting up is very high. And the operating cost depends on the fuel used. Diesel and HFO are expensive. To use coal bigger plant is required. Therefore for captive, only big plants are viable. They can produce at cheaper than the grid rate and be absolutely independent of the grid. Secondly, we are an electricity dependent process but not a power intensive industry. This means that the proportion of expenses on power of the total expense is not very high. So that means it is not so much cost wise viable for us to produce our own power. Those who are power intensive will have an economic incentive to save costs by producing cheaper power.
Note: Gave contact of Mr. Hari Mohan Reddy, 23096688, GM Virchow Labs. Has CPP

Interviewee Name: Mr. J. Dwarkanath
Details: General Manager (BD & Projects), Renewable Energy Group, HBL Power Systems
Role: Industry Actor
Date: 13-12-11
Mode: Face to Face

Venue: Kausar Villa, M.L.A. Colony, Banjara Hills, Hyderabad
Interviewer Name: Ranjan Kumar Ghosh

Q1: Do you have captive facility in your plant?

A: Yes. We have a 3.2 MW own generation.

Q: What is your own capacity requirement?

A: Around 7 MW.

Q: What do you do for the rest?

A: We buy the remaining amount from the grid and the captive facility we use for backup.

Q: What was the set up cost of the captive plant?

A: For 3.2MW, it cost us around 10 crore rupees.

Q2: Which fuel do you use for your captive plant?

A: We use heavy fuel oil (HFO). Earlier we used diesel through gensets.

Q: Why did you change?

A: It is cheaper. And the gensets are easier to get. We use old ship machines.

Q: What is the operating cost difference?

A: For diesel it was around 14-15 Rs. per unit. For HFO it is nearly 11 Rs. per unit.

Q: What are your products?

A: Engineering and electronic equipments.

Q: Do you sell any excess power to the grid?

A: No. We do not produce enough for ourselves even. And selling is messy, due to high T&D losses.

Q: Were there any other advantages for you in setting up your captive unit?

A: Yes, we have a large plant area and lot of extra space. That means we did not have to buy any extra land for the facility. That made things cheaper and easier.

Interviewee Name: Mr. M. Sreerama Murthy
Details: Chairman, Industrial Development Committee, FAPCCI

Role: Industry Expert. Government, Regulation
Date: 08.11.11,
Venue: SEC Industries, Balanagar, Hyderabad
Interviewer Name: Ranjan Kumar Ghosh, Doctoral Fellow, HU Berlin

Q. What is the main reason for firms turning captive?
A: There is dual purpose involved. First, it is needed as there is interrupted power supply. However it is not a question of unreliability, as the wider power situation needs to be also accepted and the truth is there is not enough power being produced. Second, it also creates a business opportunity for selling excess power to the grid.

Q. Is it any hassle to feed power back into the grid?
A: Not in the city or areas where grid connectivity is high. (this may be problem for units away from the city – can you get information about the grid connectivity in AP – a map would be good as a background information)
Q. What is the average cost of production for captive power?
A: Generally 12-16 Rs. per unit. Whereas buying from the grid is around 4.5 Rs. (If cost of production is 3-4 times higher - the question boils down to only reliability and assured supply).

Q: Which firms are more vulnerable?
A: Only big firms can go for captive. Main problem is with SSIs and MSIs. They go to distant locations due to land prices for setting up industries. In these places if there are no dedicated power lines then they can face problems. There is not much grid connectivity and small firms do not have enough resources to turn captive. In such situations they have to adopt illegal means (*he did not elaborate on this*).

Q: Do you know cases where firms have left the industry because of lack of power supply?
A: Yes, firms leave the industry for various reasons and one important reason for some of them could be power supply (*more credible information is needed in this matter*).

GI[1]: The establishment cost of 1 MW captive power plant is on average Rs. 5 crore.
GI: Policies should be cross functional. There is also fear or risk of other laws like the environment laws. While captive is being encouraged, issues related to grid reach and other incentives need to be also addressed.
GI: For a period of around 7 years in AP, there was no power cuts due to a reformative regime, but then there was a break.
II[2]: The factors needed for easy and effective captive trade also need to be studied.

---

[1] General Information from the conversation with the interviewee when they speak beyond direct answers to questions
[2] Interviewer Insights: These are my own thoughts based on the conversation

C. Questionnaire: Industrial Survey

Questionnaire ID

Principal Investigator

Ranjan Kumar Ghosh

(Ph.D Fellow)

Humboldt University of Berlin, Germany

Email: ghoshrak@staff.hu-berlin.de

Number _____

Date _____   *Start Time* _____ *End Time* _____

All your information will be treated confidential and it will not be shared with other people. The data will only be used in aggregate and your name will not be mentioned at any stage of the study.

Part A: Contact Details

1. Name of the company: _____

2. Interviewee's name: _____

3. Designation: _____

4. Address: _____

5. District: _____ Pin: _____

6. Telephone number: _____Fax: _____

7. Email: _____

Part B: General Information about the Company

8. How many plants does the company have?

   _____

9. What is the location of the plants?

   I: _____ II: _____ III. _____

10. What is the main product manufactured at your plant? If more than one, please state the three most important

    _____

    _____

    _____

11. What is the annual sales/turnover? *(for the latest financial year)*

    _____

12. What is the percentage of expenses on electricity to the total expense?

    _____

13. What percent of your total output do you export?

    _____

14. This manufacturing unit is

    A part of an industrial estate ☐
    (If so, the name of the estate is _____)
    A stand alone unit with no industries around ☐
    Has a small number of other factories in the neighborhood ☐
    Neither of the above ☐

15. In the total plant area, apart from your core manufacturing area, do you have any excess land area? (**this is not including** any area used for power backup generators or own power plant)

    Yes ☐   No ☐

Part C: Electricity Related Information

16. What is your power requirement?

_____ kVA/kW or MVA/MW

17. Do you procure electricity for the manufacturing unit from the grid?

Yes ☐   No ☐

18. If yes, what is the electricity sanctioned load/contracted demand (CMD) from the distribution company?

_____ kVA/kW or MVA/MW

19. The distance of the manufacturing unit from the nearest substation is between

Own Substation ☐   Less than or equal to 1 km ☐   1-5 km ☐

5-10 km ☐   More than 10 km ☐

20. If you buy from the grid, what is the average tariff for electricity that you pay to the distribution company?

_____ Rs/kWh

21. What type of power cuts do you face?

None ☐   Scheduled ☐   Unscheduled ☐   Both ☐

22. Do you face voltage fluctuations during production hours?

Yes ☐   No ☐   Once in two or three months ☐

23. How many days of power holidays do you face?

None ☐   1 day/week ☐   2 days/week ☐   More than 2 days/week ☐
Not complete holidays but peak load restrictions during shortages ☐

Now we want to understand how you respond to power shortages. So the next set of questions will be related to that.

24. What level of electricity supply does your production process require?

24 hours non stop quality supply   ☐

Atleast 18 hours supply   ☐

Atleast 12 hours supply   ☐

Less than 12 hours supply   ☐

25. Please click the option which fits your actual electricity arrangement

We have LT connection with no back up arrangement   ☐

We have LT connection and use DG sets for back up   ☐

We have HT connection with no back up arrangement   ☐

We have HT connection and use DG sets for back up   ☐

We have both HT connection and a captive facility for partial fulfilment   ☐

We have only a captive facility from which we fulfil all our power requirements   ☐

If any other arrangement, please specify   _____

26. What is the level of your HT/LT connection?

Less than 11 kV   ☐

11 kV   ☐

33 kV   ☐

132 kV   ☐

27. Did you have to migrate (or planning to migrate) to a higher connection?

Yes ☐   No ☐

28. If yes, what was (would be) the cost of shifting to the higher connection?

_____ Rs.

29. What is the capacity of the DG sets?

_____ kVa/kW or MVA/MW

30. What is the cost per unit of diesel?

_____

[If you have a captive facility (equal to or greater than 1 MW), then respond to Q.31-Q.47, otherwise please move to Question 48]

31. What is its capacity?

Unit I   _____ MW

Unit II   _____ MW

Unit III _____ MW

32. Which year was the plant set up?

Unit I   _____

Unit II   _____

Unit III _____

33. Did you get any credit financing to set up your captive power unit?

Yes ☐   No ☐

34. Is the captive plant also used for co-generation purposes?

Yes ☐   No ☐

35. What was the capital cost of setting up the captive plant (total)?

_____ Rs.

36. The captive plant is

Multi Fuel ☐   Single Fuel ☐

37. Which fuel is used and its unit cost?

Unit	Coal	Natural gas	Diesel	Heavy Fuel Oil	Bagasse (Sugarcane)	Renewable based (biomass, solar, wind)	Any other please specify
I							
II							
III							

38. What is the cost of generation (average variable cost)?

_____ Rs. / kWh

39. How many employees are dedicated for maintaining the power plant?

_____

40. Is the unit cost of generation from captive plant higher than the grid rate?

Yes ☐   No ☐

41. If yes, it is because: (please tick one or more options)

The price of contracted fuel fluctuates ☐

We do not receive the complete quota of contracted/allocated fuel ☐

We have to use expensive alternative fuel ☐

If any other reason, please specify _____

42. Do you produce excess electricity from your captive unit?

Yes ☐   No ☐   Only during off season ☐

43. Do you sell the electricity to the grid?

Yes ☐   No ☐   Only during off season ☐

44. Do you have an existing PPA (Power Purchase Agreement) with APTRANSCO?

Yes ☐   No ☐

45. What is the contracted PPA capacity?

_____ MW

46. How much do you sell?

Season: ——————

Off season: ——————

47. What tariff do you receive as per the PPA?

_____ Rs. /Unit

48. Are you part of any cooperative captive arrangement?

Yes ☐   No ☐

THANK YOU VERY MUCH FOR SPARING YOUR VALUABLE TIME!

D. Descriptive Statistics of Thermal Power Plants and Efficiency

Table D 1: State-wise share of thermal generation

	No. of Plants	Mean Installed Capacity (MW): 2010	Mean Installed Capacity (MW): 1994-2010	Mean PLF (%): 2010	S.D. of PLF: 2010	Mean PLF (%): 1994-2010	S.D of PLF: 1994-2010	S.D of PLF: 2010	Mean Power Generation (GWh): 2010	Mean Power Generation (GWh): 1994-2010
Andhra Pradesh	6	1196.50	912.50	86.07	5.2	78.55	16.61		9135.66	6791.34
Assam	3	110.00	110.00	0.00	0	13.58	14.57		0.00	76.76
Bihar/Jharkhand	6	795.00	572.53	38.49	29.6	33.34	24.01		2991.46	1936.00
Delhi	3	362.50	367.21	58.38	20.27	60.80	18.80		1977.77	2200.10
Gujarat	8	515.00	533.15	60.20	26.74	65.39	19.13		3283.91	3208.09
Haryana	2	735.00	556.47	59.22	26.33	57.62	14.45		4847.11	3175.60
Karnataka	1	1470.00	1198.24	63.90	-	78.64	8.31		8803.59	7831.61
MP/Chattisgarh	8	1196.56	963.04	75.79	16.74	71.46	15.67		8688.71	6666.09
Maharashtra	9	906.67	863.27	61.44	20.9	71.52	13.09		4908.48	5388.59
Orissa	3	1296.67	887.73	88.17	3.52	72.89	16.6		9838.07	5925.78
Punjab	3	873.33	749.57	72.96	23.35	75.20	12.51		6108.27	4943.93
Rajasthan	2	1370.00	964.67	83.87	10.16	84.68	6.48		9650.68	7027.64
Tamil Nadu	6	840.00	835.78	66.73	22.6	70.79	17.9		5617.08	5446.55
Uttar Pradesh	10	1138.20	940.20	72.65	24.66	64.33	26.73		7900.31	6016.78
West Bengal	12	673.75	590.61	59.89	24.63	55.86	21.43		3781.03	2883.71
All India	**82**	**873.08**	**740.31**	**64.45**	**25.68**	**63.16**	**24.08**		**5665.42**	**4575.88**

Source: Own compilation

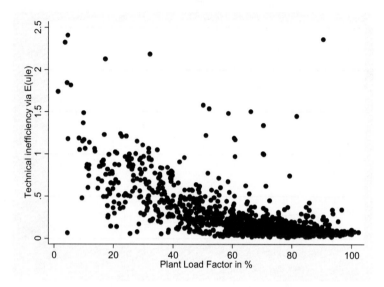

Figure D 1: Relation TIE and PLF

Source: Own compilation

Table D 2: Year-wise distribution of TIE

	Percentage of Plants in TIE Categories					
Year	0 - 10%	10% - 20%	20% - 30%	30% - 40%	40% - 50%	Above 50%
1994	38.96	20.78	10.39	7.79	7.79	14.29
1995	38.96	25.97	7.79	6.49	6.49	14.29
1996	46.75	16.88	10.39	5.19	3.90	16.88
1997	31.17	27.27	6.49	7.79	5.19	22.08
1998	42.86	27.27	5.19	10.39	5.19	9.09
1999	41.56	31.17	2.60	9.09	7.79	7.79
2000	45.45	28.57	9.09	6.49	0.00	10.39
2001	28.57	28.57	19.48	11.69	1.30	10.39
2002	66.23	15.58	9.09	1.30	2.60	5.19
2003	67.53	16.88	7.79	3.90	2.60	1.30
2004	59.74	23.38	3.90	5.19	3.90	3.90
2005	61.04	19.48	7.79	2.60	0.00	9.09
2006	68.83	15.58	3.90	0.00	2.60	9.09
2007	72.73	11.69	7.79	2.60	0.00	5.19
2008	79.22	7.79	1.30	5.19	3.90	2.60
2009	46.75	20.78	11.69	3.90	1.30	15.58
2010	55.84	15.58	10.39	0.00	1.30	16.88

Source: Own compilation

Table D 3: State-wise distribution of TIE

	Percentage of Plants in TIE Categories					
State	0 - 10%	10% - 20%	20% - 30%	30% - 40%	40% - 50%	Above 50%
Delhi	56.86	25.49	5.88	5.88	3.92	1.96
Haryana	50.00	32.35	11.76	2.94	2.94	0.00
Punjab	58.82	23.53	5.88	1.96	0	9.8
Rajasthan	76.47	5.88	0	2.94	0	14.71
Uttar Pradesh	54.71	15.88	12.35	8.82	2.94	5.29
Gujarat	61.34	27.73	5.88	0.84	1.68	2.52
MP/Chhattisgarh	65.44	22.79	7.35	1.47	0	2.94
Maharashtra	66.18	25.74	1.47	0	2.21	4.41
Andhra Pradesh	59.8	15.69	8.82	3.92	2.94	8.82
Karnataka	64.71	29.41	0	0	0	5.88
Tamil Nadu	65.69	20.59	2.94	3.92	0	6.86
Bihar/Jharkhand	12.75	14.71	10.78	16.67	9.8	35.29
West Bengal	29.41	21.08	11.76	8.82	7.35	21.57
Orissa	54.9	15.69	13.73	3.92	3.92	7.84

Source: Own compilation

Institutional Change in Agriculture and Natural Resources
Institutioneller Wandel der Landwirtschaft und Ressourcennutzung

edited by/herausgegeben von Volker Beckmann & Konrad Hagedorn

Erschienene Bände in der Reihe:

Bd. 1: BREM, Markus, *Landwirtschaftliche Unternehmen im Transformationsprozess: Ein Beitrag zur Theorie der Restrukturierung während des Übergangs vom Plan zum Markt.* 320 S., pb EUR 28,00, ISBN 978-3-8265-8656-9 (1/2001).

Bd. 2: PAVEL, Ferdinand, *Success and Failure of Post-Communist Transition: Theory and an Application to Bulgaria.* 210 S., pb EUR 28,00, ISBN 978-3-8265-8774-0 (2/2001).

Bd. 3: SCHLÜTER, Achim, *Institutioneller Wandel und Transformation: Restitution, Transformation und Privatisierung in der tschechischen Landwirtschaft.* 360 S., pb EUR 28,00, ISBN 978-3-8265-9284-3 (3/2001).

Bd. 4: BOGER, Silke, *Agricultural Markets in Transition: An Empirical Study on Contracts and Transaction Costs in the Polish Hog Sector.* 300 S., pb EUR 28,00, ISBN 978-3-8265-9634-6 (4/2001).

Bd. 5: KLAGES, Bernd: *Die Privatisierung der ehemals volkseigenen landwirtschaftlichen Flächen in den neuen Bundesländern: Grundlagen, Rahmenbedingungen, Ausgestaltung und Wirkungen.* 520 S., pb EUR 38,00, ISBN 978-3-8265-9714-5 (5/2001).

Bd. 6: VERHAEGEN, Ingrid/VAN HUYLENBROECK, Guido: *Hybrid Governance Structures for Quality Farm Products: A Transaction Cost Perspective.* 200 S., pb EUR 28,00, ISBN 978-3-8265-9774-9 (6/2002).

Bd. 7: HURRELMANN, Annette: *Land Markets in Economic Theory: A Review of the Literature and Proposals for Further Research.* 138 S., pb EUR 18,00, ISBN 978-3-8265-9844-9 (7/2002).

Bd. 8: BOGALE, Ayalneh: *Land Degradation, Impoverishment and Livelihood Strategies of Rural Households in Ethiopia: Farmers' Perceptions and Policy Implication.* 236 S., pb EUR 28,00, ISBN 978-3-8322-0214-9 (8/2002).

Bd. 9: ZILLMER, Sabine: *Arbeitsangebotsverhalten im Transformationsprozess: Eine empirische Analyse des polnischen Agrarsektors.* 334 S., pb EUR 28,00, ISBN 978-3-8322-0356-6 (9/2002).

Bd. 10: GATZWEILER, Franz/JUDIS, Renate/HAGEDORN, Konrad: *Sustainable Agriculture in Central and Eastern European Countries: The Environmental Effects of Transition and Needs for Change.* 390 S., pb EUR 28,00, ISBN 978-3-8322-0366-5 (10/2002).

Bd. 11: MILCZAREK, Dominika: *Privatisation as a Process of Institutional Change: The Case of State Farms in Poland.* 154 S., pb EUR 18,00, ISBN 978-3-8322-0364-1 (11/2002).

Bd. 12: CURTISS, Jarmila: *Efficiency and Structural Changes in Transition: A Stochastic Frontier Analysis of Czech Crop Production.* 284 S., pb EUR 28,00, ISBN 978-3-8322-0365-8 (12/2002).

Bd. 13: CLASEN, Ralf: *Jenseits des Sonderfalls: Eine vergleichende Analyse der Agrartransformation in Ostdeutschland und Estland aus der Perspektive des akteurzentrierten Institutionalismus.* 392 S., pb EUR 28,00, ISBN 978-3-8322-1004-5 (13/2002).

Bd. 14: LÜTTEKEN, Antonia: *Agrar-Umweltpolitik im Transformationsprozess: Das Beispiel Polen.* 316 S., pb EUR 28,00, ISBN 978-3-8322-1134-9 (14/2002).

Bd. 15: HANISCH, Markus: *Property Reform and Social Conflict: A Multi-Level Analysis of the Change of Agricultural Property Rights in Post-Socialist Bulgaria.* 322 S., pb EUR 28,00, ISBN 978-3-8322-2093-8 (15/2003).

Bd. 16: GATZWEILER, Franz: *The Changing Nature of Economic Value: Indigenous Forest Garden Values in Kalimanatan, Indonesia.* 250 S., pb EUR 28,00, ISBN 978-3-8322-1973-4 (16/2003).

Bd. 17: LÖW, Daniel: *Crop Farming in China: Technology, Markets, Institutions and the Use of Pesticides.* 242 S., pb EUR 28,00, ISBN 978-3-8322-2373-1 (17/2003).

Bd. 18: VANNOPPEN, Jan/VAN HUYLENBROECK, Guido/VERBEKE, Wim: *Economic Conventions and consumer valuation in specific quality food supply networks.* 202 S., pb EUR 28,00, ISBN 978-3-8322-3065-4 (18/2004).

Bd. 19: KORF, Benedikt: *Conflict, Space and Institutions: Property Rights and the Political Economy of War in Sri Lanka.* 232 S., pb EUR 28,00, ISBN 978-3-8322-3219-1 (19/2004).

Bd. 20: RUDOLPH, Markus: *Agrarstrukturpolitik im vereinten Deutschland: Eine Analyse der Gemeinschaftsaufgabe "Verbesserung der Agrarstruktur und des Küstenschutzes" im Lichte der Neuen Politischen Ökonomie.* 492 S., pb EUR 38,00, ISBN 978-3-8322-3807-0 (20/2005).

Bd. 21: NGUYEN, Tan Quang: *What Benefits and for Whom?: Effects of Devolution of Forest Management in Dak Lak, Vietnam.* 346 S., pb EUR 28,00, ISBN 978-3-8322-3905-3 (21/2005).

Bd. 22: HIDAYAT, Aceng: *Institutional Analysis of Coral Reef Management: A Case Study of Gili Indah Village, West Lombok, Indonesia.* 252 S., pb EUR 28,00, ISBN 978-3-8322-3815-5 (22/2005).

Bd. 23: THEESFELD, Insa: *A Common Pool Resource in Transition: Determinants of Institutional Change for Bulgaria's Postsocialist Irrigation Sector.* 308 S., pb EUR 28,00, ISBN 978-3-8322-3906-0 (23/2005).

Bd. 24: HURRELMANN, Annette: *Agricultural Land Markets: Organisation, Institutions, Costs and Contracts in Poland.* 262 S., pb EUR 28,00, ISBN 978-3-8322-4114-8 (24/2005).

Bd. 25: EGGERS, Jörg: *Dezentralisierung der Agrarumweltmaßnahmen in der europäischen Agrarpolitik: Hemmnisse eines institutionellen Wandels.* 300 S., pb EUR 28,00, ISBN 978-3-8322-4170-4 (25/2005).

Bd. 26: BECKMANN, Volker/HAGEDORN, Konrad: *Understanding Agricultural Transition: Institutional Change and Economic Performance in a Comparative Perspective.* 510 S., pb EUR 38,00, ISBN 978-3-8322-4795-9 (26/2007).

Bd. 27: TRAN, Thanh Ngoc: *From Legal Acts to Village Institutions and Forest Use Practices: Effects of Devolution in the Central Highlands of Vietnam.* 244 S., pb EUR 28,00, ISBN 978-3-8322-4796-6 (27/2005).

Bd. 28: HA, Thuc Vien: *Land Reform and Rural Livelihoods: An Examination from the Uplands of Vietnam.* 364 S., pb EUR 28,00, ISBN 978-3-8322-6908-1 (28/2007).

Bd. 29: DIRIMANOVA, Violeta: *Economic Effects of Land Fragmentation: Property Rights, Land Markets and Contracts in Bulgaria.* 270 S., pb EUR 28,00, ISBN 978-3-8322-6948-7 (29/2008).

Bd. 30: JUNGCURT, Stefan: *Institutional Interplay in International Environmental Governance: Policy Interdependence and Strategic Interaction in the Regime Complex on Plant Genetic Resources for Food and Agriculture.* 280 S., pb EUR 28,00, ISBN 978-3-8322-6974-6 (30/2008).

Bd. 31: BANASZAK, Ilona: *Success and Failure of Cooperation in Agricultural Markets: Evidence from Producer Groups in Poland.* 220 S., pb EUR 28,00, ISBN 978-3-8322-6995-1 (31/2008).

Bd. 32: BEYENE, Fekadu: *Challenges and Options in Governing Common Property: Customary Institutions among (Agro-) Pastoralists in Ethiopia.* 254 S., pb EUR 28,00, ISBN 978-3-8322-6375-1 (32/2008).

Bd. 33: BOENING, Frank: *Accessing Land at the Agricultural Frontier: A Case Study from the Honduran Mosquitia.* 370 S., pb EUR 28,00, ISBN 978-3-8322-6994-4 (33/2008).

Bd. 34: HUNDIE, Bekele: *Pastoralism, Institutions and Social Interaction: Explaining the Coexistence of Conflict and Cooperation in Pastoral Afar, Ethiopia.* 234 S., pb EUR 28,00, ISBN 978-3-8322-6376-8 (34/2008).

Bd. 35: THIEL, Andreas: *Environmental Policy Integration and Water Use Development in the Algarve since Portugal's Accession to the European Union.* 358 S., pb EUR 28,00, ISBN 978-3-8322-8105-2 (35/2009).

Bd. 36: BECKMANN, Volker/DUNG, Nguyen Huu/SHI, Xiaoping/SPOOR, Max/ WESSELER, Justus: *Economic Transition and Natural Resource Management in East and Southeast Asia.* 412 S., pb EUR 38,00, ISBN 978-3-8322-8107-6 (36/2010).

Bd. 37: FARRELL, Katharine N.: *Making Good Decisions Well: A Theory of Collective Ecological Management.* 332 S., pb EUR 28,00, ISBN 978-3-8322-8549-4 (37/2009).

Bd. 38: ARZT, Katja: *Lokale Partizipation und nachhaltige Ressourcennutzung: Eine institutionelle Analyse von Agrar-Umwelt-Foren.* 326 S., pb EUR 28,00, ISBN 978-3-8322-8604-0 (38/2009).

Bd. 39: SCHLEYER, Christian: *Institutioneller Wandel von Meliorationssystemen: Eine vergleichende Studie in Ostdeutschland und Polen.* 332 S., pb EUR 28,00, ISBN 978-3-8322-8726-9 (39/2009).

Bd. 40: WEDAJOO, Aseffa Seyoum: *Microeconomics of Wild Coffee Genetic Resources Conservation in Southwestern Ethiopia: Forest zoning and economic incentives for conservation.* 206 S., pb EUR 28,00, ISBN 978-3-8322-8841-9 (40/2010).

Bd. 41: MARGARIAN, Anne: *Die regionale Spezifität des Agrarstrukturwandels: Eine theoretische und empirische Analyse.* 346 S., pb EUR 28,00, ISBN 978-3-8322-9493-9 (41/2010).

Bd. 42: RAUCHENECKER, Katharina: *Institutioneller Wandel im Bereich Jagd und Wildtiermanagement: Das Beispiel der Jagdgenossenschaften.* 288 S., pb EUR 28,00, ISBN 978-3-8322-9587-5 (42/2010).

Bd. 43: VON BOCK UND POLACH, Carlotta: *Die Bedeutung von Sozialkapital und Netzwerken für die saisonale Migration polnischer Arbeitskräfte nach Deutschland: Am Beispiel des brandenburgischen Spargelanbaus.*
260 S., pb EUR 28,00, ISBN 978-3-8440-0314-7 (43/2011).

Bd. 44: IRAWAN, Evi: *The Effect of Labor Organization on Integrated Pest Management (IPM) Adoption: Empirical Study of Durian and Tangerine Production in Thailand.*
ca. 192 S., pb EUR 28,00, ISBN 978-3-8440-0630-8 (44/2012).

Bd. 45: DENEKE, Tilaye Teklewold: *Water Governance in Amhara Region of Ethiopia: An Institutional Analysis.*
234 S., pb EUR 28,00, ISBN 978-3-8440-0725-1 (45/2012).

Bd. 46: HERNÁNDEZ RIVERA, José: *Analysis of Economic Driving Forces in Crop Protection: A Case Study of Apple Production in the EU.*
184 S. pb EUR 28,00, ISBN 978-3-8440-1137-1 (46/2012)

Bd. 47: SRIGIRI, Srinivasa Reddy: *Institutions of collective action and property rights for natural resource management: Participation of rural households in watershed management initiatives in semi-arid India.*
190 S., pb EUR 28,00, ISBN 978-3-8440-1165-4 (47/2014).

Bd. 48: KIMMICH, Christian: *Networks of Coordination and Conflict: Governing Electricity Transactions for Irrigation in South India.*
198 S., pb EUR 28,00, ISBN 978-3-8440-1947-6 (48/2013).

Bd. 49: CHALIGANTI, Raghu: *Biofuel promotion in India: Analyzing the policy process from a discursive-institutional perspective.*
268 S., pb EUR 28,00, ISBN 978-3-8440-2718-1 (49/2014).

Bd. 50: STUPAK, Nataliya: *Institutional Analysis of Black Earth Soil Degradation and Conservation in Ukraine.*
280 S., pb EUR 28,00, ISBN 978-3-8440-2734-1 (50/2014).

Bd. 51: GHOSH, Ranjan Kumar: *Towards Transaction Cost Regulation: Insights from the Indian Power Generation Sector.*
218 S., pb EUR 28,00, ISBN 978-3-8440-3263-5 (51/2014).